CONVIVIUMPRESS

Roland Meynet

Called to freedom

Translated by Patricia Kelly

CONVIVIUMPRESS
GREGORIAN UNIVERSITY PRESS

SERIES RHETORICA SEMITICA

2009

Called to freedom

Original Title: *Appelés à la liberté*

Translation: *Called to freedom*

http://www.conviviumpress.com
sales@conviviumpress.com
ventas@conviviumpress.com
convivium@conviviumpress.com

7661 NW 68th St, Suite 108,
Miami, Florida 33166. USA.
Fax: +1 (305) 8875463

Edited *by* Rafael Luciani
Translated *by* Patricia Kelly
Tables translated *by* Vitus Rubianto Solichin
Designed *by* Eduardo Chumaceiro d'E
Series: *Rhetorica semitica*

ISBN: 978-1-934996-08-9

Printed in Colombia
Impreso en Colombia
D'VINNI, S.A.

Convivium Press
Miami, 2009

ESTE LIBRO
HA SIDO PUBLICADO
CON EL APOYO
EDITORIAL DE LA
R B S

SOCIETY FOR THE STUDY OF BIBLICAL AND SEMITIC RHETORIC (RBS)

Several learned societies exist whose objective is the study of rhetoric. The «Society for the Study of Biblical and Semitic Rhetoric» (RBS) is the only one

- that is devoted exclusively to the study of Semitic literature, in particular the Bible, but also others texts, for example of Muslim origin;
- that consequently is dedicated to listing and describing the particular laws of a rhetoric that have governed the composition of texts which are of no less importance than those of the Greek and Latin world, of which modern Western civilization is the heir.

It must not be forgotten that this same Western civilization is also heir to the Judeo-Christian tradition, which has its origin in the Bible, that is to say, in the Semitic world.

More broadly, the texts that we study are the foundational texts of the three great monotheistic religions: Judaism, Christianity and Islam. Such academic study, the primary condition for better mutual knowledge, can contribute to a rapprochement between those who belong to these diverse traditions.

Founded in Rome, where its headquarters are situated, the «Society for the Study of Biblical and Semitic Rhetoric» (RBS) is a not-for-profit organization, under Italian law, that promotes and sustains research and publications

- especially in the Biblical field, both the New and Old Testaments;
- but also of other Semitic texts, in particular those of Islam.

The essential objective of the RBS is to promote research projects, exchanges between Universities and publications in the area of Biblical and Semitic Rhetoric, thanks especially to the collection of necessary funds for financing these diverse projects.

The «Society for the Study of Biblical and Semitic Rhetoric» first and foremost welcomes and brings together Scholars and University Professors who, in different Universities and Institutes, both in Italy and abroad, work in the area of Biblical and Semitic Rhetoric. It is open also to those who are interested in research and are intent on supporting it. For more information on the RBS, see:

www.retoricabiblicaesemitica.org

RHETORICA SEMITICA

Series directed by Roland Meynet s.j.

Many people think that classical rhetoric, inherited from the Greeks via the Romans, is universal—this is what seems to govern modern culture, which the West has spread through the whole world. But the time has come to abandon this ethnocentrism— classical rhetoric is no longer alone in the world. We cannot judge everything according to the small village where we were born and which we have never left, whether that little «village» is Paris, Rome, Berlin, or even New York.

The Hebrew Bible, whose texts were mostly written in Hebrew, but also in Aramaic, uses a very different rhetoric from Greco-Roman rhetoric, so we need to acknowledge that there is another rhetoric, which we refer to as «Hebrew Rhetoric».

Other biblical texts from the Old and New Testaments, which were translated into or written directly in Greek broadly follow the same rules; we can therefore rightly talk not just about Hebrew rhetoric but more broadly about «Biblical Rhetoric».

Furthermore, these same laws were later recognized to be at work in Akkadian, Ugaritic and other texts which were earlier than the Hebrew Bible, and then in Arabic texts from the Muslim tradition and the Qur'an, later than the biblical literature. This rhetoric, then, is not only biblical, and we might even say that all these texts, which come from the same cultural sphere, belong within the same rhetorical style which we refer to as «Semitic Rhetoric».

Contrary to the inevitable impression of western readers, these texts from the Semitic tradition, whether the Prophets, the Gospels, or the Qur'an, are carefully composed, providing that they are analyzed according to the rhetorical laws which govern them. We know that the text's form and arrangement is the main gate which gives access to its meaning; although its composition does not directly and automatically provide the meaning. However, when formal analysis leads to a thoughtful division of the text, defining its context more objectively, emphasizing the way it is organized at its different structural levels, then the conditions which allow the work of interpretation come together on less subjective and fragmentary bases.

Contents

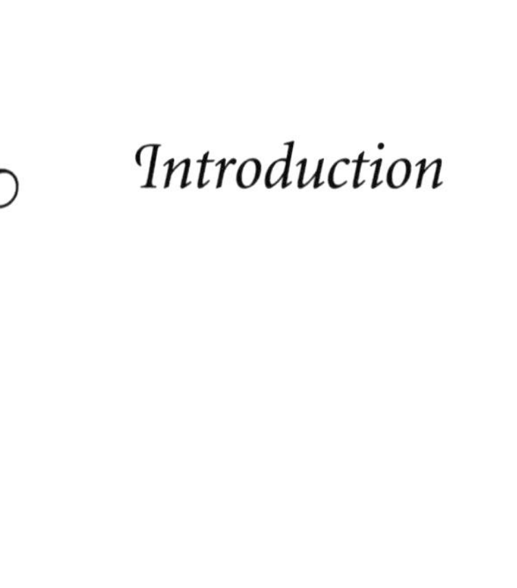

Introduction

The crossing of the sea signals the birth of the people of Israel. Everything which had preceded it — the patriarchal saga of Abraham, Isaac and Jacob — merely somehow represents its pre-history. When Jacob-Israel's children multiplied in Egypt, to the extent that they filled the country, they began to attain the size of a people, rather than the family they had been until then[1]. But they could never have become a real people, that is, an independent nation just like any other, if they had not been expelled from the very nation where they were provided for, but in which they had been reduced to slavery. They had to separate themselves from the land where they had grown to reach the independence and freedom which mark any people worthy of the name. This is what happened when, crossing the Red Sea, they crossed the boundary which divided the reassuring house of slavery from the formidable desert of freedom. In the book of Exodus, the account of the crossing of the sea (Exod 14) is immediately followed by the «Song of the Sea» (Exod 15). As soon as they realized that the Egyptians had perished, drowned in the sea which they themselves had crossed dry-shod, the children of Israel intoned this canticle which celebrates both the freedom they hardly knew and also, looking to the future, the later events which will lead them towards what their purpose is, serving God in the liturgy of the Jerusalem Temple. These two inseparable texts make up the first part, with the title, «The gift of freedom».

As long as the children of Israel were no more than immigrants, reduced to slavery by the land which had welcomed their ancestors, they could not be free actors, since they were subject to the law of force and coercion. Once they were free and had become an independent people, however, they were to receive on Mount Sinai the Law which sought to govern their relationship with their God and among themselves, condensed into the Decalogue, the «ten words», which ordain and consecrate the freedom of the people as a whole as well as each individual. As a result, the second part is entitled «The law of freedom». The Torah contains two versions of the Decalogue, one in Exodus 20 and another in Deuteronomy 5. This is the subject of the second part: having analyzed the two texts, we will try to answer the question raised by the fact that there are two, not one, Decalogues.

Finally, in the third part we will analyze and comment on each of the seven psalms which, following on from the Song of the Sea, celebrate the foundational event of the crossing of the sea during the paschal meal: the «Hallel», or «Praise»,

1 Deut 10:22.

the group of psalms numbered 113 to 118, to which are added Psalm 136, known as the «Great Hallel». The words of praise were to resound in the Temple at the moment when the paschal lambs were sacrificed, and in each house where they would later be consumed, as a sort of answer to the words of the Law received on Mount Sinai, to celebrate the founding event of the leaving of Egypt. This is why this third part is entitled «Hymns to freedom».

We thus have twelve chapters, the same number as the sons of Israel. All bar one are given to the study of a text. First of all, we offer a literal translation, which follows the Hebrew very closely in order to enable an initial contact with the biblical text. For the crossing of the Sea and the two Decalogues, which are prose, there is no division apart from the division of sentences imposed by syntax. The Song of the Sea and each of the seven psalms in the last part, however, are presented in such a way as to respect their most basic poetic rhythm: each member takes up one line and the segments — which are mostly two members, sometimes three and occasionally one — are separated by a white line[2].

We then analyze the text's composition in detail following the process of rhetorical analysis[3]. Various re-writings allow us to see how the text is constructed at different levels, and a description of the composition describes and justifies this.

Then we present the biblical context, relating the text under examination to other texts in the Bible which shed light on it and enable it to be better understood. Finally, we offer an interpretation which is the fruit of the previous work on composition and intertextuality.

The attentive reader may be surprised that the biblical text is not always translated in the same way. The first reason for this is that the translation is not the text — no translation could replace the original. Using several translations helps us to remain aware of this essential fact. The second reason is that the translation is purely functional. The translations in this volume are not for reading in public, but are working translations. They are different because of the textual level where the work of analysis is carried out. When a text is studied at the lower levels, the level of a piece or a part, a «carbon-copy translation» is needed, which follows the original very closely — we might almost say that it is Hebrew with English words. This can be seen with the third part of the Exodus version of the Decalogue (Exod 20:12):

2 See «Glossary of technical terms», p. 15.
3 For a detailed account of this methodology, see our *Traité de rhétorique biblique.*

– [12] Honor	the FATHER	of you	and the mother	of	**you**,
– so that	are prolonged		the days	of	**you**,
– on the land	that YHWH THE GOD	of **you**	donates	to	**you**.

However, at the superior level, the level of the passage and, particularly, the sequence, it is not necessary to be so literal; we can offer a more readable translation which is further from the source-language but closer to the target-language[4]. So, for the same text, Exod 20:12, here is the translation adopted at the level of the Decalogue as a whole (see p. 125):

[12] HONOR	**YOUR FATHER**	and **YOUR MOTHER**,
so that your *days*	are prolonged,	
on the land that		THE LORD YOUR GOD donates to you.

I would like to thank those who have encouraged me to write this short volume which would probably never have seen the light of day but for their friendly insistence. This work was commissioned by the editor and secretary of the Hervé Renaudin association, which funded the collection in which it was published in French. Other volumes, which will also be published in Spanish and English by Convivium Press, such as *L'Évangile de Luc* and *La Lettre de Jacques*, the study on sura 5 of the Qur'an, *Le Festin, une lecture de la sourate* al-Mâ'ida, and the *Traité de rhétorique biblique* had to be published alongside a book which presented an Old Testament text, or the collection would not have deserved its name! Given the time-frame, it was out of the question to undertake a whole book, however short, and even less to commission another author. I therefore had to resort to what one dreams of once one reaches a certain age — a collection of articles. But from among my publications on Old Testament texts I had to choose some which would be coherent. The first and second parts return to works which I have already published but which I have reviewed and extended as appropriate. The seven chapters of the third part are unpublished, although in the *Traité* I had already given the composition of the first two psalms. Given the particular circumstances of its writing, the reader will understand why some chapters of this book are much more documented than others. Those which appeared earlier in a scholarly journal had to quote secondary literature as widely as possible[5],

4 See *Traité*, 155.533-547.

5 The case for the work on the Song of the Sea and the two Decalogues.

but whatever the interest in this type of work, I did not think it necessary to do the same for the other chapters. To avoid lengthening the work, for the seven psalms in the last part, I had to give up the discussion of the positions defended in specialist articles and be content to refer to a limited number of authorized commentaries.

I am also delighted to thank the editors of the journals in which the three articles, re-published here, originally appeared for generously giving me permission to re-use them. Finally, I will like to thank the editors of *Convivium Press* for this beautiful designed publication of *Called to freedom*. It only remains for me to hope that the reader has as much pleasure and profit from reading these pages as I have had in writing them.

1
Note to the reader: how to read this Book?

Some might be put off by the technical nature and scientific appearance of this book. To be convincing, commentaries on biblical texts need to be based on precise, rigorous analysis. The scientific nature of the work is its own guarantor. The demanding reader will not be happy with pious thoughts which are not based on serious study. This is why usually, the reading of this kind of work demands great attention and serious concentration: this kind of book is not to be read as one would read a novel.

However, this book has been designed for two readerships, or at least, for two kinds of use.

THE FIRST WAY OF READING THIS BOOK

The first, lighter way, within everyone's reach, is to only read the biblical text as it is re-written in the tables, followed by the paragraphs entitled «*Biblical context*» and «*Interpretation*». This kind of «cursory reading» does not burden itself with all the «rhetorical» technique, and goes straight to the point. In brief, it is a *spiritual reading* for those who wish to meditate on biblical texts with a guide. The work has been designed to make this kind of use possible.

THE SECOND WAY OF READING THIS BOOK

The second use is clearly more onerous, but also much more profitable, and consists of using this book as a tool for work. Rather than contenting oneself with reading the tables attentively, the reader will take the time to *color* them in. Such advice may seem childish, but anyone who wishes to work seriously on texts, whether biblical texts or others, knows very well that this is one of the most effective ways of appropriating them. Rather than re-writing the text oneself[6], a good coloring in will enable a similar result to be obtained. The greatest saints were not reluctant to undertake this kind of exercise[7].

6 «Every man in Israel has the duty to acquire a book of the Torah; *and if he writes it himself*, he is worthy of praises. Did not our Elders say: "*If he has written it himself*, it is as though he had received it at Sinai? If this is not possible for him, let him acquire a scroll from one who has written it. This is how our elders interpret the verse "and now, *write this hymn for yourself*, that it be taught to the children of Israel"» (Deut 31:19). Cf. *Sefer Ha-Hinukh.*

7 «As he really enjoyed his books, the thought came to him to draw out in summary some of the most essential points of the life of Christ and the saints. This is how he began writing with great care (for he was beginning to get up a little in the house): the words of Christ in red ink, those of Our Lday in blue ink, the paper was smooth and lined, and it was well written, for he was a very good calligrapher. He spent part of the time writing and part of it in prayer» (Cf. Ignace de Loyola, *Récit écrit par le Père Louis Gonçalves aussitôt qu'il l'eut recueilli de la bouche même du Père Ignace*, 65-66).

Abbreviations

1

Abbreviations

Alonso Schoekel et Carniti — ALONSO SCHOEKEL Luis and CARNITI Cecilia, *I Salmi*, Commenti biblici, I-II, Roma 1992-1993.

Amos — BOVATI Pietro and MEYNET Roland, *Le Livre du prophète Amos*, Éd. du Cerf, RhBib 2, Paris 1994.

Beaucamp — BEAUCAMP Évode, *Le Psautier*, Gabalda, Sources bibliques, Paris 1979.

BetM — *Beth Mikra*

JB — *The Jerusalem Bible*, Darton, Longman & Todd, London 1966.

Bovati — *Giustizia e ingiustizia nell'Antico Testamento*, duplicated, Pontificio Istituto Biblico, Roma 1996.

Deissler — DEISSLER Alphonse, *Le Livre des Psaumes*, I-II, Verbum Salutis, Beauchesne, Paris 1968.

ed. — edited by

Ed. — Editions

EDB — Edizioni Dehoniane Bologna

ex. — for example

f. — following

ff. — following

Gerstenberger — GERSTENBERGER Erhard S., *Psalms. Part I with an Introduction to Cultic Poetry. Part II and Lamentations*, The Forms of the Old Testament Literature 14-15, Eerdmans, Grand Rapids, MI 1988-2001.

Ibid. — *Ibidem*

Id. — Idem

Jacquet — JACQUET Louis, *Les Psaumes et le cœur de l'homme. Étude textuelle, littéraire et doctrinale*, Gembloux, Duculot, I-III, 1975-1979.

Joüon — JOÜON Paul, *Grammaire de l'hébreu biblique*, Institut Biblique Pontifical, Rome 1947.

Luc — MEYNET Roland, *L'Évangile de Luc*, Lethielleux, RhSem 1, Paris 2005.

MT Masoretic Text
n. note
Osty *La Bible*, Osty, Éd. du Seuil, Paris 1973.
p. page
pp. pages
PUG Pontificia Università Gregoriana (Pontifical Gregorian University)
Ravasi RAVASI, Gianfranco, *Il libro dei Salmi. Commento e attualizzazione*, Lettura pastorale della Bibbia 17-19, I-III, EDB, Bologna 1985.
StRh *Studia Rhetorica* (www.retoricabiblicaesemitica.org)
TOB Traduction œcuménique de la Bible
Trans. translation
Traité MEYNET Roland, *Traité de rhétorique biblique*, Lethielleux, RhSem 4, Paris 2007.

2 *Books of the Bible*

Abbreviations for books of the Bible are those used by *Biblica*.

3 *Commentaries*

References to commentaries give the name of the author followed by page number, e.g., Ravasi, III, 740.

4 *Abbreviations for journals and collections*

AJSL *American Journal of Semitic Languages and Literatures*
AnB Anchor Bible

AnBib Analecta biblica
Aug *Augustinianum*
Bib *Biblica*
BiTod *Bible today*
BN *Biblische Notizen*
CBQ *Catholic Biblical Quarterly*
CEv Cahiers Évangile
EstBib *Estudios Biblicos*
EThL *Ephemerides Theologicae Lovanienses*
Gr. *Gregorianum*
JBL *Journal of Biblical Literature*
JETS *Journal of the Evangelical Theological Society*
JNES *Journal of Near Eastern Studies*
JQR *Jewish Quarterly Review*
JSOT.S Journal for the Study of the Old Testament. Supplement series
JTC *Journal for Theology and the Church*
LeDiv Lectio Divina
MUSJ *Mélanges de l'Université Saint-Joseph*
NRTh *Nouvelle Revue Théologique*
OTWSA *Ou Testamentiese Werkgemeenskap in Suid-Afrika*
RB *Revue Biblique*
ReBib Retorica biblica
RevSR *Revue des sciences religieuses*
RhBib Rhétorique biblique
RhSem Rhétorique sémitique
RSR *Recherches de Science Religieuse*
RThL *Revue théologique de Louvain*
RTLu *Revue théologique de Lugano*
SC Sources chrétiennes
StRh *Studia Rhetorica*
VD *Verbum Domini*
VT *Vetus Testamentum*
WBC Word Biblical Commentary

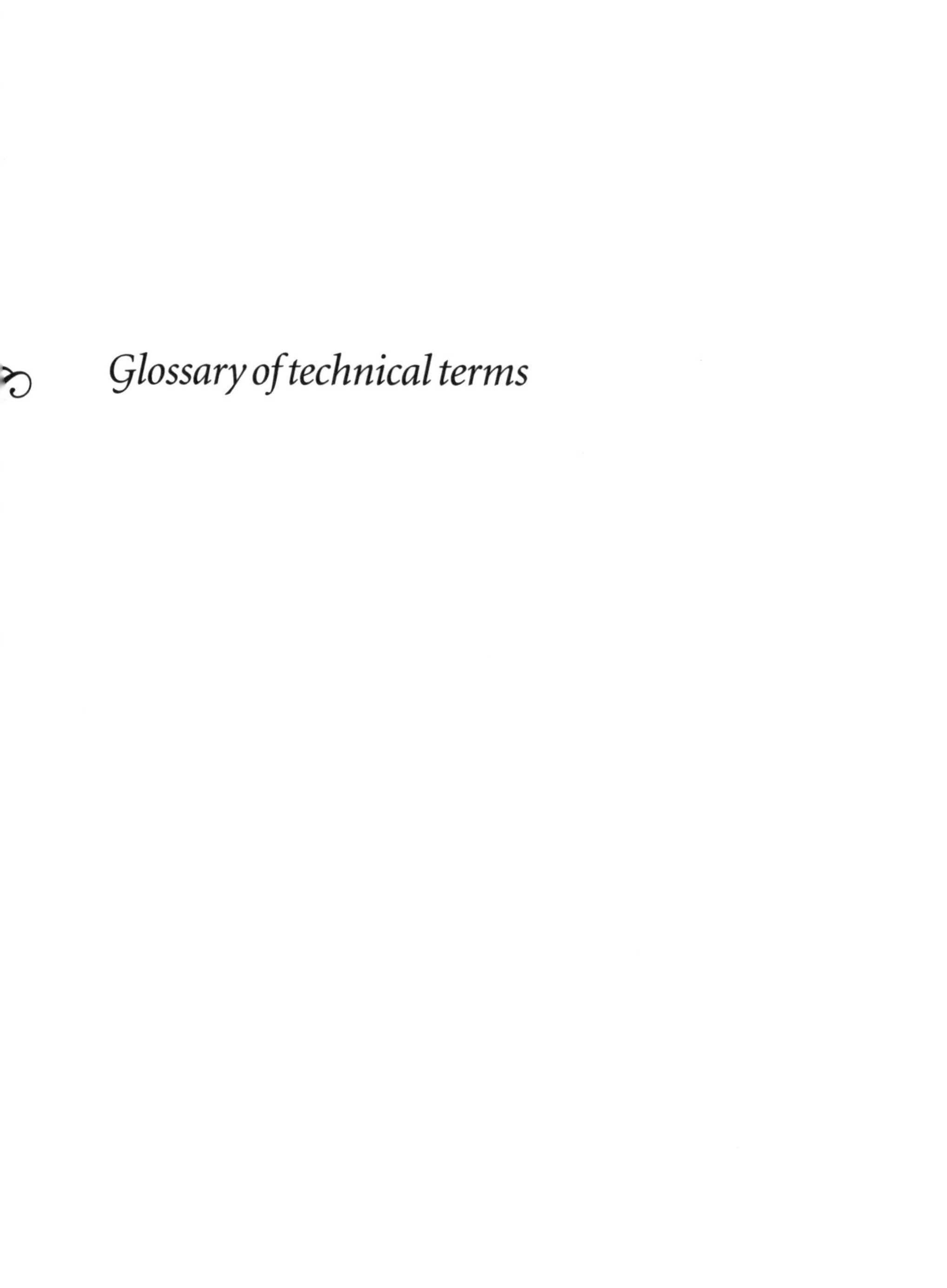

Glossary of technical terms

1

Terms signifying the rhetorical units

Very often, in works of exegesis, the terms «section», «passage» and, especially «piece» and «part» are used unequivocally. Here is a list of terms, which in the present methodological exposition, signify the textual units at each successive level.

THE «INFERIOR» (NON-AUTONOMOUS) LEVELS

Apart from the first and second (Term and Member), the units of inferior levels are formed of *one*, *two* or *three* units of the preceding level.

TERM the term usually corresponds to a lexeme, or word that belongs to the lexicon — noun, adjective, verb, adverb.

MEMBER the member is a syntagma, or group of «terms» linked closely together syntactically. The «member» is the minimal rhetorical unit. Sometimes the member can include only one term (the original Greek term is «stich»).

SEGMENT the segment counts one, two or three members, and there are unimember segments (the Greek terms is «monostich»), bimember segments (or «distichs») and trimember segments (or «tristichs»).

PIECE the piece counts one, two or three segments.

PART the part counts one, two or three pieces.

THE «SUPERIOR» (OR AUTONOMOUS) LEVELS

They are all formed of either *one* or *several* units from the previous level.

PASSAGE the passage — the equivalent of the exegetes' «pericope» — is formed of one or several parts.

SEQUENCE the sequence is formed of one or more passages.

SECTION the section is formed of one or more sequences.

BOOK finally, the book is formed of one or more sections. Sometimes it is necessary to use intermediary levels such as the «sub-part», «sub-sequence» and «sub-section»; these intermediary units have the same definition as the part, sequence and section.

SIDE the side is the part of text which precedes and/or follows the center of a construction; if the center is composed of two parts the side corresponds to each of the two halves of the construction.

2
Terms signifying the relations between symmetrical units

TOTAL SYMMETRIES

PARALLEL CONSTRUCTION figure of composition where the elements in paired relations are arranged in a parallel manner: A B C D E | A'B'C'D'E'.

When two parallel units frame a unique element, we talk about parallelism to indicate the symmetry between these two units but the whole (the superior unit) will be considered as a concentric construction: A | X | A'.

«Parallel construction» can also be described as «parallelism» (which is the opposite of «concentricism»).

CONCENTRIC CONSTRUCTION figure of composition where the symmetric units are arranged in a concentric manner: A B C D E | X | E'D'C'B'A', around a central element (which can be a unit of any level of textual organization).

«Concentric construction» can also be described as «concentrism» (which is opposite to «parallelism»).

MIRROR CONSTRUCTION figure of composition similar to concentric construction, but without the central element: A B C D E | E'D'C'B'A'.

When the construction only has four units, we also speak about «chiasmus»: A B | B'A'.

PARTIAL SYMMETRIES

INITIAL TERMS identical or similar terms or syntagmas which mark the beginning of symmetrical textual units; anaphora in classical rhetoric.

FINAL TERMS identical or similar terms or syntagmas which mark the end of symmetrical textual units; epiphora in classical rhetoric.

OUTER TERMS identical or similar terms or syntagmas which mark the outer parts of a textual unit; «inclusio» in traditional exegesis.

MEDIAN TERMS identical or similar terms or syntagmas which mark the end of a textual unit and the beginning of the unit which is symmetrical to it; «link word» in traditional exegesis.

CENTRAL TERMS identical or similar terms which mark the centers of two symmetrical textual units.

PRINCIPLE RULES FOR RE-WRITING

- within the member, terms are usually separated by spaces;
- each member is usually on a single line;
- segments are separated from one another by a blank line;
- pieces are separated by a broken line;
- parts, and sub-parts, are limited by two continuous lines.
- within the passage, the parts are framed (unless they are very short, for instance an introduction or conclusion); the sub-parts are arranged in adjoining frames;
- within the sequence or sub-sequence the passages, re-written in prose, are arranged in frames separated by a blank line;
- within the sequence, the passages of a sub-sequence are arranged in adjoining frames.

For details, see R. MEYNET, *Traité de rhétorique biblique*, Paris, Lethielleux, RhSem 4, 2007. See *Traité*, ch. 5, 283-344 on the rules for re-writing (on the re-writing of synoptic tables, see ch. 9, 471-506).

Part One

The gift of freedom

In Egypt, Jacob-Israel and his twelve sons had been welcomed with open arms by the Pharaoh, whose right-hand man Joseph, previously sold by his brothers, had become. Thus ends the book of Genesis. The next book begins by reporting that «Joseph died, and his brothers, and all that generation» (Exod 1:6), that the children of Israel had increased in numbers, and that «there came to power in Egypt a new king who knew nothing of Joseph» (Exod 1:8). Pharaoh, concerned by the increasing numbers of the people of the Hebrews, tried to curb this growth by any means — having failed to control births by killing male babies, he finally subjected the children of Israel to hard labor.

Moses, saved from the waters, and brought up by Pharaoh's daughter, had taken refuge in the country of Midian, having defended one of his Hebrew brothers and killed the Egyptian who was mistreating him; this had come to Pharaoh's attention, and he had decided to have Moses killed. After several years, the Lord, God of Abraham, Isaac and Jacob appeared to Moses in a burning bush and, having revealed his name, «Yhwh», to him, sent him back to Egypt with the mission of freeing his people and bringing them out of the land of Egypt.

«During this long period» of Moses' absence, «the children of Israel *groaning* in (the depths of) their slavery, *cried-out-for-help* and from the depths of their slavery their *cry* came up to God. God heard their *groaning*»[1] (Exod 2:23-24). This is the one and only time, prior to the crossing of the sea in ch. 14, when the narrator mentions the Israelites' cry. He does so using four terms, two verbs, «to groan» and «to cry», and two nouns, «cry-for-help» and «groaning» (or «sighing»). This last term will be repeated by God when he says he has heard their «groaning» (6:5). In 3:7.9 he uses a further word, «cry» (translated as «appeal» in v. 7 JB). All these terms share the fact that they describe vocal sounds which are not articulated in words. The people cry, they do not speak; they cry without addressing their cry to anyone; these are simply sighs and groans, like the cries of animals, for only human beings are capable of speech. This suggests that as long as they are not free, neither will their speech be free. The sign that they will have been freed is that they will acquire the gift of speech.

We have to wait until ch. 14 which comes after the long account of the ten plagues on Egypt, before we hear the first words spoken by the children of

1 Osty prefers the translation «sighs».

Israel[2], at which point, seeing themselves trapped between the sea and Pharaoh's army, «they cried out to Yhwh» (Exod 14:10). This is most significant, as it is the first time that their cries have been addressed to anyone. But the narrator does not report any of their words, if indeed any were spoken. Immediately afterwards, however, comes a flurry of infuriated, rebellious questions addressed to Moses; and it happens that these questions, along with Moses' response, take central place in the account of the Crossing of the Sea (Exod 15:11). It is likely that they were unable to speak even words of rebellion until they had left the land of Egypt.

However, we still have to wait until they have crossed the sea, leaving their former masters «dead on the shore» behind them for a song to resound in the mouths of Moses and the children of Israel in which they celebrate their freedom (Exod 15:1-5) and which ends with them managing to address their liberator — «Your right hand, Yhwh, shows majestic in power, your right hand, Yhwh, shatters the enemy» (15:6). Right in the middle of their song resounds a question, the counterpart of those which they addressed to Moses while complaining in the center of the Crossing of the Sea:

> Who is like you
> among the gods, Yhwh?
>
> Who is like you,
> shining of holiness,
> terrible in praises,
> maker of miracles? (Exod 15:11).

The account of the Crossing of the Sea in Exod 14 and the Song of the Sea which follows it in Exod 15 form a kind of diptych. It is impossible to read one without the other; this would be like reading the accounts of Jesus' Resurrection without having read those of his Passion first. We need to have crossed the sea with the children of Israel to be able to sing their song of exultation and gratitude with them.

2 Apart from the words of Moses and of Aaron his brother, the only words spoken by an Israelite are those of Moses' sister, who offers to find a nurse for the baby whom Pharaoh's daughter has found among the reeds on the banks of the Nile (2:7), and those of the man who struck another Hebrew — «And who appointed you to be prince over us, and judge? Do you intend to kill me as you killed the Egyptian?» (2:14).

Chapter 1

The crossing of the sea

Exod 14

An earlier version of this chapter was published as «Le passage de la mer (Exod 14). Analyse rhétorique» in *RTLu* 9 (2004) 569-590, in which only the text's composition was analyzed.

Exod 14

1 *And Yhwh spoke to Moses saying:* 2 *«Speak to the sons of Israel to turn back and*
camp before Pi-Hahiroth between Migdol and between the sea; before Baal-Zephon
in front of it you shall camp by the sea. 3 *And Pharaoh will say of the sons of Israel:*
"They are entangled in the land; the desert enclosed upon them!" 4 *And I will*
harden the heart of Pharaoh and he will pursue after them and I will glorify myself
against Pharaoh and against all his army and the Egyptians have to know that I
am Yhwh». And they did so. 5 *And it was told to the king of Egypt that the people*
had fled; and the heart of Pharaoh and his servants turned against the people. And
they said: «What is this we have done, that we have let Israel go from serving us?».
6 *And he harnessed his chariot and he took his people with him;* 7 *and he took six*
hundred best chariots and all the chariots of Egypt, with a third-man[1] *on each of*
them. 8 *And Yhwh hardened the heart of Pharaoh king of Egypt and he pursued*
after the sons of Israel; and the sons of Israel were marching out with bold hand 9 *and*
the Egyptians pursued after them. And they overtook them camping by the sea all
horses of Pharaoh's chariots and his horsemen and his army near Pi-Hahiroth be-
fore Baal-Zephon; 10 *and Pharaoh drew near. And the sons of Israel lighted up the*
eyes and behold Egypt was marching after them; and they feared greatly and the
sons of Israel cried out to Yhwh. 11 *And they said to Moses: «Is it because there were*
no graves in Egypt that you have taken us to die in the desert? What is this you have
done to us that you have brought us out of Egypt? 12 *Is it not this word that we have*
told you in Egypt saying: "Leave-us alone that we may serve Egypt, because it is
better for us to serve Egypt than to die in the desert"?» 13 *And Moses said to the*
people: «Do not be afraid, stand still and see the salvation of Yhwh which he will do
for you today, because the Egyptians whom you see today you will never see them
again. 14 *Yhwh will fight for you, and you, you have to keep still».* 15 *And Yhwh*
said to Moses: «Why are you crying out to me? Speak to the sons of Israel to march on!
16 *And you, lift your staff and stretch out your hands over the sea and divide it; and*
that the sons of Israel may come into the midst of the sea on dry land! 17 *And I, be-*
hold I will harden the heart of the Egyptians and they will come after them; and I
will glorify myself against Pharaoh and all his army, against his chariots and against

1 According to Tournay («Recherches»,342), the *šālîš* (or «third» occupant of the chariot, in addition to the driver and the shield-bearer) was an officer of a certain rank, often a noble whose role was to fight. It is often translated as «officer» or «captain».

*his horsemen. 18 And the Egyptians have to know that I am Yhwh, when I glorify
myself against Pharaoh, against his chariots and against his horsemen». 19 And
the angel of Elohim who went before the camp of Israel marched on and moved behind them; and the pillar of cloud marched on before them and stood behind them.
20 And it came between the camp of the Egyptians and between the camp of Israel.
And it was cloud and darkness and it enlightened the night; and no one approached
the other all the night. 21 And Moses stretched out his hand over the sea and Yhwh
made the sea moved by a strong wind of east all the night; and he turned the sea
into dry land and the waters were divided. 22 And the sons of Israel came into the
midst of the sea on dry land and the waters were to them a rampart on their right
and on their left; 23 and the Egyptians pursued and came after them all the horses
of Pharaoh, his chariots and his horsemen into the midst of the sea. 24 And it was
at the morning watch Yhwh looked down to the camp of the Egyptians through the
pillar of fire and of cloud and he threw confusion in the camp of the Egyptians; 25 and
he clogged the wheels of their chariots and they drove them with difficulty. And the
Egyptians said: «Let us flee from the face of Israel, because Yhwh fights for them
against Egypt». 26 And Yhwh said to Moses: «Stretch out your hand over the sea
and that the waters may turn back over the Egyptians over their chariots and over
their horsemen». 27 And Moses stretched out his hand over the sea; and the sea
turned back to its course at daybreak and the Egyptians marched toward its coming; and Yhwh shook off the Egyptians into the midst of the sea. 28 And the waters
turned back and covered the chariots and the horsemen and all the army of Pharaoh
who were coming in after them into the sea. And there was no left of them even one.
29 And the sons of Israel have gone on dry land into the midst of the sea and the waters were to them a rampart on their right and on their left. 30 And Yhwh saved
in that day Israel from the hand of the Egyptians; and Israel saw the Egyptians
dead on the seashore 31 and Israel saw the great arm which Yhwh did against the
Egyptians; and the people feared Yhwh and they believed in Yhwh and in Moses his
servant.*

It is not unheard of, in introductions to the critical study of the Bible, for the crossing of the sea in Exodus 14 to be used as a clear and simple example to illustrate the documentary theory[2]. Examining the tensions in the account, considered to be incoherent or even contradictory, the noting of repetitions considered to be doublets, the variety of divine names used, allows the current text to be disentangled. In this way we can distinguish two very different texts, one Yahwist, the other Priestly, at the root of the final narrative, to which we must add snatches from a third tradition, that of the Elohist.

Leaving the redaction history to one side, many people have sought to study the final text to detect its composition and coherence[3]. There is no room here to offer a systematic critique of these analyses; I aim merely to re-examine the text in a different way through the application of the now well-known and rigorous process of biblical rhetorical analysis[4].

Exodus 14 forms a unit whose limits are agreed by most scholars. The end of the previous chapter recounts how the children of Israel leave freely for the desert, guided by the pillar of cloud. Chapter 14 begins with a sudden about-turn — the Lord gives Moses a counter-command, Moses makes the people turn back, which leads to the pursuit by the Egyptian armies and finally leads to the salvation of the children of Israel and the destruction of their enemies, just as if it had been necessary for the liberation of the people to be accompanied by the humiliation of those who had reduced them to slavery, and who, right up to the end, had refused to let their servants leave; as if the coming to freedom of the people of Israel could not confront and pass over death. Chapter 15 begins with the long song of victory by Moses and the children of Israel, after they had crossed the see and seen their enemies dead on the shore (Exod 15:1-8). Furthermore, the regularity of the text's internal composition, and its coherence, are almost certainly major criteria for its unity, and thus its limits.

A. FIRST HYPOTHESIS

A systematic listing of those words, and particularly those expressions, which are used more than once led us to an initial hypothesis — vv 1-10 and 15-31 could form two parallel units, despite a notable difference in length.

2 For example, CHARPENTIER É., *Pour lire l'Ancien Testament*, 28-28; WIENNER C., *Le livre de l'Exode*, 22-25; SKA J.-L., *Introduction à la lecture du Pentateuque*, 101-111, 113-114.

3 GALBIATI E., *La struttura letteraria dell'Esodo*, 158-160; AUFFRET P., «Essai sur la structure littéraire d'Ex 14»; SKA J.-L., *Le Passage de la mer*. See too VERVENNE M., «The Sea Narrative Revisited».

4 See R. MEYNET, *Traité de rhétorique biblique*.

• *Initial terms:* one sentence within the account introduces an address by God (1a and 15a)[5]; both use the same order («Speak to the sons of Israel»), followed by another, very similar, order («to turn back»; «to march on»). A little later, v. 4 and vv. 17-18 are almost identical.

• *Central terms:* the only two phrases spoken by the Egyptians are found at the center of each passage (5cd and 25bc)[6].

• *Final terms:* what the children of Israel «see» is reported at the end of these passages (30c.31a); «they raised [lighted up] their eyes» (10b) is another way of saying the same thing. What they see leads to «fear» (10c.31b). The «cry» sent «to the Lord» at the start is replaced by «faith» in «the Lord and in Moses» at the end:

And they feared	greatly	and **cried out** the sons of Israel to Yhwh.
And feared	the people to Yhwh	and **they believed** in Yhwh and in Moses his servant.

• *Median terms:* the first passage ends with the children of Israel's «cry» (10e: «and the sons of Israel *cried out* to Yhwh»), and the final passage begins with a question to the Lord, related to this cry (15b: «Why *are you crying out* to me?»)

Just as in the Hebrew, the letter «p» at the end of 25 and 31 indicates the end of the second and third *parashâ*, or units for reading established by the Masoretes. The first ends at v. 14, before the start of the second passage we are examining. The Masoretic division of the text, adopted by Jean-Louis Ska, follows the scansion marked by the Lord's three interventions, introduced using the narrative phrases, «And Yhwh spoke to Moses saying» (1a), «And Yhwh said to Moses» (15a.26a). These three phrases undeniably play a role in the composition of the chapter. The problem, which always arises when faced with repetitions, particularly obvious ones, is to establish at what level of the text's organization they are operating. For Jean-Louis Ska, they are operating at the same level, as they indicate the start of three stages of the narrative. I personally think that the first two (1a.15a) operate at the level of the sequence, indicating the start of its outer passages, and that the latter two (15a.26a), which we noted were identical, operate within the final passage (15-31), where they indicate the start of its outer parts (15-25; 26-31), because they introduce the order given to Moses to stretch out his hand over the sea (16a.26ab), which was not the case at the start of the

5 The letters which follow the verse numbers refer to lines of the tables.

6 To describe the Egyptians' only words as «central terms» is merely hypothetical at the moment; it will be verified below.

[1] **And Yhwh spoke to Moses saying:**

[2] «**Speak to the sons of Israel** *to turn back*
and camp before Pi-Hahiroth between Migdol and the see; before Baal-Zephon in front of it you shall encamp by the sea. [3] And Pharaoh will say of the sons of Israel: "They are entangled in the land, the desert enclosed upon them!"

[4] And
I will harden the heart of Pharaoh
and they will pursue after them
and I will glorify myself
against Pharaoh and against all his army

AND THE EGYPTIANS HAVE TO KNOW
THAT I AM YHWH».

And they did so [5] and it was told to the king of Egypt that the people had fled. And the heart of Pharaoh and his SERVANTS turned against the people.

And they said: «What is this we have done that we have let **Israel** go from **SERVING** us?»

---

[6] And he harnessed his chariots and he took his people with him [7] and he took six hundred best chariots and all the chariots of Egypt, and a third-man on each of them. [8] And Yhwh hardened the heart of Pharaoh king of Egypt and he pursued after the sons of Israel and the sons of Israel were marching out with bold hand [9] and the Egyptians pursued after them and overtook them camping by the sea *all horses of Pharaoh's chariots and his horsemen and his army* near Pi-Hahiroth before Baal-Zephon; [10] and Pharaoh drew near.

And **the sons of Israel** ***LIFTED UP THEIR EYES***
and behold ***Egypt*** was marching after them.

AND THEY FEARED greatly
and **the sons of Israel** ***cried out*** to YHWH.

[15] **And Yhwh said to Moses**:
«Why are ***you crying out*** to me?
Speak to the sons of Israel *to march on*
[16] And you, lift up your staff and stretch out your hand over the sea and divide it and that the sons of Israel may come into the midst of the sea on dry land.

[17] **And I behold**
I will harden the heart of the Egyptians
and they will come after them
and I will glorify myself
against Pharaoh and all his army,
against his chariots and against his horsemen.
[18] AND THE EGYPTIANS HAVE TO KNOW
THAT I AM YHWH
when I glorify myself against Pharaoh,
against his chariots and against his horsemen».

---

[19] And the angel of God who went before the camp of Israel marched on and moved behind them and the pillar of cloud marched on before them and stood behind them. [20] And it came between the camp of the Egyptians and between the camp of Israel. And it was cloud and darkness and it enlightened the night and no one approached the other all the night. [21] And Moses stretched out his hand over the sea and Yhwh made the sea moved by a strong wind of east all the night and it turned the sea into dry land and the waters were divided. [22] And the sons of Israel came into the midst of the sea on dry land and the waters were to them a rampart on their right and on their left. [23] And the Egyptians pursued and came after them all the horses of Pharaoh, his chariots and his horsemen into the midst of the sea. [24] And it was at the morning watch Yhwh look down to the camp of the Egyptians through the pillar of fire and of cloud and he confused the camp of the Egyptians [25] and he clogged the wheel of their chariots and they drove them with difficulty.

And Egypt said: «Let us flee before **Israel**, because Yhwh fights for them against Egypt».

---

[26] **And Yhwh said to Moses**: «Stretch out your hand over the sea that the waters may return *over the Egyptians and over their chariots and over their horsemen.*»
[27] And Moses stretched out his hand over the sea and the sea turned back to its course at daybreak. And the Egyptians marched toward its coming and Yhwh shook off the Egyptians into the midst of the sea
[28] And the waters came back and cover *the chariots and the horsemen and all the army of Pharaoh* who came after them into the sea and there was no left even one. [29] And the sons of Israel have gone on dry land into the midst of the sea and the waters were to them a rampart on their right and on their left [30] And Yhwh saved in that day Israel from the hand of the Egyptians.

And **Israel** ***SAW the Egyptians*** dead on the seashore
[31] and **Israel** ***SAW*** the great arm by which Yhwh do against ***the Egyptians***.

AND THEY FEARED **the people** to YHWH
and they believed in YHWH and in Moses his **SERVANT**.

chapter. So we see that the same occurrence, here of the narrative phrase of 15a, can have two different functions at two different levels — at 1a at the level of the sequence (1-31), and at 26a the level of the final passage (15-31).

Clearly the coherence of the final unit and the regularity of its composition allow us to confirm what we have just suggested. My hypothesis will be that the two units under examination are the size of a passage.

B. THE FIRST PASSAGE (1-10)

COMPOSITION

This passage is made up of three parts, organized concentrically.

The first part (1-4)

+ [1] And spoke YHWH to *Moses* saying:

: [2] «Speak	to **the sons of Israel**	and that they turn back	
. *and that they camp*	before Pi-Hahiroth,	between Migdol	and the sea;
.	before Baal-Zephon	in front of it *you shall camp*	by the sea.
[3] And *Pharaoh* will say of **the sons of Israel:**		"Entangled they are in the land;	
		enclosed on them the desert!"	
. [4] And I will harden	the heart of *Pharaoh*	and he will pursue after them	
. and I will glorify myself against	*Pharaoh*	and against all his army	
: and shall know	**the Egyptians**	that I am YHWH.»	

+ And they did so.

The first part is made up of three sub-parts. The outer sub-parts, both of which are narrative, only have one unimember segment. In the last one (4d) the children of Israel «do» what the Lord «talked about» in the first (1). The central part (2-4c), which is discourse, is made up of three pieces. The first and the last (2 and 4abc) each have three bimembers which are arranged in mirror formation. The first says what «the sons of Israel» are to do, and the other what the Lord will do to «the Egyptians». The central piece, (3), an ABB trimember, which reports the words of the Egyptians in advance, provides the movement from the first piece to the third.

The second part (5-7)

The second part is shorter, and made up of three pieces. The first (5ab) reports the change which has come into Pharaoh's heart, and the last piece reports his acts (6-7). In the center (5cde) are the Egyptians' words, with a question in the center, in which they express their regret at having let their slaves go. «People» is repeated at the end of the two segments of the first piece (5a.5b), and in the second member of the last piece (6); but while it refers to the people of Israel at the start, it refers to the Egyptians at the end. «Egypt» is twice repeated, in the outer parts (5a.7); «servants» in 5b heralds «serving us» in the center (5e)[7]. The second member of the last piece (the end of 6) recalls the second members of the segments of the first piece (end of 5a and 5b).

: 5 And it was told	to the king	**of Egypt**		that had fled	**the people**;
: and was changed	the heart	of Pharaoh	and his SERVANTS	against	**the people**.

And they said: «What is this we have done,
that we have sent away Israel from SERVING us?»

: 6 And he harnessed his chariot	and **his people** he took with him;
: 7 and he took six hundred best chariots, and all the chariots of **Egypt**,	and a third-man on each of them.

The third part (8-10)

This part is made up of three pieces, which correspond to three time-frames — Pharaoh pursues the children of Israel (8-9), and catches up with them (9-10a), which leads to their cries when they notice. The second members of the two segments of the first piece are very similar — the first names what is being pursued, and the second the pursuer. The last piece (10bc) also has two bimembers — the first reports the children of Israel's awareness of what is happening to them (10b) and then their reaction (10c). At the center (9b-10a) is a piece constructed of a long trimember and a very short and rather abrupt unimember (10a). The outer verbs of the central piece, «overtook» and «drew near», belong to the same semantic field.

7 To be more precise, the first piece is made up of a bimember (5a) and a unimember (5b); the last piece is made up of a bimember (6) and a trimember (7).

The two occurrences of «Yhwh» make an inclusio (8a.10c). We might say that «pursue» and «drew near» fix the two first pieces together, because these two verbs are consecutive (see, for example, Exod 15:9; Deut 19:6; Josh 2:5).

.[8] And YHWH hardened the heart of Pharaoh king of *EGYPT* — and he pursued after THE SONS OF ISRAEL;
. and THE SONS OF ISRAEL were going out with a high hand — [9] and the *EGYPTIANS* pursued after them.

: And they overtook them camping by the sea
- all the horses of Pharaoh's chariots and his horsemen and his army
: near Pi-Hahiroth before Baal-Zephon;

= [10] and Pharaoh drew near.

. And THE SONS OF ISRAEL lifted up the eyes — and behold *EGYPT* was marching after them;
. and they feared greatly — and cried out THE SONS OF ISRAEL to YHWH.

The first passage as a whole (1-10)

The three parts which we have analyzed up to now form a single passage (1-10). The first part includes the Lord's address to Moses and, very briefly at the end, the mention of the orders received being carried out (4d). The second part (5-7) reports the Egyptians' reaction and their army being mobilized. The subject of this part is therefore at the center of the passage, the only subject of the passage as a whole. In the third part (8-10) we see the promise the Lord had made in the first part being fulfilled — the Egyptians pursue and overtake the children of Israel on the seashore; the part — and, therefore, the passage — ends with the children of Israel's agony as they cry out to the Lord (10bc).

The relationship between the outer parts is marked by a number of connections:

- «Yhwh's» initiative is indicated at the very start of both parts: «And Yhwh spoke» (1a), «And Yhwh hardened» (8a);
- Yhwh's promise, «And I will harden Pharaoh's heart» (4a), at the start of the second section of the first part, is carried out at the start of the third (8a);
- «that they camp before Pi-Hahiroth ... before Baal-Zephon, in front of it you shall camp by the sea», at the start of the Lord's address (2) is repeated in the middle of the last passage as «camping by the sea ... near Pi-Hahirtoh before Baal-Zephon» (9b.9d);
- the announcement that «he will pursue them» (4a) becomes fact in 8.9a.10b.
- the name of «Yhwh» is repeated at the outer parts of both parts (1a.4c; 8a.10c).

+ [1] And YHWH spoke to Moses saying:

: [2] «Speak to ***the sons of Israel*** and that they turn back
. AND THAT THEY CAMP **before Pi-Hahiroth** between Migdol and the sea;
. **before Baal-Zephon** in front of it YOU SHALL CAMP BY THE SEA.

[3] And Pharaoh will say of ***the sons of Israel***: "They are entangled in the land;
the desert enclosed upon them!"

. [4] And I will harden **the heart of Pharaoh** *AND HE WILL PURSUE* ***AFTER*** *THEM*
. and I will glorify myself against Pharaoh and against all his army
: and **the Egyptians** shall know that I am YHWH».

+ And they did so.

: [5] And it was told to the king **of Egypt** that the people had fled;
: and was changed **the heart of Pharaoh** and his servants against the people.

And they said: «What is this we have done,
that we have sent away ***Israel*** from serving us?»

: [6] And he harnessed his CHARIOT and he took his people with him;
: [7] And he took six hundred best CHARIOTS, all the CHARIOTS **of Egypt** and a third-man on each of them.

. [8] And YHWH hardened **the heart of Pharaoh** king **of Egypt** *AND HE PURSUED* ***AFTER the sons of Israel***;
. and ***the sons of Israel*** were going out with a high hand [9] *AND* **the Egyptians** *PURSUED* ***AFTER*** *THEM.*

: And they overtook them, (while they were) CAMPING BY THE SEA,
- all the horses of Pharaoh's CHARIOTS and his horsemen and his army
: **near Pi-Hahiroth before Baal-Zephon**;

= [10] and Pharaoh drew near.

. And ***the sons of Israel*** lifted up the eyes and behold **Egypt** *WAS MARCHING ON* ***AFTER*** *THEM;*
. and they feared greatly and ***the sons of Israel*** cried out to YHWH.

The central part is marked by the fact that the name of «Yhwh» only appears once, and also by the fact that those who are called «the sons of Israel» in the other two parts (2a.3a; 8a.8b.10b.10c) are called «the people» at the start of the central part (5a.5b) and «Israel» in the center (5e). «Pharaoh's heart» is «changed» in the center (5b), and «hardened» in the outer parts (4a, 8a).

INTERPRETATION

The Egyptians' change of heart

The whole account hinges on the question the Egyptians ask themselves at the center of the passage—«What is this we have done, that we have let Israel go from serving us?» The master regrets having freed the slave. The tenth plague, the striking down of the first-born, had driven them to letting the Israelites go.

They had even gone as far as urging them to go, and had chased them out (Exod 12:31-33). Now those who are fleeing are to be caught and put back on the right path of «service», that is serving, which also marks Pharaoh's people, who are described as «his servants» (5b).

«The heart of Pharaoh turned»

The central part begins, unusually, with two passive verbs — «It was told to the king of Egypt» (5a) and «the heart of Pharaoh [was] turned» (5b). The children of Israel's leaving is presented to the king of Egypt as a «flight», although things did not happen like that. Someone, therefore, has chosen to describe events with the very particular aim of making the king of Egypt change his mind, «turn his heart». Having heard the words the Lord spoke to Moses in the first part, the reader understands that it is God himself who has intervened to lead to Pharaoh's change of mind. The maneuver he ordains aims to lead the king of Egypt to express himself in the words the Lord gives to him at the heart of the piece itself (3). In this way, the events narrated in the second part happen exactly according to the plan outlined in the first — it is God who is in charge of the game.

The trap closes

Pharaoh had finally agreed to free his slaves (center of the passage, 5c, d), even though their leader had to force this decision during a long battle. Just as God had planned, the Egyptians think that the fleeing Israelites have been driven back into the desert which has closed around them (center of the first part), and so think that they, too, will be able to «close» their hands around the children of Israel, who will be unable to resist the cavalry and chariots of the army of a power is far greater than their strength. When, in the center of the last part, Pharaoh's army, at full strength, «overtakes» its prey (9b) and Pharaoh in person «draws near» (10a), the hunt reaches its end. The children of Israel, caught by surprise, are paralyzed by fear — although not to the extent of being speechless: they still have the reflex to turn to their God. Who knows if he will release them from the snare of the fowler? (Ps 91:3; 124:7-8).

c. THE LAST PASSAGE (15-31)

COMPOSITION

The third and last passage is the longest. It is made up of four parallel parts framing a fifth, very brief, part.

Yhwh orders Moses to stretch out his hand to *divide* the sea	15-18
Israel crosses the sea dry-shod	19-25a
The Egyptians' cry	25b
Yhwh orders Moses to stretch out his hand to *turn back* the sea	26
Egypt is swallowed up by the sea	27-31

The first part (15-18)

15 And said	YHWH	to Moses:	
: «Why are you-crying-out	to me?		
:: Speak	***to the sons-***	***of Israel***	and *that they may go on*!
– 16 **And you,**	lift up	your staff	
– and stretch out	your hand	over *the sea* and divide-it;	
:: and *that may go*	***the sons-***	***of Israel***	
: into the midst of	*the sea*	on dry land!	
+ 17 **And I, behold**	I will harden	the heart	**of the Egyptians**
+ and they will come	after them;		
= and I WILL GLORIFY MYSELF	*AGAINST PHARAOH*		and all his army,
= *AGAINST HIS CHARIOTS*	*AND AGAINST HIS HORSEMEN.*		
+ 18 And	shall know		**the Egyptians**
+ that I (am)	**YHWH,**		
= when I WILL GLORIFY MYSELF	*AGAINST PHARAOH,*		
= *AGAINST HIS CHARIOTS*	*AND AGAINST HIS HORSEMEN.*»		

In addition to the introductory account, the first part has two other sub-parts. The three bimember segments of the second part (15b-16) seem to be arranged concentrically. The central segment (16ab), which says what Moses is to do to make the sea open up, is preceded by the calling of the people (15bc), and followed by what they are then to do (16cd). 15c and 16c are very closely linked.

The last sub-part (17-18) is made up of two parallel pieces. In the first segments, the Lord says what he will do to the Egyptians (17ab), and then what their reaction to him will be (18ab). The second segments (17cd; 18cd) are almost identical.

The first sub-part announces what Moses and the people have to do, and the second what the Egyptians will do. The name of «Yhwh» returns at the start (15a) and almost at the end (18b).

The second part (19-25a)

This part is made up of three sub-parts (19-20; 21-23; 24-25). The first sub-part reports the angel of the Lord's intervention, separating the two battle camps; the second recounts how Moses and the Lord opened up the sea (21) to allow the children of Israel to cross it (22), followed immediately by the Egyptians (23);

:: 19 And *marched on*	the angel	OF ELOHIM	who went	*before*	**THE CAMP** OF ISRAEL
.			and *he moved*	**behind**	them;
:: and *marched on*	THE PILLAR	OF CLOUD	*from*	*before*	them
.			and it stood	**behind**	them.
20 **And it came**	between	**THE CAMP** *OF THE EGYPTIANS*	and	between	**THE CAMP** OF ISRAEL.
:: And it was	CLOUD	and darkness	and it enlightened		***the night***
:: and not approached	one	to the other		***all***	***the night***.
+ 21 And stretched		Moses	his hand out		over *the sea*
+ and *made*	*to move*	YHWH	*the sea*		
– by a wind		of east	strong	***all***	***the night;***
+ and it turned			*the sea*		into dry land
– and *THE WATERS*	were divided .				
+ 22 **And came**	THE SONS OF ISRAEL		*into the midst of the sea*		on dry land
- and *THE WATERS*	to them	a rampart	on their right		and on their left;
+ 23 and pursued	*THE EGYPTIANS*		**and they came**		**behind** them
- all the horses	of Pharaoh,	his chariots	and his horsemen		*in the midst of the sea.*
:: 24 And it was				at	the morning watch;
.. and looked down		YHWH			**THE CAMP** *OF THE EGYPTIANS*
.. THROUGH THE PILLAR		of fire	and OF CLOUD		
.. and he confused					**THE CAMP** *OF THE EGYPTIANS*;
= 25 and he clogged		the wheels	of their chariots		
= and they let them proceed		with difficulty.			

finally, the third part reports the Lord's intervention sowing confusion in Egypt's camp.

The first sub-part (19-20) is made up of three pieces. The first is made up of two segments, a trimember and a bimember segment, parallel to one another. Their initial and final terms are identical — «the pillar of cloud» is parallel to and identified with «the angel of Elohim». The third piece (20bc) is made up of two segments, a bimember and a unimember segment, which both finish with the word «night»[8]. The central piece (20a) has a single segment, whose two members parallel one another; so the separation between the two camps is expressed at the center.

8 20b raises a problem — the «pillar of cloud» mentioned in 19c becomes both «cloud and darkness» (which could be understood as a hendiadys and translated as «dark cloud»), a darkness which «enlightens the night». The traditional interpretation is that the same cloud is light for the Israelites and darkness for the Egyptians (see J.-L. SKA, *Le Passage de la mer*, 17-18; 102-103).

The second sub-part (21-23) is made up of two pieces. The two segments of the first piece, a trimember and a bimember segment, describe the joint work of Moses and God (21abc) followed by its result (21de). The second piece is made up of two bimembers, the first of which (22) reports what the children of Israel do, and the second of which (23) reports what the Egyptians do immediately afterwards. Here we note that the second members match, «the waters» defending the children of Israel against Pharaoh's armies «like a rampart»[9]. Both occurrences of «the waters» (21e and 22b) play the part of median terms.

The third sub-part (24-25) is made up of three segments — a unimember segment, which gives the time (24a), followed by a trimember aba' segment, whose outer members end identically. The third segment (25ab) is a bimember segment which explains the last member of the previous segment.

:: 19 And *marched on*	the angel	OF ELOHIM	who went	*before*	**THE CAMP** OF ISRAEL
.			and *he moved*	**behind**	them;
:: and *marched on*	THE PILLAR	OF CLOUD	*from*	*before*	them
.			and it stood	**behind**	them.
20 **And it came**	between	**THE CAMP** *OF THE EGYPTIANS*	and	between	**THE CAMP** OF ISRAEL.
:: And it was	CLOUD	and darkness	and it enlightened		***the night***
:: and not approached	one	to the other		*all*	***the night.***
+ 21 And stretched		Moses	his hand out		over *the sea*
+ and *made*	*to move*	YHWH	*the sea*		
– by a wind		of east	strong	*all*	***the night;***
+ and it turned			*the sea*		into dry land
– and *THE WATERS*	were divided .				
+ 22 **And came**	THE SONS OF ISRAEL		*into the midst of the sea*		on dry land
- and *THE WATERS*	to them	a rampart	on their right		and on their left;
+ 23 and pursued	*THE EGYPTIANS*		**and they came**		**behind** them
- all the horses	of Pharaoh,	his chariots	and his horsemen		*in the midst of the sea.*
:: 24 And it was				at	the morning watch;
.. and looked down		YHWH			**THE CAMP** *OF THE EGYPTIANS*
.. THROUGH THE PILLAR		of fire	and OF CLOUD		
.. and he confused					**THE CAMP** *OF THE EGYPTIANS*;
= 25 and he clogged		the wheels	of their chariots		
= and they let them proceed		with difficulty.			

9 This double «rampart» is often imagined to be solid, like a wall of water (from which the fish would watch people go past); the image refers to the image of the Lord protecting his people — «The Lord is the fortress of my life, of whom should I be afraid?» (Ps 27:1 and context; 31:4; 71:3, etc).

The outer sub-parts match, with the repetition of the «pillar of fire/cloud» (19c, matched by 20b.24c), and the three occurrences of «the camp of the Egyptians» (20a.24bd), opposed by the two occurrences of the «camp of Israel» (19a.20a). «At the morning watch», at the start of the last sub-part (24a) is opposed by «all the night», at the end of the first sub-part (20c), which takes on the role of median terms at a distance.

«All the night», at the end of the first sub-part (20c) is repeated in the first of the two pieces of the central sub-part (21c), so, like the first one, this piece goes through «all the night», which suggests that the second piece (22-23) takes place, like the last sub-part, «at the morning watch».

The third part (25b)

+ And said the Egyptians:

: «**Let us flee**	from the face of		ISRAEL,
: because Yhwh	**fights**	for them	against- *EGYPT*».

This part is very short, since it is made up of a single piece, a narrative unimember and a bimember of speech.

The fourth part (26)

+ [26] and said Yhwh to Moses:

– «Stretch out	your hand	**over** the sea
:: and may come back	the waters	**over** the Egyptians
:: **over** their chariots	and **over** their horsemen».	

This part is the length of a piece — a narrative unimember is followed by an abb' trimember of a speech.

The fifth part (27-31)

This final part is made up of three sub-parts. The first (27) reports what Moses and Yhwh do; the second (28-29), how the Egyptians are lost while the children of Israel are saved; and the third (30-31) Israel's reaction to what Yhwh has done for them.

: 27 And stretched out	MOSES	HIS HAND	over *THE SEA*;
= *and came back*	*THE SEA*	at turning of the morning	to its course
= and *THE EGYPTIANS*	fled ahead	toward its coming;	
: and shook off	**YHWH**	*THE EGYPTIANS*	in the midst *THE SEA*.
- 28 *And came back*	***the waters***		
- and covered	the chariots	and the horsemen	and all the army of Pharaoh
. **who were coming in**	after them		into *THE SEA*.
AND THERE WAS LEFT	NONE OF THEM EVEN ONE.		
. 29 And THE SONS OF ISRAEL	**have gone**	on dry land	in the midst of *THE SEA*
- and ***the waters*** (were)	to *them* a rampart	on their right	and on their left.

+ 30 And saved	**YHWH**	in that day	ISRAEL from the HAND		*OF THE EGYPTIANS*;
. and saw	ISRAEL	*THE EGYPTIANS*	dead on the shore		of *THE SEA*
. 31 and saw	ISRAEL	THE HAND	great which did	**YHWH**	*AGAINST THE EGYPTIANS*;
+ and feared	THE PEOPLE	to **YHWH**	and they believed in	**YHWH**	and in MOSES his servant.

The first sub-part (27) is the size of a piece. The outer segments are unimembers (27a.27d) with the same syntactical structure, one reporting what Moses does, and the other what Yhwh does. In the center (27bc), is a bimember which shows the two «partners», the sea and the Egyptians, moving towards one another.

The second sub-part (28-29) is also the size of a piece. It is made up of a trimember and a bimember framing a unimember (28d). The initial trimember and the final bimember are mirrored — at the outside, the Egyptians are submerged by «the waters» (28ab), which protect the children of Israel (29b); 28c and 29a both talk of movement (note the movement verbs translated by «come» and «go»). Finally, at the center (28d) a brief unimember tells of the death of all the enemies. The entire part is focused on this segment.

The third sub-part (30-31) is made up of three pieces. The two outer segments first describe God's acts for Israel (30a) and then Israel's reaction towards their savior (31b). The two central segments begin in the same way — «and Israel saw». The first segment describes what Israel physically, and the second what they saw through faith, and how they understood what they had observed.

The names «Moses» and «Yhwh», which frame the first sub-part (27a and 27d) are not repeated in the central sub-part, which only reports the acts of the two peoples and of the sea-waters. In the last sub-part, the people of Israel recognize the joint action of «Yhwh», whose name is repeated four times and of «Moses his servant» in what has happened; so Moses' name is an inclusio for the whole part, and we might also say that the last two occurrences of Yhwh's name in the final segment (31b), with the one in 27d, play the role of final terms for the outer sub-parts. In addition, Moses' «hand» (27a) and the Lord's «hand» (31a) are inclusios[10].

10 The expression «the great arm which the Lord did» seems strange, the more so since it does not recur often (see Deut 34:10-12 — «Since then never has there been such a prophet in Israel as Moses, the man Yhwh knew face to face. What signs and wonders Yhwh caused him to *perform* in the land of Egypt against Pharaoh and all his servants and his whole land! How mighty the *hand* and *great* the fear that Moses *wielded* in the sight of all Israel!»; see too Deut 4:3-4; 7:19). This is why the JB translates «Israel witnessed the *great act* that Yhwh had performed against the Egyptians»; Osty, whose translation is often more literal, suggests, «Israel saw the great *power* which Yhwh used against the Egyptians».

The third passage as a whole (15-31)

The first two parts (15-18; 19-25a)

What the Lord announces to Moses in the first part takes place in the second. «Moses stretched out his hand over the sea» (21a) as the Lord had commanded him (16b); «the Egyptians pursued» the children of Israel and «came after them» (23), as the Lord had foretold in 17a. Note that «And Yhwh» (15a) and «And the angel of Elohim» (19a) act as initial terms — it is still he who takes the initiative, and Moses only intervenes after him (21a).

The last two parts (26 and 27-31)

Once again, what the Lord says to Moses in the fourth part happens in the following part. «Moses stretched out his hand over the sea» (at the start of the first sub-part of the last part, 27a), as the Lord had commanded him (26b), and «the waters turned back» over the Egyptian army (at the start of the second sub-part of the last part, 28a), just as the Lord had told him (26c). The two occurrences of «hand» at the start (26b.27a) are echoed at the end with two other occurrences of the same word (20a.31a) — at the start, it is the hand of Moses, at the end, that of the Egyptians and of the Lord.

The links between the five parts

As we have just seen, the Lord gives Moses the same order to stretch out his hand over the sea in the first and fourth parts (15-18; 26), but while the first time he is to «divide» it (16b), the second time it is to cover the Egyptians (26b). The second and fifth parts (19-25b; 27-31) recount the carrying out of the orders given to Moses and the Lord's promises being realized. The Lord's command, «and that the sons of Israel may come into the middle of the sea on dry land» (16c, in the first part), takes place in 22a, in the second part, this time accompanied by the amplification «and the waters were to them a rampart to their right and to their left» (22b). The two segments are repeated in the final part in 29b. The Lord's prediction, «and they will come after them» in the first part (17a) comes true in the second part (23), but it is also repeated in the fifth part (28b).

In the central part (25bc), the Egyptians' words begin with a decision, «Let us flee», which takes place in the final part, while the reason for flight refers to the previous part.

15 **And Yhwh said to Moses**:
«Why are you-crying-out to me? Speak to the sons of Israel and that they may march on! 16 And
you, lift up your staff and STRETCH OUT YOUR HAND OVER THE SEA and divide-it;
and that the sons of Israel may come *into the midst of the sea* on dry land!

17 And I, behold I will harden the heart of the Egyptians *and they will come **after** them*; and
I will glorify myself *AGAINST PHARAOH AND ALL HIS ARMY, AGAINST HIS CHARIOTS AND AGAINST HIS HORSEMEN*. 18 And the Egyptians shall
know that I am Yhwh, when I will glorify myself *AGAINST PHARAOH, AGAINST HIS CHARIOTS AND AGAINST HIS HORSEMEN*».

19 And the angel of Elohim who went before the camp of Israel marched on *and it moved
behind them*; and the pillar of cloud marched on before them *and it stood **behind** them*.
20 And it came between the camp of the Egyptians and between the camp of Israel. And it was
cloud and darkness and it enlightened the night and no one approached the other all the night.

21 And *MOSES STRETCHED OUT HIS HAND OVER THE SEA* and Yhwh made the sea
moved by a strong wind of east all the night; and it turned the sea into dry land and the
waters were divided.
22 **And the sons of Israel came *into the midst of the sea* on dry land**
AND THE WATERS WERE TO THEM A RAMPART ON THEIR RIGHT AND ON THEIR LEFT;
23 and the Egyptians *pursued* them and *ALL THE HORSES OF PHARAOH, HIS CHARIOTS AND HIS HORSEMEN* *came **behind**
them **into the midst of the sea***.

24 And it was at the morning watch Yhwh looked down to the camp of the Egyptians through the
pillar of fire and of cloud and he confused the camp of the Egyptians; 25 and he clogged the wheels
of their chariots and they let them proceed with difficulty.

And the Egyptians said:

«Let us flee — from the face of Israel,
because Yhwh fights for them — against the Egyptians!»

26 **And Yhwh said to Moses**:
«STRETCH OUT YOUR HAND OVER THE SEA
that the waters may come back OVER THE EGYPTIANS, OVER THEIR CHARIOTS AND OVER THEIR HORSEMEN».

27 And *MOSES STRETCHED OUT HIS HAND OVER THE SEA*; and at turning of the morning the
sea came back to its course and the Egyptians marched toward its coming; and Yhwh shook off the
Egyptians ***into the midst of the sea***.

28 ***And the waters came back*** and covered *THE CHARIOTS AND THE HORSEMEN AND ALL THE ARMY OF PHARAOH* *who were
coming in **behind** them* into the sea.
And there was no left of them even one.
29 **And the sons of Israel have gone on dry land *into the midst of the sea***
AND THE WATERS WERE TO THEM A RAMPART ON THEIR RIGHT AND ON THEIR LEFT.

30 And Yhwh saved in that day Israel from THE HAND of the Egyptians; and Israel saw the Egyptians
dead on the seashore 31 and Israel saw THE HAND great which did Yhwh against the Egyptians; and
the people feared Yhwh and they believed in Yhwh and in Moses his servant.

«The Lord fights for them»

Throughout the whole of this long scene, the children of Israel do not open their mouths; even Moses does not say a word. With the exception of the Lord, who twice addresses Moses (15-18; 26), the Egyptians are the only ones who speak; and their words resound at the very center of the passage (25cde). This is no order to retreat given by Pharaoh, but a panic-stricken cry of disarray which seems to issue from every mouth — «let us flee in Israel's face». But this cry is motivated by a statement which could be mistaken for a confession of faith — «for the Lord fights for them against Egypt». Of course, the narrative ends with the mention of Israel's faith — «the people believed in the Lord and they believed in the Lord and in Moses his servant» (31). However, the location of the Egyptians' declaration needs to be assessed — it is as though they come before Israel in faith. It is not, of course, faith as faith — that conviction whose substance is to give confidence, to have confidence in the one in whom we have faith, because we recognize that we owe salvation to him. But victory would not be complete if those who had shown themselves to be the as much God's enemy as his people's did not recognize the strength and greatness of the one who had ordered events to their cost. In reality, their words are the opposite of faith, because they do not accept God — on the contrary, they think they can still escape the judgment which is ready to strike them, by their own strength. At the same time, their cry represents the accomplishment of what the Lord promised at the end of his first address to Moses — «The Egyptians will know that I am the Lord» (18). Even though «know» rhymes with «believe», they are not at all the same thing, unfortunately for the Egyptians.

«Stretch out your hands over the sea and divide it»

Moses says nothing, but is happy to do what he is told, which in fact is not much. Curiously, the narrator, in reporting the facts, abridges them in relation to what the Lord had commanded at the start — «lift your staff and stretch out your hands over the sea, and divide it» (16). Afterwards, there is no further mention of the staff — even God makes no mention of it in his second intervention (26); and nowhere does it say that Moses «divides» the sea. The same verb is repeated at the center of the second part, but in a form which removes any active role from Moses — «the waters were divided»[11]. Moses stretches out his hand,

11 This is the reflexive form of the verb (niphal), which also often has the meaning of the passive (Joüon, § 51c).

but the cloud and light (19-20), and the wind and the sea (21) obey the Lord; it is God alone who «shakes off the Egyptians in the middle of the sea» (27) to save Israel from their hands (30). While Moses seems to do nothing except raise his hands, in fact this gesture shows his faith. Had he not believed in the word of the Lord, had he not believed that he could divide the sea, he would not have stretched out his hand, twice. Everything is done by God — but what would have happened if Moses had not stretched out his hand over the sea? Faith without divine power can do nothing, but all the divine power without Moses' faith would have been worthless, unable to find a way out.

D. THE CENTRAL PASSAGE (11-15)

Now it only remains to study the few verses which separate the two passages analyzed so far. We must first examine them on their own, and then in their role of binding or joining the two other passages.

COMPOSITION

The passage is made up of two parts[12]: the people's address to Moses (11-12) and his response to them (13-14). Each part is made up of two sub-parts — the narrative phrases (11a.13a), followed by the addresses which they introduce. Each address is constructed concentrically.

11 *And they said*	*to Moses:*			
+ «Is it because there were no graves	IN EGYPT	that you have taken us	TO DIE	IN THE DESERT?
: What is this you have done to us		that you have brought us out	OF EGYPT?	
12 Is not this the word		that we have told you	IN EGYPT saying:	
: "Leave us alone		that we may serve	EGYPT,	
+ because it is better for us to serve	EGYPT	than	TO DIE	IN THE DESERT?"».

13 *And Moses said*	*to the people:*		
= «Do not be afraid,		stand still	
. and you see the salvation of YHWH		which he will do **for you**	today
	- for THE EGYPTIANS	whom you see	today
	- you will add no more	to see them again	forever.
. 14 YHWH will fight **for you**			
= and you, you shall keep still».			

12 The first part is longer than the second — 38 words, in Hebrew, as opposed to 32 words (the words linked by the *maqqep* are counted as two words). The difference is more important if we count the number of members (eleven versus eight).

[11] *And they said*	*to Moses:*			
+ «Is it because there were no graves	IN EGYPT	that you have taken us	TO DIE	IN THE DESERT?
: What is this you have done to us		that you have brought us out	OF EGYPT?	
	[12] Is not this the word	that we have told you	IN EGYPT saying:	
: "Leave us alone		that we may serve	EGYPT,	
+ because it is better for us to serve	EGYPT	than	TO DIE	IN THE DESERT?"».

[13] *And Moses said*	*to the people:*		
= «Do not be afraid,		stand still	
. and you see the salvation of YHWH		which he will do **for you**	today
	- for THE EGYPTIANS	whom you see	today
	- you will add no more	to see them again	forever.
. [14] YHWH will fight **for you**			
= and you, you shall keep still».			

The first address (11b-12) is made up of three pieces. The outer pieces, made up of two bimember segments, oppose the action for which Moses is criticized, coming out of Egypt (11bc), to the wish which the children of Israel had already expressed to leave the country, that is, to stay there (12bc). The link between the outer pieces is formed by the central piece (12a), which is the length of a single bimember. Coming out of Egypt is opposed by «serving» it. At the end of the outer segments, «dying in the desert» is the inclusio. Note the regular appearance of the name «Egypt», which is repeated five times.

The second address is also made up of three pieces. The first has two bimembers, the other two are both the length of a bimember. The «salvation» which «Yhwh» will do «for you» (13c.14a), is specified in the center. The outer members (13b.14b) both deal with the calm attitude of expectation which the people should have.

The people's cry in the first part is completely directed towards the past (the verbs are in the past tens, the name «Egypt» repeated five times), while Moses' response, in the second part, is totally directed towards the future. In this second part, the name Egypt is repeated again, but only once, while the name «Yhwh» appears twice as the subject of the verbs, while he was only mentioned once in the people's words.

Egypt or death

We are not told what the children of Israel «cried out» to the Lord (10); however, the words they speak to Moses are reported at length (11-12). With their back to the desert, like the snake's prey, they are fascinated by Egypt to the extent that it is all they see; they repeat its name no less than five times, while they only say the Lord's name once, as though he does not exist for them. So the only solution is to give oneself up, to capitulate immediately, to avoid death — slavery or death! They have chosen to live. They had already said, before leaving their masters, that they preferred the security of slavery to the risks of freedom. The break has finished, and it is time to go back to brick-making.

The Lord and salvation

Moses will not be flustered by the accusation his people bring against him; he will not join in the debating game. He answers, of course, but does not go on the attack. He does not use the first person once. He is not the one under discussion — his whole address is made to «you». Above all, he only mentions the Egyptians at the very center of his words to emphasize that they will be caught in the net the Lord is throwing around them, and that, therefore, the children of Israel have no reason to «be afraid», and can «keep still» (14b).

E. THE SEQUENCE AS A WHOLE (EXOD 14:1-31)

COMPOSITION

At the end of the analyses we have carried out so far, we can say that our initial hypothesis has been shown to be true — Exodus 14 is a sequence made up of three passages.

- The first passage (1-10) tells how Israel was led to find itself cornered between the sea and the Egyptian army.
- The second passage (11-14) is noticeably shorter — this is the dialogue between Moses and the people, one asking questions (11-12), the other answering to encourage and promise God's salvation (13-14).
- The third passage (15-31) is the longest, recounting how Israel was saved from its enemies by the Lord and Moses. While the children of Israel cross the sea dry-shod, the Egyptians are swallowed up by it.

ISRAEL IS CAUGHT IN THE TRAP	1-10

The children of Israel complain to Moses for having made them come out of Egypt	11-12
Moses answers that the Lord will free them from the Egyptians	13-14

ISRAEL IS FREED FROM THE TRAP	15-31

We have already described the parallelism of the outer passages (p. 34). The first parts (1-4; 15-18) have many points in common, as do the last parts (8-10; 27-31). We have indicated the connections between the centers (5c and 25c) as our hypothesis, which has been proven by the analysis of the two passages.

In the first part of the central passage (11-12), the people's speech is made up of a series of questions, which once again proves the laws of biblical rhetoric, which require that a question be at the center of a concentric construction[13]. In addition, it is not unknown that the central question is sometimes joined to its answer, which is the case here.

The usual function of the center of a concentric construction is to join the whole text together, in other words, to bind the other passages together. This is the only place of the whole sequence where words are exchanged between Moses

13 See *Traité*, 417-435.

[1] ***And Yhwh spoke to Moses saying***: [2] «**Speak to the sons of Israel** *and that they may turn back* and camp before Pi-Hahiroth between Migdol and between the sea; before Baal-Zephon in front of it you shall camp by the sea. [3] And Pharaoh will say of the sons of Israel: "They are entangled in the land; the desert enclosed upon them!" [4] **And I will harden the heart of Pharaoh** and he will pursue after them *and I will glorify myself against Pharaoh and against all his army* AND THE EGYPTIANS HAVE TO KNOW THAT I AM YHWH». And they did so.

[5] And it was told to the king of Egypt that the people had fled; and was turned the heart of Pharaoh and his servants against the people.

• And they said: «WHAT IS THIS WE HAVE DONE, THAT WE HAVE LET ISRAEL GO FROM SERVING US?»

[6] And he harnessed his chariot and he took his people with him; [7] and he took six hundred best chariots and all the chariots of Egypt, with a third-man on each of them.

[8] And Yhwh hardened the heart of Pharaoh king of Egypt and he pursued after the sons of Israel; and the sons of Israel were marching out with bold hand [9] and the Egyptians pursued after them. And they overtook them camping by the sea *all horses of Pharaoh's chariots and his horsemen and his army* near Pi-Hahiroth before Baal-Zephon; [10] and Pharaoh drew near. And **the sons of Israel** LIFTED UP THE EYES and behold ***Egypt*** was marching after them; and they FEARED greatly and **the sons of Israel *cried out*** to Yhwh.

[11] And they said to Moses: «Is it because there were no graves in Egypt that you have taken us to die in the desert? WHAT IS THIS YOU HAVE DONE TO US THAT YOU HAVE BROUGHT US OUT OF EGYPT? [12] Is not this word that we have told you in Egypt saying: "Leave-us alone that we may SERVE Egypt, because it is better for us to SERVE Egypt than to *DIE* in the desert?"».

[13] And Moses said to the people: «DO NOT BE AFRAID, stand still and SEE the SALVATION of Yhwh which he will DO for you today, for the Egyptians whom you SEE today you will not SEE them again forever. [14] *YHWH WILL FIGHT FOR YOU* and you, you have to keep still».

[15] ***And Yhwh said to Moses***: «Why are ***you crying out*** to me? **Speak to the sons of Israel** *and that they may march on*! [16] And you, lift up your staff and stretch out your hand over the sea and split it; and that the sons of Israel may come into the midst of the sea on dry land! [17] And I, behold **I will harden the heart of the Egyptians** and they will come after them *and I will glorify myself against Pharaoh and all his army, against his chariots and against his horsemen.* [18] AND THE EGYPTIANS HAVE TO KNOW THAT I AM YHWH *when I will glorify myself against Pharaoh, against his chariots and against his horsemen*».

[19] And the angel of Elohim who went before the camp of Israel marched on and moved behind them; and the pillar of cloud marched on before them and stood behind them. [20] And it came between the camp of the Egyptians and the camp of Israel. And it was cloud and darkness and it enlightened the night; and no one approached the other all the night. [21] And Moses stretched out his hand over the sea and Yhwh made the sea moved by a strong wind of east all the night; and it turned the sea into dry land and the waters were split. [22] And the sons of Israel came into the midst of the sea on dry land and the waters were to them a rampart on their right and on their left; [23] and the Egyptians pursued and came after them all the horses of Pharaoh, his chariots and his horsemen into the midst of the sea. [24] And it was at the morning watch Yhwh looked down to the camp of the Egyptians through the pillar of fire and of cloud and he confused the camp of the Egyptians; [25] and he clogged the wheels of their chariots and they drove them with difficulty.

• And the Egyptians said: «Let us flee from the face of Israel, for *YHWH FIGHTS FOR THEM* against Egypt».

[26] And Yhwh said to Moses: «Stretch out your hand over the sea and that the waters may turn back over the Egyptians over their chariots and over their horsemen».

[27] And Moses stretched out his hand over the sea; and the sea turned back at daybreak to its course and the Egyptians marched toward its coming; and Yhwh shook off the Egyptians into the midst of the sea. [28] And the waters turned back and covered *the chariots and the horsemen and all the army of Pharaoh* who were coming in after them into the sea. And there was no left of them even one. [29] And the sons of Israel have gone on dry land into the midst of the sea and the waters were to them a rampart on their right and on their left. [30] And Yhwh SAVED in that day Israel from the hand of the Egyptians; and **Israel** SAW ***the Egyptians*** *DEAD* on the seashore [31] and **Israel** SAW the great arm which Yhwh DID against the Egyptians; and **the people** FEARED Yhwh and they believed in Yhwh and in Moses his SERVANT.

and the children of Israel. At the start of the outer passages (1 and 15), the Lord orders Moses to «speak to the sons of Israel», but the narrator does not report Moses' words.

The most solid fact is the link established between the central passage of the sequence with the outer passages.

• in the first part of the central passage of the sequence the words of the children of Israel recall those of the Egyptians at the center of the first passage:

5c	*What is this we have done,*		that we have sent away Israel	**from** serving us?
11b	*What is this you have done*	*to us,*	that you have brought us out	**of** Egypt?

• in the same way, Moses' words in the second part of the central passage prepare for the Egyptians' words at the center of the last passage:

14	*Yhwh will fight*	*for you*	
25c	*Yhwh fights*	*for them*	*against* Egypt.

In addition, Moses' answer heralds the end of the last passage — «salvation» (13) is repeated by «saved» (30); «do» is repeated in 31 as in 13; the three «see»s in 13 herald the two in 30-31; «do not be afraid» (13) heralds «feared» in 31.

The first part of the central passage is linked to the first passage by the double repetition of «desert» (11.12, like 3) and by the double repetition of the root of «serve» (12, like the center of the passage, at 5); furthermore the double occurrence of «die» in 11 and 12 heralds «dead» at the end of the last passage (30).

INTERPRETATION

We should probably examine the «difficulties which prevent [the current text] from being read as a single coherent account» step by step[14]. Whatever the text's pre-history, it is difficult to imagine that the final text is not coherent, the more so since its composition, as it has been drawn out, is simply remarkable at every level of its organization. It seems that nothing can «prevent» it from being read according to its own unity and coherence.

14 J.-L. SKA, *Introduction à la lecture du Pentateuque*, 102.

Such an important text is obviously likely to have several interpretations. It is possible to read it as the account of the birth of Israel, now a people entirely apart, having come out of another people[15]. The reading, which will be given here, aims to base itself first and foremost on the composition.

«They feared and they believed»

The end of a story reveals what its issue is. This one ends by talking about Israel's faith — «Israel saw… and they feared the Lord and they believed in the Lord and in Moses his servant» (31). It is no exaggeration to say that the narrative does not so much report the defeat of the Egyptians as Israel's victory over its own unbelief. Of course, Yhwh «saved Israel in that day from the hand of the Egyptians» (30), but the greater miracle is not the routing and death of the external enemies as much as the coming to recognize the saving presence of God which finally manages to overcome all interior resistance.

There is fear …

Both the outer passages end in fear, but there is a gulf between them. It is a gulf in the true sense of the word, because nothing less than crossing the sea and death was needed to go from one to the other. It is at the sight of Egypt appearing suddenly and unexpectedly that the children of Israel are struck by «fear» (10). This fear is none other than fear and fear of death — it is the terror of the one who sees himself delivered into the hands of his enemies with no chance of defense. It is blind fear, unable to see anything except the men who wish them dead. However, a glimmer of hope is among the shadow — the children of Israel «cry out to the Lord». He has not completely disappeared from their view. We do not hear their voice, however, as though their cry is that of an inarticulate hunted animal. The words we hear are questions, addressed not to God but to Moses, words obsessed with the enemy's name, in which the Lord is absent — in short, words where their total lack of faith is obvious.

15 On this see in particular WÉNIN A., «Naître à la liberté et à la vie. Le passage de la Mer (Exod 14)».

... and fear

We can see the problem which the first words the Lord addresses to Moses at the start of the last part present — «Why do you cry out to me?» (15). Nowhere, in fact, does it say that Moses himself has cried out to the Lord. Of course, it might be thought that he had brought the people's complaints to the Lord (11-12). However, when we take the text's composition seriously — the distant median terms which represent the only two occurrences of «to cry» in 10 and 15 — we understand that either Moses had himself cried out with all the other children of Israel, or that God treats him as their representative. Whatever is meant, such a «cry» is not pleasing to the Lord — this is not what he wishes to hear. The end of the account is clearly opposed both to the start of the last passage, where God rejects the Israelites' cry, and, particularly to the end of the first passage. It is still fear, but not the same fear — it is, in fact, exactly the opposite. It is no longer fear of the enemy and of death, but fear of the Lord, «the trembling certainty of love»[16]. The text gives another name for this «trembling certainty» — faith.

There is serving ...

Two other key words have three strategic places in the text. «Serve» is twice repeated in the children of Israel's complaints in the center (12), «serving us» is used in the center of the first passage (5c), and «servant» is the very last word of the text (31c)[17]. The «serving us» mentioned by the Egyptians is the slavery described in the first chapter of Exodus — «they made their lives unbearable with hard *slavery*, work with clay and with bricks, all kinds of *service* in the fields, all the *services* that they *served on* them with force» (Exod 1:14)[18]. The Egyptians missed the slaves who served them and sought to get them under their thumb again. In the midst of the account, the former slaves, too, miss their serving — «Leave us alone that we may serve Egypt, for it is better to serve Egypt than to die in the desert» (12).

16 BEAUCHAMP P., *L'Un et l'Autre Testament*, I, 272.

17 This is an example of Lund's third («Identical ideas are often arranged in such a way that they appear at the outer parts and center and nowhere else in the system») and fourth laws («There are also many examples where ideas appear at the center of one system and the outer parts of a connecting system, the second system clearly having been constructed to go with the first. This we call the *law of the center's displacement* to the outer parts»); see *Traité*, 98.

18 This literal translation allows us to focus on the emphasis of the root *"bd*, «serve», which is repeated four times in a single verse, compared with the translation of the JB, for example.

… and serving

Israel is called to serve, but in a totally different way. Just as with fear, its service is to change both its object and its reason. To recognize Moses as the Lord's «servant» is to call him to serve in his image. The crossing of the sea makes Israel go from servitude to service, from the forced slavery of Egypt to the free service of its Lord, a service which has nothing to do with slavery, since the Lord is precisely the one who has delivered them from their slavery, imposed on them by Egypt, and the one they had interiorized to the extent of preferring it to freedom. How could the one who made them find the path of freedom with such effort wish to hold them in the net of another slavery? Such service would be the worst of all, the total denial of the divine nature. Moses is called the Lord's «servant», but his service is both of God and of his people — it is the collaboration which his faith has offered to the work of salvation of freedom accomplished by God.

To cry out or to sing

«Then Moses and the children of Israel sang this song to the Lord…» The Song of the Sea can and must be distinguished from the account which goes before it and prepares for it. However, it cannot be separated from it, if only because it shows how the miracle ends — through the Lord's grace, the cry of the children of Israel is transfigured into the most beautiful song of victory.

Chapter 2

The song of the sea

Exod 15

This chapter reworks and updates
part of «Le cantique de Moïse et
le cantique de l'Agneau (Ap 15 et Ex 15)»
in *Gr.* 73 (1992), 19-55.

Exod 15

1 *Then sang Moses and the sons of Israel this song to Yhwh*
and they said, saying:

«I sing to Yhwh,
for he is exalted highly;

the horse and its rider
he has cast into the sea.

2 *My strength and my song, is Yah;*
he has become for me the salvation.

He is my God, I praise him,
the God of my father, I exalt him.

3 *Yhwh is a man of war,*
Yhwh is his name.

4 *The chariots of Pharaoh and his army*
he has thrown into the sea;

the elite of his captains
are drowned into the sea of Reeds;

5 *the depths cover them,*
they went down into the deeps like a stone.

6 *Your right hand, Yhwh,*
shining of power,

your right hand, Yhwh,
shatters the enemy.

7 *In abundance of your greatness*
you overthrow your adversaries;

you loose your wrath,
it devours them like straw.

8 At the breath of your nostrils
piled up the waters,

stood up like a heap the floods,
congealed the depths in the heart of the sea.

9 The enemy said:
«I will pursue, I will overtake,

I will divide the spoil,
will fill up of them my gorge;

I will draw out my sword,
will dispossess them my hand.»

10 You have blown your breath:

covered them the sea,
they sank like lead
into the waters tremendous.

11 Who is like you
among the gods, Yhwh?

Who is like you,

shining of holiness,
terrible in praises,
maker of miracles?

12 You have stretched out your right hand:
swallowed them the earth.

13 You have led in your faithfulness
this people whom you have redeemed,

whom you have guided in your strength
to the dwelling of your holiness.

14 Have heard the peoples, they tremble.
Pangs seize the inhabitants of Philistia;

15 then dismayed the chiefs of Edom,
the leaders of Moab, trembling seizes them;

melted away are all the inhabitants of Canaan.

16 Fall upon them terror and dread.

By the greatness of your arm
they are still like a stone,

till pass over this people, Yhwh,
till pass over this people whom you have purchased.

17 You will bring them and will plant them
on the mountain of your inheritance,

on the place of your habitation
that you have made, Yhwh,

on the sanctuary, Lord,
that have established your hands».

18 Yhwh reigns forever and ever!

This canticle has given rise to many studies of poetry, meter and strophe. Flavius Josephus thought it was written in hexameters (*en hexametrō tonōį*)[1], and Eusebius of Caesarea, who was more precise, in hexameters of sixteen syllables[2]. According to Philo of Alexandria, the canticle was sung by two choirs with a wonderful refrain[3]. The idea that the canticle follows a regular meter found supporters during the last century, and, indeed, even in our own day. For Gerhard Gietmann, for instance, it is composed of heptasyllbic verse[4]. This preoccupation with finding a mathematical regularity in the canticle's composition is found in many commentators, particularly those at the end of the nineteenth and start of the twentieth centuries. So Paul Haupt organized the canticle into three sections, each made up of three strophes which each had two «couplets», in turn made up of two hemistiches, each with two accents[5]. Some years earlier, M.-J. Lagrange[6], following Felix Perles' analysis[7] on David Heinrich Müller's principles[8], had seen three 10-line strophes in Moses' canticle (1-5, 7-10, 12-15, divided into two parts given to two different choirs), each followed by a refrain (6, 11, 16b), whose characteristic was that both stichs began with a repeated word (vv. 17-18, which were not part of this schema, were considered to be an envoi «which could in fact be removed»[9]).

More recently, Raymond Tournay has stated that «the Song's rhythm is binary; each stich has 2 + 2 accents»[10], even if this corrects the text[11]; the verses are now grouped in threes — «verses 1 and 18 between them form a tercet, framing another twelve tercets», «on condition [however] that 7b goes just before v. 10 where it is perfectly suited to both meaning and grammar»[12]. Each group of two tercets forms a strophe, each group of two strophes a stanza; and in this way,

1 *Jewish Antiquities*, II.16.4. See GAROFALO S., «L'Epinicio di Mosè (Esodo 15)».
2 *Preparation for the Gospel*, XI.5; for a study of the ancients' attitude to Hebrew poetry see CASTELLINO G., «Il ritmo ebraico nel pensiero degli antichi» (for Exodus 15 see pp. 510-511).
3 *De agricultura*, I, 79-82.
4 *De re metrica hebraeorum*, 68.
5 «Moses Song of Triumph». To get this result, he changed the verse order (157). Haupt reviewed previous studies and presented their divisions of the text (150 ff.).
6 «Deux chants de guerre».
7 *Zur Althebraïschen Strophik*.
8 *Die Propheten in ihrer ursprünglicheren Form*; an introduction to Müller's theory in CONDAMIN A., *Poèmes de la Bible*, 3.
9 LAGRANGE M.-J., «Deux chants de guerre», 539.
10 «Recherche sur la chronologie des Psaumes», 336 (he refers to Flavius Josephus in a note).
11 For example, by suppressing «Yah» from 2a (343), considering «his army» in 4a to be an addition (340.345), ommitting «like a stone» at the end of 5 with no justification.
12 «Recherches», 337.

«the poem is easily divided into three stanzas, framed by the hymnic prelude (v. 1) and the final acclamation (v. 18)»; «it is difficult to find a more uniform structure from one end to the other»[13].

Two much deeper analyses deserve special attention — James Muilenburg's[14] and David Noel Freedman's[15]. Unlike previous studies, which tended to remain at a more general level, with little argument, these two analyses abound with pertinent observations which pick up all sorts of symmetries marking a remarkable progression in the canticle's analysis. However, it must be acknowledged that they are still broadly dependent on strophic theory and aim to extract a measurable organization of regularity and balance — that is, logic — which seems foreign to biblical rhetoric, as we can see in the following tables which summarize their analysis:

J. Muilenburg:

+ *Hymnic introduction*	1b
First division (2-5)	
: Hymnic confession	2-3
—Epic narrative	4-5
HYMNIC RESPONSE	6
Second division (7-10)	
: Hymnic confession	7-8
—Epic narrative	9-10
HYMNIC RESPONSE	11
Third division (12-16ab)	
: Hymnic confession	12-14
—Epic narrative	15-16ab
HYMNIC RESPONSE	16cd[16]
+ *Final acclamation*	18

13 «Recherches», 337.

14 «A Liturgy on the Triumphs of Yahweh».

15 «Strophe and Meter in Exod 15». J.J. BURDEN's analysis («A Stylistic Analysis of Exodus 15:1-21; Theory and Practice») partly concurs with Freedman's; however he does not seem to be aware of Freedman's work, or Muilenberg's, but only Rozelaar's (see below, n. 18) and Watts' (see below, n. 42). M. HOWELL's work, «Exodus 15,1b-18; A Poetic Analysis», applies the procedures suggested by W.G.E. WATSON, *Classical Hebrew Poetry*.

16 Verse 17 is taken to be «a hymnic celebration of YHWH's occupation of the country and his enthronement in the sanctuary» (248).

D.N. Freedman:

+ *Introductory refrain*	1b
Exhortation	2
Introduction	3-5
REFRAIN A	6
STROPHE I (7-10)	
A	7-8
B	9-10
REFRAIN B	11
STROPHE II (12-16a)	
A	12-14
B	15-116a
REFRAIN C	16b
Conclusion	17-18
+ *Concluding refrain*	21[17]

The merit of these studies is their emphasis of some precise points of composition: (for example, caesuras at the end of vv. 5, 10, 13 and 17[18], and the symmetry of vv. 6, 11 and 16b)[19]. They still all tend to find Greco-Latin structures of regularity in the poem. It seems that we need to completely abandon the idea that Hebrew poetry might obey the laws of Western poetry. Of course, like all poetry, Hebrew poetry is essentially made up of parallelism[20], which does not exclude a certain regularity — on the contrary. However, observing the facts makes us acknowledge that this is no mathematical regularity, but, rather, most of the time, combined with skillful disequilibrium, at every level of the text's organization.

17 Freedman considers Miriam's words in v. 21 to form an inclusio with v. 1b. It seems more natural to see them, not as extreme terms, but rather as initial terms: after Moses and the sons of Israel had finished singing, it was the turn of the women to repeat the same song. Among the different understandings of the verb *'nh* at the start of v. 21, P. JOÜON («Respondit et dixit») leans towards «repeat».

18 TOURNAY R., «Recherches», 337; similarly ROZELAAR M., «The Song of the Sea (Exodus XV,1b-18)», although his organization is different — between a Prologue (1) and an Epilogue (18) two large parts are sub-divided into two sub-parts which are parallel (the first part 2-5, 6-10; the second part is 11-13, 14-17).

19 See to LOHFINK N., «De Moysis Epinicio (Exod 15,1-18)» (who identified the limits of part 8-10) and COATS G.W., «The Song of the Sea».

20 G.M. HOPKINS, quoted in JAKOBSON R., «Closing Statements: Linguistics and Poetics», trans. RUWET N., *Essais de linguistique générale*, 235.

The Song of the Sea (see «The canticle as a whole», p. 86) has two long parts (1b-10 and 12-17) which frame a short central part (11) whose basic characteristic is that these are the canticle's only two subjects.

A. THE FIRST PART (1b-10)

The first part (see p. 75) is made up of three sub-parts, two longer (1b-5 and 8-10) ones framing a shorter sub-part (6-7).

1. THE FIRST SUB-PART (1b-5)

COMPOSITION

This sub-part has three pieces (1b-2b; 2c-3 and 4-5) arranged concentrically.

The first piece (1b-2b)

: [1b] I SING			to YHWH,
+ for HE is exalted			highly.
	+ *The horse*	*and its rider*	
	+ *he has cast*	*into the sea.*	
: [2] My strength		and my SONG	is YaH:
+ HE has become		for me	the salvation.

This piece has three bimember segments[21]. The outer segments (1bc and 2ab) are similar; the second members express the reason for the song[22] for «YHWH / «YAH». The central segment (1de) explains God's acts mentioned in the second members of the other two segments. It may be noted that the construction of the central segment resembles the other two — in fact, the second member also describes one of God's acts, but this time against an army of warriors.

21 «He is exalted highly»: literally, «to raise himself he raised himself», an expression formed by the verb and the infinitive absolute from the same root *gā'ōh gā'â*.

22 «My song» corresponds to «I sing». The construction of this piece, particularly the symmetry between 1b and 2a, seems to be an argument in support of translating *zimrāt* by «song» and not by «strength» (to make it a synonym for «my vigour»). See R. TOURNAY's discussion, «Recherches» (343); GOOD's E.M., «Exodus XV 2», 358-2599; and LŒWENSTAMM's S.E., «The Lord is my Strength and my Glory». BAR TURA A., «Uzzî vezimrat Yah», 330, interprets it as «Yah is my force for attack and my force for defense».

The second piece (2c-3)

+ He	(is)	my GOD,	*I praise him,*
+ the GOD	of	my father,	*I exalt him.*
+ 3 YHWH	(is)	a man	of war,
+ YHWH	(is)	his name.	

This piece only has two segments. These two bimembers identify the subject of the song—the first segment identifies God in relation to «me» and «my father», and the second in relation to the enemies he fights. The name of «God» is repeated in each member of the first segment, while his proper name, «YHWH», is repeated at the start of both members of the second segment. The final member, which only has two terms, while the first three each of three, seems to be emphasized by its very brevity.

The third piece (4-5)

: 4 The chariots		of Pharaoh	and his army,
– he has	*thrown*	into the **sea**:	
: the elite		of his captains	
– are	*drowned*	into the **sea**	of Reeds;
– 5 the **depths**		cover them,	
– they	*went down*	into the **deeps**	like a stone.

The last piece also has three segments[23]. All three are given to the drowning of the Egyptians, or more precisely, the most important elements, «the chariots», the «elite of his captains», which follow one another in chronological fashion. The two members of the final segment (5) correspond to the second members of the previous segments: «the depths» and «the deep» are synonyms for «the sea» (twice, 4b and 4d).

23 These have a variable rhythm, 3 + 2, then 2 + 3, finally 2 + 3; the fact that the outer members are three terms could be interpreted as a phenomenon of closure.

The sub-part as a whole (1b-5)

· [1b] I sing to YHWH,	for HE IS EXALTED highly;
the horse and its rider	*HE HAS CAST* *into* ***the sea.***
· [2] My strength and my song, is YaH:	he has become for me the salvation.
He is my GOD, I praise him,	the GOD of my father, I EXALT HIM.
[3] YHWH is a man of war,	YHWH is his name.
: [4] *The chariots of Pharaoh and his army,*	*HE HAS THROWN* *into* ***the sea:***
: *the elite of his captains*	*ARE DROWNED* *into* ***the sea*** *of Reeds;*
- [5] *The depths cover them,*	*THEY WENT DOWN* *into the deeps like a stone.*

The final piece (4-5) repeats and develops the central segment of the first piece (1c)[24]. «He is exalted highly» at the start (1b) is opposed to the whole series of verbs which express downward movement: «he has cast» (1c) and «he has thrown» (4a), «are drowned» (4b) and «they went down» (5)[25].

The start of the central piece (2b) uses «I», like the piece which precedes it[26]; and in addition «I exalt» recalls «he is exalted highly» in 1b[27]. Conversely, the end of the central piece (3) prepares for the final piece—the subject of these two members, «YHWH», will be the subject of 4a; the Lord has shown he is a «man of war» by destroying Pharaoh's army.

INTERPRETATION

By pulling all Pharaoh's forces, his horses and riders, chariots, officers and whole army down to the depths of the sea (1c; 4-5), Yhwh «has been greatly exalted» (1b). Those he has saved joyfully recognize that the humiliation and destruction of their enemies is the work of their God, and that their strength comes from him alone (1b, 2a), so they can join in the movement of exalting their savior by «exalting» him by the song of praise (2b-3).

24 4a, in particular, has the same syntactical structures as 1c, apart from the expansion «of Pharaoh».

25 The play on words between the verbs which describe falling, *rmh* = «he has cast» (1c), *yrh* = «he has thrown» (4a), *yrd* = «they went down» (5) on the one hand, and, on the other hand, *rwm* = «I exalt him» (2b) reinforce the semantic opposition.

26 It uses both the first person, at the end of each member («I praise him», «I exalt him») like the first members of the outer segments (1b and 2a) and the third person, whose referent is God, at the start of the members («Him», «Yhwh»), like the second members of the outer segments (1b and 2a).

27 Words with the same root as these two verbs are often used synonymously elsewhere, eg Isa 2:12 and Jer 48:29.

2. **THE SECOND SUB-PART (6-7)**

COMPOSITION

The central sub-part has two pieces, each made up of two bimember segments; all the members have two terms:

= [6] Your *right hand,*		*YHWH,*
	: shining	of POWER,
= your *right hand,*		*YHWH,*
	: shatters	the ENEMY.
= [7] In abundance of		your GREATNESS
	: you overthrow	your ADVERSARIES,
= you loose		your ***wrath***:
	: it devours them	like straw.

The first members of the first piece (6a.c) are identical, while the second members (6b.d) match one another. One describes God's power and the other the effect of this power on the enemy. The two segments of the second piece (7) both repeat the same logic — God's action in the first members, the effects of this action on the adversaries. «Power» in 6b heralds «greatness» in 7a; «enemy» in 6d is synonymous with «adversaries» in 7b. A new image, of fire, is introduced in the final segment: the two representations of the «right (hand)» and «wrath» (this word is often used in the expression «the wrath of your nostrils» to mean «your anger») match one another[28].

INTERPRETATION

God's omnipotence, described at length with a very concrete image by the power of his hand (6) and the wrath of his anger which comes from his nostrils[29] (7cd), is, as it were, further reinforced by the fact that it is opposed to the image of the straw devoured by the fire, an even more striking contrast for its brevity and appears at the end (7d). Such a fall emphasizes the vanity of Israel's «enemy» (6d), described as those who in fact oppose the Lord's power («your adversaries» in 7b).

28 In 6b the two images seem condensed; effectively just as «power» in 6b previews «greatness» in 7a, it can be said that «wrath» in 7c is previewed by «shining» in 6b.

29 The term translated by «wrath», *ḥārôn*, is often accompanied by *'ap*, usually translated by «the burning» or «fierce anger of Yhwh», literally, «the wrath of your nose» (eg, Num 25:4; 1Sam 28:18, etc.)

3. THE THIRD SUB-PART (8-10)

COMPOSITION

+ 8 *AT THE BREATH*	of your nostrils,	
. piled up	***THE WATERS***,	
. stood up	LIKE a dam	the floods,
. congealed	the depths	in the heart of **THE SEA**.
– 9 The enemy	said:	
– "I will pursue,	I will overtake;	
. I will divide	the spoil,	
- will fill up of them	*MY GORGE;*	
. I will draw out	my sword,	
- will dispossess-them	*my hand*".	
+ 10 You have blown	*YOUR BREATH:*	
. has covered them	**THE SEA**,	
. They sank	LIKE lead	
. into ***THE WATERS***	tremendous.	

The third sub-part has three pieces. The first (8) has one unimember, an adverbial phrase of means, and a trimember, which juxtaposes the three main clauses. The final piece (10) is composed in a similar way, with God's breath (10a) leading to the enemies' drowning (10bcd). These two pieces parallel one another—the same «breath» (8a and 10a) first of all makes the waters draw back (8; see Exod 14:21-22), and then makes them surge back over the Egyptians (10; see Exod 14:27-28). «How» is repeated in the third members, while «waters» and «sea» mirror one another in the second and fourth members.

The central piece (9), which reports the words of those who pursued Israel into the dried-out sea-bed, is therefore the second time-frame of the narrative. It has three bimember segments of the same rhythm (2 + 2 terms in each segment). It is in ABB' form: effectively the last two segments parallel one another (the first members are in the first person singular and the second members end with subjects which belong to the same semantic field, that of parts of the body («my throat», and «my hand»).

At the center of the central piece (9d) «throat» is part of the same semantic field as «breath» (8a and 10a)[30].

30 Note that *napšî* («throat») is a play on words with *nāšaptā* («you have exhaled») at the start of the third piece (10a).

INTERPRETATION

Caught between two sovereign demonstrations by God, who, as the absolute ruler, commands the most uncontrollable forces (8 and 10), the claims of the enemy who brandishes his sword (9ef) to get his hands on his loot (9cd) appear as derisory as they really are.

4. THE FIRST PART AS A WHOLE (1b-10)

COMPOSITION

1b I sing to YHWH, for **he is exalted greatly**;
the horse and its rider he has cast into the sea.
2 My strength and my song, is YaH: he has become for me the salvation.

He is *my God*, I praise him, *the God* of my father, I exalt him.
3 YHWH is a man of war, YHWH is his name.

4 The chariots of Pharaoh and his army, he has thrown into the sea:
the elite of his captains are drowned into the sea of Reeds;
= 5 *COVER THEM the* **DEPTHS**,
they went down *into the deeps* LIKE a stone.

6 Your RIGHT HAND, YHWH, glorious in power,
your RIGHT HAND YHWH, shatters ***the enemy***.
7 In abundance of **your greatness**, you throw down your adversaries,
you loose your wrath, it devours them LIKE straw.

8 At the breath of your nostrils,
piled up the waters,
stood up the floods LIKE a heap,
congealed the **DEPTHS** in the heart of *the sea*.

9 ***The enemy*** said: "I will pursue, I will overtake,
I will divide the spoil, my gorge will fill up of THEM;
I will draw out *my sword*, my **HAND** will dispossess THEM".

10 You have blown your breath:
= *HAS COVERED THEM the sea*,
they sank LIKE lead
into the waters tremendous.

The expressions «like a stone» (5b), «like straw» (7b) and «like lead» (10c) act as final terms for each of the three sub-parts. Verses 5 and 10bcd fulfill the function of final terms for the outer two sub-parts. Both occurrences of «depths» (5a and 8d), like the syntagmas «like a stone» (5b) and «like a heap» (8c) can be considered as distant median terms.

1b I sing to YHWH, for **he is exalted greatly;**
the horse and its rider he has cast into the sea.
2 My strength and my song, is YaH: he has become for me the salvation.

He is *my God*, I praise him, *the God* of my father, I exalt him.
3 YHWH is a man of war, YHWH is his name.

---

4 The chariots of Pharaoh and his army, he has thrown into the sea:
the elite of his captains are drowned into the sea of Reeds;
= 5 *COVER THEM the* **DEPTHS,**
they went down *into the deeps* LIKE a stone.

---

6 Your RIGHT HAND, YHWH, glorious in power,
your RIGHT HAND YHWH, shatters ***the enemy.***
7 In abundance of **your greatness,** you throw down your adversaries,
you loose your wrath, it devours them LIKE straw.

---

8 At the breath of your nostrils,
piled up the waters,
stood up the floods LIKE a heap,
congealed the **DEPTHS** in the heart of *the sea.*

---

9 ***The enemy*** said: "I will pursue, I will overtake,
I will divide the spoil, my gorge will fill up of THEM;
I will draw out *my sword,* my **HAND** will dispossess THEM".

---

10 You have blown your breath:
= *HAS COVERED THEM the sea,*
they sank LIKE lead
into the waters tremendous.

The outer sub-parts are both composed concentrically. Their centers (2b-3 and 9) match one another, with verbs in the first person singular, whose subject is the psalmist in 2b and the enemy in 9. Both are speaking, one to praise God, the other to express their destructive desire. The same person, Israel, is present, first of all relating to God as the subject of the praising («I», twice), secondly relating to the enemy as the object of their chase («they», twice). «My God» in the psalmist's mouth in 2b could be opposed to «my sword» in the enemy's mouth in 9c, to the extent that they represent what gives each person their strength, where they each put their trust.

The start of the central sub-part (6) refers both to the center of the first sub-part (the name of «YHWH» is repeated twice in 6, just as in 3) and at the center of the third sub-part (v. 6 ends with «enemy» and v. 9 begins with the same word; «hand», at the end of v. 9 is synonymous with «right» at the start of 6, repeated at the start of 6b). The end of the central sub-part (7) refers to the start of the other two sub-parts: on the one hand 7a's «your greatness» repeats 1b's «he is exalted highly» (literally, «he has grown in his greatness»)[31] and on the other, v. 7's construction is very similar to v.8's[32]. The central sub-part switches the passage into the second person singular: while the whole of the first sub-part speaks about God in the third person, the final sub-part addresses him in the second person (with, of course, the exception of v. 9 in the center).

INTERPRETATION

«The Lord is a man of war!» (3). The whole of this part is strongly marked by images which are characteristic of war. The power which throws men with their chariots and horses (1c, 4-5 and 6) is joined by fire which sends all protection up in smoke (7b): «The Lord of hosts [Sabaoth] says this: The wide ramparts of Babylon will be razed to the ground and her high gates will be burnt down. Thus the laboring of the peoples comes to nothing, the toiling of the nations ends in fire» (Jer 51:58).

The powers which are present are, on the one hand, Pharaoh's, his horses and chariots, his army and officers (4), who have thrown themselves into the pursuit of booty (9). On the other hand the power which oppose the Egyptian's strength is not that of those they are chasing, but God's, the only one whose «name» is spoken (2-3) against that of «Pharaoh» (4a)[33]: his right hand does not brandish a sword, but the fire of anger which devours everything, the breath of his nostrils raising the storm which pushes back the sea and then makes it surge back over the enemy. The fighting reaches cosmic proportions, as the primordial elements of wind, waters and fire are employed by God in the battle. The Egyptians oppose the Lord's all-powerful strength in vain, using what was strongest and swiftest at the time, horses and chariots; they are still transformed into the most inert, heavy elements there are, «stone» (5b) and «lead» (10c). Is-

31 «Enemy» and «greatness» are the only two lexcial repetitions between the central sub-part and the other two.

32 For this reason, J. Muilenburg («A Liturgy», 243) places vv. 7 and 8 in the same strophe. However, due to the image of fire in 7b, which is not coherent with the image of the waters in v. 8 (and in the rest of the part, vv. 1bc, 4-5 and 10), v. 7 belongs to a more general line than the exact action mentioned in the two outer parts. At this level of analysis, therefore, the central sub-part, 6-7, therefore can be understood, at as a description of God's usual behavior towards the enemies of his people.

33 Neither the «I» of the first sub-part (1-2) nor the «they» of the third sub-part (9) are formally identified within these verses.

rael does not take part in the fighting, Israel is at stake. The Egyptians want to raise their hands over Israel to dispossess them and swallow them up (9); but God's right hand saves them (6) and it is the enemy who will be consumed by fire (7).

B. THE SECOND PART (11)

= 11	**Who is**	**like you**
	. among the gods,	YHWH?
=	**Who is**	**like you,**
	. shining	of holiness,
	. terrible	in praises,
	. maker	of miracles?

This part has two pieces. The first (ab) is made up of a single bimember segment, and the second is made up of two segments, one unimember (11c) and one trimember (11def). Each of the members has two terms. The first members of each piece are identical. The last trimember seems to be opposed to the second member of the first piece (b) — in fact, God's attributes are described at length and in detail at the end while nothing is said about the attributes of the «gods» mentioned at the start.

As often happens, the center of the Song of the Sea is taken up with a question[34], a double question, in fact[35], which the rest of the text allows us to answer.

C. THE THIRD PART (12-17)

The last part has three sub-parts which are grow in length (12-13; 14-16a and 16b-17; see p. 84).

1. THE FIRST SUB-PART (12-13)

COMPOSITION

This sub-part, the size of a piece, has three bimembers, each member of which has two terms. These three segments follow one another chronologically — having destroyed his enemies, God guides his people into the desert, to lead them, at the end of the journey, to the place they will remain. At the outer parts, «your

34 See *Traité*, 417-435.

35 On binarity, a basic characteristic of biblical rhetoric, see *Traité*, 15-21; other examples of a double question in the center are found in Amos 6:8-14; Luke 12:25-26; Mark 8:36-37 (see *Traité*, 425.431.434).

right hand» and «your strength» both express power (against enemies), while «your faithfulness» in the center indicates love (of his «people»)[36]; God's two attitudes match one another.

+ 12	**You have** stretched out	YOUR RIGHT HAND:
=	has swallowed them	*the earth.*
+ 13	**You have** *led*	***in*** YOUR FAITHFULNESS
–	this people	whom you have redeemed,
+ whom	**you have** *guided*	***in*** YOUR STRENGTH
–	to *the dwelling*	*of your holiness.*

BIBLICAL CONTEXT

Verse 12 is problematic — for some it is still about the Egyptians' defeat[37], «the earth» being taken in a general sense, rather than «the sea»[38], while for others it is a way of describing Sheol[39]. For others, however, this verse alludes to the punishment of Korah's sons, Dathan and Abiram (Num 16:30-34), swallowed up by the earth[40]. Similarly, Tournay observes that the image of fire in v. 7 recalls the expression «the fire consumed them» in Num 16:35[41]. The commentators' choice seems to depend broadly on their opinion about the date of the canticle's composition, which for Freedman is ancient (12th-10th century)[42], while for Tournay it is more recent (under Josiah, probably in 622)[43]. The canticle's insertion into the Book of Exodus, just after the account of the crossing of the sea could tip the balance in favor of the interpretation which sees Moses' song as simply the celebration of God's victory over the Egyptians. However, vv. 14-15 introduce four other peoples alongside the Egyptians, whose presence might also seem out of place just after the crossing of the sea. This is to say nothing of the double mention of the introduction of the people's being led «towards the dwelling of your holiness» in 13, to which the canticle returns at length in 17. While Korah's

36 This could tip towards a concentric construction, especially since «the earth» which swallows up the enemies is somehow opposed to «the dwelling of your holiness», towards which the people will be raised up. However, the last two segments are much closer to one another in terms of content («led» is synonymous with «guided») and from the point of view of their structure (the first two members have exactly the same construction). In addition, they seem to form only one phrase.

37 So, for example, Lagrange, Muilenburg, Freedman.

38 M.-J. LAGRANGE, «Deux chants», 537.

39 TOURNAY R., «Recherches», 346; see too LEVINE E., «*Neofiti* 1, A Study of Exodus 15», 314.

40 See J.D. WATTS's opinion in «The Song of the Sea, Exod XV».

41 «Chronologie», 346.

42 «Strophe and Meter», 171.

43 «Recherches», 357.

sons are not explicitly named, it seems that we can keep the reference to the account in Num 16, at least as a reasonable hypothesis. We will return to this later.

However, within this sub-part we can already observe a relationship between the second member of the first segment («the earth has swallowed them», repeated word for word in Num 16:30.32), and the second member of the last segment («the dwelling of your holiness»). Words from the same root as «holiness» are repeated several times in the narrative in Numbers 16, where they have the function of keywords: the aim of the revolt was to know who, out of Moses and Aaron, or Korah's sons, was «holy» or «consecrated» (Num 16:3.5.7), that is, who, of the people, represented God's authority?

INTERPRETATION

Out of love for his people the Lord has redeemed them from slavery and led them out of the place of slavery. By contesting Moses' and Aaron's authority, by demanding consecration for themselves, Dahan and Abiram question God's choice (Numbers 16). They even fight his plans: «Was it not enough to take us from a land where milk and honey flow to die in this wilderness...?» (Num 16:13). Out of love for his people, the Lord could not allow his work to be ruined — those who refused to acknowledge the power of his right hand must experience that power; those who look behind them and call the land of slavery by the very name of the promised land (Num 16:13-14) do not deserve to enter it and the earth is to swallow them. Only those who have recognized his holiness may pass into the dwelling of his holiness.

2. THE SECOND SUB-PART (14-16a)

COMPOSITION

This sub-part, the length of a piece, is made up of three bimembers. The first and the third bimembers mirror one another. The outer members (14a.16a) are general — they deal with the «peoples» as a whole (14a), described later; «they», in 16a, seems immediately to refer to «all the inhabitants of Canaan» in the previous member, but from its position, it could also refer to «the peoples» at the beginning (14a). The second member of the first segment (14b) and the first member of the final segment (15e) deal with «the inhabitants» of Philistia and Canaan, to the west of the Jordan.

The central segment no longer deals with «the inhabitants» but the «chiefs» and «leaders» of Edom and Moab, both countries located to the east of the Jordan. This segment is in mirror construction, with the verbs at the outside and the subjects in the center. A similar phenomenon marks the other two segments — in the first «the peoples» and «the inhabitants of Philistia» are at the outside, while the corresponding terms, «they tremble» and «pangs» are in the center; this is reversed in the last segment, which accentuates the mirror nature of these two segments.

The verb «they tremble» in 14a previews the two verbs, «dismayed», in 15a, and «melted away» in 15e, as they both have «the peoples» as their subject, generally at the beginning, then of Edom and Canaan. Conversely the two occurrences of «seize» with «pangs» and «trembling» as subjects (14b, 15d), preview the final member where «fall» refers back to «seize» and where «terror and dread» adapt «pangs» (14b) and «trembling» (15d). Note the accumulation of seven terms to describe fear[44].

= 14 have heard	THE PEOPLES	they TREMBLE;		
+ PANGS	seizes	*the*	*inhabitants*	of PHILISTIA.
– 15 Then	DISMAYED			
		THE	*CHIEFS*	of Edom;
		THE	*LEADERS*	of Moab
– TREMBLING	seizes them.			
+ MELTED AWAY		*all the*	*inhabitants*	of CANAAN;
= 16 *fall*	UPON THEM	TERROR and DREAD.		

BIBLICAL CONTEXT

The list of peoples seems to follow the chronological sequence of Israel's peregrinations between leaving Egypt and settling the Promised Land. Even before the people cross the sea, «God did not let them take the road to the land of the *Philistines*, although that was the nearest way. God thought that the prospect of fighting would make the people lose heart and turn back to Egypt» (Exod 13:17). Having crossed the desert, the people wished first to cross the country of *Edom*, which refused to allow them to cross (Num 20:14-21) and then camped on the plains of *Moab* (Num 22-24), finally crossing the Jordan to take possession of the land of *Canaan* (Num 33:50f).

44 See B. COSTACURTA, *La vita minacciata*, 56, 225-228.

INTERPRETATION

The generalized panic which afflicts all the peoples might appear to contradict the facts reported in the different accounts in Exodus. Philistia is presented here with one of the more characteristic and strongest images of fear and anguish, the woman seized by the pangs of childbirth[45] — this is a total reversal compared to the Exodus account, where God himself thinks that the children of Israel would be afraid of the «war» which the Philistines would surely wage on them. At the same time, according to Numbers, it was not Edom which was horrified by Israel, but the other way around. The re-reading of ancient events which the canticle carries out in the light of later history is coherent with the way in which the crossing of the sea has been interpreted — the one who was weakest has overcome those who are stronger, through the radical reversal which only the all-powerful Lord can effect.

3. THE THIRD SUB-PART (16b-17)

COMPOSITION

:: 16b By the greatness of	YOUR ARM	
:: they are still	like a stone,	
: *till pass over*	**this people,**	YHWH,
: *till pass over*	**this people**	whom you have purchased.
+ 17 You will bring them	and you will plant them	
– **upon the mountain**	*of your inheritance,*	
– **on the place**	*for your habitation*	
: you made,	YHWH,	
– **on the sanctuary,**	Lord,	
: established	YOUR HANDS.	

45 B. COSTACURTA, *La vita minacciata*, 209-210, 232-233, 162-167.

Each of the two pieces of this sub-part makes up a single phrase. The first piece (16b-e) is made up of two bimembers, the first is the main clause which describes the enemies being immobilized[46], the second, which juxtaposes two temporals (16de) whose first terms are identical, reports the people's crossing[47]. The second piece (17) is made up of three segments. The last two (17cd and 17ef) are objects of place, in apposition to the object of the second member of the first segment (17b). The last two segments parallel one another — objects of place followed by a relative clause whose verbs, «you made» and «established», are synonymous. The two apostrophes, «YHWH» and «Lord» are median terms[48].

At the end of the first member «your arm» (16b) and «your hands» at the end of the last member (17f) make an inclusio for the sub-part as a whole.

INTERPRETATION

Through the power of his arm, the Lord petrifies and silences the enemy (16ab); with the strength of his hand he builds the shrine (17ef), the place where his people's praise will resound. Here is the place where Israel will celebrate the mighty deeds of He who snatched them from the hand of their enemies, who led them, who made them cross the waters of the river and planted them in the inheritance he granted them.

46 The third person plural of *dmh* («to bring together») and *dmm* («to be unmoving, in silence») are homophones (*yidᵉmû*); TOURNAY («Recherches»,353) emphasizes the parallel with Zeph. 1.11: «The whole brood of Canaan has been destroyed»; see too WALDMANN N., «A Comparative Note on Exodus 15:14-16». It is this interpretation which we follow and this is why the verb has been translated by «they are still».

47 In «Recherches» (p. 353), TOURNAY writes: «The verb "to cross" is used in the older and in the more recent parts of *Deuteronomy* about Israel's crossing of the Jordan (Deut 9:1; 12:10; End of the Exile, 4:21-22; 30:18; 21:2, etc) and also, more generally, as here, for the entry into the promised land (Deut 6:1; 11:8.11.31; 27:4,12; 31:13, etc)».

48 In addition the noun «place» (17c) has the same root as the verb «to establish» (17f).

- [12] You have stretched out YOUR RIGHT (HAND):
- has swallowed them the earth.

+ [13] You have led in your faithfulness
+ **THIS PEOPLE WHOM YOU HAVE REDEEMED.**

. *You have guided* in YOUR STRENGTH
. *TO YOUR DWELLING of your* *HOLINESS.*

+ [14] have heard the ***PEOPLES***, they tremble;
– the pangs seizes the inhabitants of Philistia.

. [15] Then dismayed the chiefs of Edom;
. the leaders of Moab, seizes them the trembling.

– Melted away are all the inhabitants of Canaan;
+ [16] fall upon ***THEM*** terror and dread.

- By the greatness of YOUR ARM,
- they become still like a stone,

+ till pass over **THIS PEOPLE**, YHWH,
+ till pass over **THIS PEOPLE WHOM YOU HAVE PURCHASED.**

. [17] *You will bring them* and will plant them
UPON THE MONTAIN of your inheritance,

. *ON THE PLACE of your habitation*
that you have made, YHWH,

. ON *THE SANCTUARY*, Lord,
that have established YOUR HANDS.

The outer sub-parts (12-13 and 16b-17) parallel one another. The initial bimembers (12ab and 16bc) match — their first members end with «your right hand» and «your arm». Both describe God's act against enemies — at the start of the final sub-part (16bc), these are obviously the peoples listed in the central sub-part, petrified by «terror and dread», while those whom «the earth has swallowed» at the start of the first part (12) are Korah's sons.

The second segments (13ab and 16de) also match — their second members end with two synonymous syntagmas, «the people you have redeemed» in 13b and «the people you have purchased» in 16e.

The last segments (13cd and 17) are different lengths, but their content is identical. The initial terms, «you have led» and «you will bring them» are synonymous. «Towards the dwelling of your holiness» (13d) heralds the three objects of place in 17 and, in particular, «on the sanctuary» in 17e, which has the same root as «holiness» in 13d.

The synonymous terms «your right hand» (at the end of 12a) and «your arm» (at the end of 16b) act as initial terms for the outer sub-parts. In the same way, «your hands» (end of 17f) and «your strength» (end of 13c), just like «holiness» (13d) and «sanctuary» (17e) act as final terms.

The central sub-part (14-16a) is the hinge of the other two sub-parts, particularly due to the first word, «they have heard». The news of God's acts, described in the first sub-part, is the *cause* of the other peoples' terror; this terror, in turn, paralyzes the peoples, which, *consequently* enables the people of God to «pass over» until they reach the land which was promised to them as inheritance. We should note that this same word, «people» (*'ammîm*) is used in all three sub-parts to describe both Israel and the foreign peoples (not the synonymous «nations» (*gōyîm*), which is often used to describe other peoples).

INTERPRETATION

While the peoples are paralyzed by fear and petrified by anguish, the People of God advance, guided by the Lord, and pass unhindered into the land given to them. While the rebels are swallowed up by the earth and go down to Sheol, Israel is planted on God's mountain. They can praise the God who has redeemed them in the sanctuary, while their enemies will remain dumb — «The dead cannot praise Yhwh, they have gone down to silence; but we, the living, bless Yhwh, henceforth and evermore» (Ps 115:17-18). To God alone belongs praise, for he alone has destroyed the rebel with his right hand and paralyzed the enemy with the strength of his arm; he alone has redeemed and purchased his people; he alone has guided them and led them to the place of his dwelling, which he himself makes in the sanctuary he establishes with his own hands. In their joy, the people acknowledge that everything has been given freely.

D. THE CANTICLE AS A WHOLE (15:1-18)

COMPOSITION

1 Then sang Moses and the sons of Israel this song to YHWH and they said, saying:

«I sing to YHWH, for he is exalted greatly;
the horse and its rider he has cast into the sea.
2 My strength and my song, is YaH; he has become for me the salvation.
He is my God, I praise him,
the God of my father, I exalt him.
3 YHWH is a man of war, YHWH is his name.
4 The chariots of Pharaoh and his army he has thrown ***into the sea;***
the elite of his captains are drowned ***into the sea of Reeds.***
5 The depths cover them, they went down ***into the deeps*** LIKE A STONE.

6 Your right hand, YHWH, *SHINING* of power,
your right hand, YHWH, shatters the enemy.
7 In abundance of your greatness you overthrow your adversaries;
you loose your wrath, it devours them like straw.

\+ 8 **At the breath of YOUR nostrils** piled up the waters,
stood up like a heap the floods, congealed the depths in the heart of the sea.
9 The enemy said: "I will pursue, I will overtake,
I will divide the spoil, will fill up of them my gorge;
I will draw out my sword, will dispossess them my hand."
= 10 **You have blown YOUR BREATH: covered them THE SEA**,
they sank like lead into the waters tremendous.

11 Who is like you among the gods, YHWH?
Who is like you, *SHINING of HOLINESS*,
terrible in praises, maker of miracles?

= 12 **You have stretched out YOUR RIGHT HAND: swallowed them THE EARTH.**
13 You have led in your faithfulness this people whom you have redeemed,
\+ **whom you have guided in YOUR strength** to the dwelling of your *HOLINESS.*

14 Have heard the peoples, they tremble;
pangs seizes the inhabitants of Philistia.
15 Then dismayed the chiefs of Edom;
the leaders of Moab trembling seizes them.
Melted away are all the inhabitants of Canaan;
16 fall upon them terror and dread.

By the greatness of your arm they are still LIKE A STONE,
till pass over this people, YHWH, till pass over this people whom you have purchased.
17 You will bring them and will plant them ***on the mountain of your inheritance,***
on the place of your habitation that you have made, YHWH,
on the SANCTUARY, Lord, that have established your hands.

18 YHWH reigns forever and ever!

The outer parts (1b-10 and 12-17) are long — 38 members in the first, 22 in the second — while the central part (11) is very short (6 members)[49]. This central part is made up of the only two questions in the canticle, which is one example among many of a law of organization of biblical texts[50]. The outer parts are also arranged concentrically.

The sub-parts which frame the central part (8-10 and 12-13) match. Segments 10a (at the end of sub-part 8-10) and segment 12 (at the start of sub-part 12-13) are parallel term for term:

You have blown *your breath:*	THE SEA	has covered them	10a
You have stretched out *your right (hand):*	THE EARTH	has swallowed them	12

They act as median terms[51]. Both sub-parts also share the fact that God's name is not mentioned here.

The centers of the outer parts (6-7 and 14-16a) also relate to one another — «the enemy» in 6b and «the adversaries» in 7a correspond to the «peoples» listed in 14-16a, even though these are different groups.

In the outer sub-parts (1b-5 and 16b-17) the only two occurrences of «like a stone» act as distant median terms, at the end of the last segment of one (5), and the end of the first segment of the other (16b). The first sub-part ends with the triple mention of the place where the Egyptians were swallowed up, «into the sea» (4a), «into the sea of Reeds» (4b), «into the depths» (5). Similarly, the last sub-part ends with the triple mention of the place the people will be planted, «on the mountain of your inheritance» (17a), «on the place of your habitation» (17b), «on the sanctuary» (17c). These places are clearly opposed: the Egyptians «go down into the depths», while the children of Israel will be settled «on the mountain».

49 We might also observe that in the first part, the first sub-part (1b-5) is longer than the symmetrical sub-part (8-10: 16 members to 14), while in the last part the balance is reversed — the first sub-part (12-13) has 6 members and the last (16b-17) has 10.

50 See p. 78, n. 35.

51 A parallel segment at the other end of the sub-parts matches these two segments (8a and 13b).

The link between the central part (11) and the other two parts is initially marked by two lexical repetitions — «shining» (11b) was already used at the center of the first part (6a); «holiness», linked to «shining» in 11b, is repeated at the outside of the last part, in an identical way at the end of 13, with «sanctuary» in the last segment (17c)[52].

Next, «praises» (11c) corresponds to the outer parts of the canticle — it recalls part of the series in the first verses («I sing», 1b; «song» in 2a; «I will praise him» in 2c), and on the other hand the «sanctuary» of the final verse (17c), which is the perfect place where God's praises should be sung for the wonders he has worked. Finally, we should observe the play on words between *ʾēlîm* (the plural of *'ēl*) = «gods» in 11a and *ʾēlê* (a plural constructed from *ʾayil*; the absolute plural is either *ʾēlîm* or *ʾēlîm*) = «nobles», «princes», in 15b. The word «captains» in the first part (4b) corresponds to «princes», itself parallel to «leaders» in 15ab; this wordplay between homophones suggests that the relationship between the Lord and the «gods» is somehow connected to the relationship between God and the leaders of nations.

We have not yet dealt with v. 18. First of all it must be recognized that this verse is not part of the composition either of the last part (12-17) or of the body of the canticle (1b-17). However, this final verse seems to correspond to the narrative phrase which introduces the words of the canticle (1a), which are inseparable from it. It would seem to be important not to remove the canticle from the context in which it is integrated — while the episodes which it mentions and to which it alludes go beyond simply the leaving of Egypt, the crossing of the sea remains the foundational event. So far from being foreign to the canticle, this acclamation is a sort of summary — from the start to the end, in fact, the only object of Moses' and the children of Israel's praise is the absolute and eternal majesty of God, which has been demonstrated all along the way that he has made his people journey, from their liberation from their state of slavery until their settlement in the place where the service of their God can be carried out[53].

52 This is a good example of the third law emphasized by LUND N.W., *Chiasmus in the New Testament*, 41: «Identical ideas are often distributed in such a fashion that *they occur in the extremes and at the centre* of their respective system, and nowhere else in the system».

53 «In like manner, the creation of the cultic metropolis and the temple of Esagila makes the keystone of the work of creation of the king-god in the Babylonian epic of creation and enthronement, *Enuma êliš*. It seems to have been a widespread idea that creation culminates with the creation of the sanctuary; in Ugarit the enthronement of Baal is likewise combined with the erection and consecration of his temple; the temple has a cosmic meaning» (MOWINCKEL S., *The Psalms in Israel's Worship*, II, 247); see too CROSS F.M., «The Song of the Sea and Canaanite Myth», and CROSS F.M. and FREEDMAN D.N., «The Song of Miriam».

Crossing the sea (Exod 14)

The last part of the Song refers to events much later than leaving Egypt. Verse 13 first of all mentions how God guided his people (in the desert), v. 16c mentions «crossing» the Jordan, and the whole of the central part (14-16a) lists four peoples whom the children of Israel will meet much later on.

The first, most developed part tells of what has just happened in the previous chapter, crossing the sea.

The earth swallows up Korah's sons (Deut 11:1-7)

We need to return to the problem posed by v. 12 of how to identify the people «swallowed up by the earth». The connection between Moses' song and Deut 11:1-7 is particularly striking — here what God has done to the Egyptians, submerged beneath the waters of the sea, is paralleled by what he did to Dathan and Abiram, swallowed by the earth:

---

[2] And you shall know today and not your sons,
who have not known, nor *seen* the lesson of YHWH your God,
his *greatness*, his mighty hand and his outstretched arm,

+ [3] the signs and the deeds *WHICH HE HAS DONE* IN THE MIDST OF EGYPT,
– to Pharaoh, king of Egypt,
– and to ALL his land,

+ [4] and that *WHICH HE HAS DONE*
– to the army of Egypt,
– to its horses and its chariots,

by causing to flow upon them **the waters of the sea** of Reeds
when they were pursuing you,
and YHWH destroyed them to his day;

- - - - - - - - - - - - - - - - - - - -

+ [5] and that *WHICH HE HAS DONE* FOR YOU IN THE DESERT
– until your coming in unto this place;

+ [6] and that *WHICH HE HAS DONE*
– to Dathan
– and to Abiram, the sons of Eliab the Reubenite,

when the **earth** opened her mouth and swallowed them,
with their families, their tents and all their belongings IN THE MIDST OF ALL ISRAEL.

---

[7] It is your own eyes that have *seen* these *great* deeds which YHWH has done.

---

2 And you shall know today and not your sons,
who have not known, nor *seen* the lesson of YHWH your God,
his *greatness*, his mighty hand and his outstretched arm,

+ 3 the signs and the deeds			*WHICH HE HAS DONE*	IN THE MIDST OF EGYPT,
–	to	Pharaoh,	king of Egypt,	
– and	to	ALL his land,		
+ 4 and that			*WHICH HE HAS DONE*	
–	to	the army of Egypt,		
–	to	its horses and its chariots,		

by causing to flow upon them **the waters of the sea** of Reeds
when they were pursuing you,
and YHWH destroyed them — to his day;

- -

+ 5 and that			*WHICH HE HAS DONE*	FOR YOU IN THE DESERT
– until your coming in				unto this place;
+ 6 and that			*WHICH HE HAS DONE*	
–	to	Dathan		
– and	to	Abiram,	the sons of Eliab the Reubenite,	

when the **earth** opened her mouth and swallowed them,
with their families, their tents and all their belongings — IN THE MIDST OF ALL ISRAEL.

---

7 It is your own eyes that have *seen* these *great* deeds which YHWH has done.

Note the mention of «this place» at 5b which recalls «the dwelling of your holiness» in Exod 15:13.

In addition, after the earth had swallowed Korah's sons, it is reported that «fire from YHWH» «consumed» the two hundred and fifty incense carriers (Num 16:35). This punishment, which matches that of being swallowed by the earth, can be linked to the image of Exod 15:7. The link is the more justified because the same verb (in the participle in 7a, translated by «adversaries»), is used at the start of the account of Korah's sons to describe their rebellion: «they *rebelled* against Moses» (Num 16:2, repeated by a synonym in v. 11 — «Against YHWH himself you have joined forces»)[54]. The translation therefore should be corrected, with «adversaries» changed to «rebels» or «opponents». So the first part of the canticle implicitly links the Egyptian enemy punished by the waters (into which they descend «like a stone») and the Israelite rebel punished by fire (which con-

54 See BOVATI P., *Ristabilire la giustizia*, 217-219.273.

sumes them «like straw»). In the same way the last part links the enemy «peoples» (who have become «like stone») and the Israelite rebels «swallowed by the earth». God's enemies are not only external, Egyptians, Philistines, Edomites, Moabites and Canaanites, but also the rebels within the people of Israel itself.

To the extent that the canticle's relationship with texts known to be later are founded, this cannot but have a bearing on the problem of its dating[55]. Tournay observes that «the imperfect *tippol* [«falls» in v.16] is followed by two imperfects»; the entry into Canaan is thus supposed, as a literary fiction, to still be in the future; Moses and Israel may not talk about it. But the poet betrays himself by using perfects in v. 13. Israel is already well settled in the promised land»[56]. The literary fiction, which is surely real, might indicate a *Sitz im Leben* which would not itself be fictitious, the time of the Exile when being in Canaan and the Temple celebrations were, once again, to come in the future. Whatever the poem's date, it seems to be more important to deal with the tension between «already there» and «not yet». The canticle's position in the Exodus account, on leaving the sea, means this — liberation has taken place, but it is only the beginning of a long path. The canticle's redaction situates those who sing it much later on the road to the Promised Land, when they «pass over» to take possession of it, but, it appears, before they have been settled on Mount Sion and before they can worship the Lord in his Temple.

Accounts of creation

Finally there is a dimension of the canticle which links it to the creation accounts. To effect the salvation of his people, God orders the world's great elements, just as he did in the beginning. With the breath of his nostrils he overturns the order which he had instituted, making the sea solid so that Israel could pass through, removing the earth's solidity to make it swallow up the rebels. Finally, he himself makes the sanctuary with his own hands. The birth of his people is thus presented as a sort of new creation. God's reign truly extends «from the beginning and for ever».

55 For different opinions on this see CRAIGIE P.C., «An Egyptian Expression in the Song of the Sea», 83. M.L. BRENNER (*The Song of the Sea, Exod 15:1-21*) places it after the return from the Exile and the rebuilding of the Temple.

56 «Recherches», 353.

Moses' song and the song of the Lamb

At the other end of the Christian Bible is another song, referred to as «the hymn of Moses and of the Lamb» (Rev 15:3-4), which appears as the final echo of the Song of the Sea.

. [3] And *they sing*	the song of Moses,		the servant of God,
. and	the song of Lamb		*saying*:
+ «Great	and amazing		your works,
– Lord	God		*All*-Mighty;
+ *just*	and true		your ways,
–	KING		of the NATIONS.
	[4] Who	shall not fear you,	LORD,
	or	shall not glorify	YOUR NAME?
+ For	(you) only		(is) holy,
– for	*all* the NATIONS		shall come
– and	PROSTRATE THEMSELVES		before you,
+ for	your *judgments*		have been manifested.

The phrase «they were singing the hymn of Moses, the servant of God, and of the Lamb» in Rev 15:3 presents difficulties for commentators. Do «those who had fought against the beast and won, and against his statue and the number which is his name» (v. 2) sing two distinct hymns, Moses', on the one hand, and the Lamb's, on the other, or is the hymn in vv. 3-4 that of both Moses and the Lamb? Furthermore, whatever the answer to this first question, a further difficulty arises from the fact that nowhere does the text of Revelation seem to say explicitly which of Moses' hymns is meant. Exegetical opinion is not unanimous on this latter point — traditional interpretation views it as the «Song of the Sea», reported after the account of the crossing of the sea in Exod 15:1-18[57], and this remains the most frequent exegesis[58]. However, some modern authors prefer to see it as the canticle of Deuteronomy 32[59]. It is also commonly acknowledged that «the canticle itself is a mosaic of Old Testament phrases»[60].

57 WALVOORD J.F., *The Revelation of Jesus Christ*, 227.

58 For example, SWETE H.B., *The Apocalypse of St John*, 195 («It is surely the song of victory which is in view here rather than the swan-like song ascribed to the dying Lawgiver»); LOISY A., *L'Apocalypse de Jean*, 281.

59 BULLINGER E.W., *Commentary on Revelation*; similarly FORD J.M., *Revelation*, 257.

60 HARRINGTON W.J., *Revelation*, 159, gives almost the same references as SWETE, H.B. *The Apocalypse*, 196; see too DRIVER S.R., *The Book of Exodus*, 131.

The canticle of Revelation 15 is much shorter than that of Exodus 15, but it so happens that their general composition is very similar. In both cases, in fact, two parts frame a double question. In addition, the content of the canticle in Revelation 15 is very close to the content of the canticle in Exodus 15[61].

Unlike the canticle of Exodus 15, that of Revelation 15 does not appear to have given rise to many studies of its rhetoric[62].

The narrative phrase which introduces the song (3ab) is a bimember segment — the verb «they were singing» at the start of the first member is not repeated but is offset by «saying» at the end of the second segment. Moses is described as «the servant of God», while the Lamb is not described. «The hymn of Moses» is paralleled with «the song of the Lamb». The song itself has three parts.

The first part (3c-f) is the length of a piece. The two bimembers parallel one another[63]. The first members have the same syntactical structure, predicates formed by two compound adjectives, followed by the subject nouns which are governed by the same possessives. The second members are apostrophes addressed to the same person. We note a sort of complementarity between the two segments — the first seems to look towards the creator God in himself (his «works», beautiful in themselves); the second views him in relation to humanity (he is «king» whose way of acting and whose «ways» are «just and true» towards «the nations».

The central part (4ab) has the canticle's only double question. Both members of this segment parallel one another — both verbs are affected by the negative. «Your name» matches «Lord»; the interrogative pronoun «Who» is the only subject of the two verbs.

61 For A. Loisy (*L'Apocalypse*, 281), «the martyrs' song only offers a limited analogy to Moses', if not in content at least in situation».

62 This analysis is linked to U. Vanni's, *La struttura letteraria dell'Apocalisse*, 161-162. J.M. Alcacér's detailed study («La historia de la salvación celebrada come Pascua. El "otro" paso del mar: Ap 15,3-4») is more recent.

63 Within each segment the symmetry between the two members is not obvious, but the parallelism is revealed at the next level up, the level of piece.

The last part (4c-f) is not constructed in parallel like the first part, but concentrically[64]. It is also the size of a piece, made up of three segments. Given that the second and third members are linked by «and» and are constructed in chiasmus (the actors on the outside, their actions in the center), they make up a bimember segment:

+ for **all the nations**
: SHALL COME
: and SHALL PROSTRATE THEMSELVES
+ before **you.**

We should therefore think of the outer members as unimembers — they are related to one another, since both begin with the same «for» (just as the central segment of the rest does) and they describe God and his actions, while the central segment describes the people's reactions to this description of God. Thus the same opposition as in the first part is repeated, with God described as himself (4c) and in his relationship to the nations (4f).

There are many links between the outer parts. The repetition of «nations» (3f.4d), «judgments» (4f) corresponding to «the just» (3e), the use of «all» (4d) which recalls «All-Powerful» (3d), and finally «will prostrate» (4e), which refers to «king» (3f), since one prostrates oneself before the king.

The «name» of the «Lord» in the center (4ab) has already been mentioned in the first part — «Lord, almighty God» and «king of the nations» (3d.3f). «Holy», in the last part (4c) can also be seen as a divine title.

We can see a sort of progression between the three parts of the hymn — initially (3c-f) only those who have triumphed over the Beast acclaim God; then (4ab) they ask a question in which they themselves are clearly implicated, but which also refers to others; and finally (4c-f) they announce that «all the nations will prostrate themselves» before the Lord. «Fear», in the first member of the central question, seems to herald the last part to the extent that those who fear will prostrate themselves. «Glorify», in the second member of the central part, would seem to suit the first part, which praises the Lord, better.

The most obvious link is the one which the Revelation text itself establishes with «Moses' song» (3a).

64 This phenomenon, which seeks to match a unit of parallel construction with a unit of concentric construction is often to be found in biblical texts.

This is the only time in the whole of the Apocalypse that an Old Testament passage is explicitly indicated and one of its characters named, which emphasizes the importance given by the author to this passage[65].

Those who have triumphed over the beast stay close to «a glass lake suffused with fire» (Rev 15:2). Similarly, in the Exodus account, Moses and the children of Israel sing after they have crossed the sea. The canticle's introduction presents Moses as God's «servant», just as in Exod 14.31 (this is the last word of the account which precedes Moses' song). We must not forget the mention of the «Lamb», recalling the paschal lamb[66] linked to the commemoration of the crossing of the sea.

In terms of the canticle itself, the first thing to note is that the canticle in Revelation, like that of Exodus, is based on a question[67]. Although the interrogative pronoun «Who», which the questions begin with, does not have the same subject in the two canticles, «fear» and «glorify» in Rev 15:4 can recall the expression «terrible in praise» of Exod 15:11.

On the other hand, there are many connections in vocabulary between the two canticles (here we only give those established by the Septuagint[68], following the order of the reading of the canticle in Revelation 15):

— «great»	(3c):	Exod 15:16	(lit. «the greatness of your arm»)
— «admirable»	(3c):	Exod 15:11	(«terrible»)
— «works»	(3c):	Exod 15:11	(«maker of miracles»)
— «Lord»	(3d)		translates «YHWH» and «God» *ĕlōhîm*
— «just»	(3e) and		
— «judgments»	(4f):	Exod 15:13	(«your faithfulness»)
— «your ways»	(3e):	Exod 15:13	(«you have led»)
— «king»	(3f):	Exod 15:18	(«reign»)
— «the nations»	(3f, 4d):	Exod 15:14	(«the peoples»)
— «shall fear»	(4a):	Exod 15:16	(«terror»)

65 VANNI U., *La struttura*, 161-162.
66 VANNI U., *L'Apocalisse*, 177-184.
67 The central question of the Revelation 15 canticle is a literal repetition of Jer 10:7. It so happens that in the long diatribe against idols in Jer 10:1-16 this question is found in the central piece (6-7). On the question of the center, see *Traité*, 417-435; and on the quotation in the center see 436-453.
68 Although the author of Revelation follows the Masoretic Text more than the LXX (see VANHOYE A., «L'utilisation du livre d'Ézéchiel dans l'Apocalypse»).

— «glorify» (4b): Exod 15:11 (*dedoxasmenos* = «shining»)
(*doxais* = «glories»)
Exod 15:1 («he is exalted highly»)
Exod 15:2b («I exalt him»)
—«your name» (4b): Exod 15:3 («The LORD is his name»).

It would be awkward not to add *hosios*' synonym.

— «holy» (3c): Exod 15:11.13.17: *hagios.*

Along with those who sing the hymn, «the nations» «shall fear» and «will glorify» the «holy» «name» of the «Lord», «king» of the «nations», because «his works» are «great» and «admirable», because «his ways» and his «judgments» are «just».

However, these many lexical repetitions (16 out of the 22 lexemes in the canticle in Revelation 15 are found in the canticle in Exodus 15) are not in themselves absolute evidence of a literary connection between the two canticles, for this vocabulary is characterized by its master-key aspect — there is no exact reference to any of the Lord's works. Just as the canticle in Exodus 15 is circumstantial, describing the events of the Exodus to which it clearly more or less alludes, so the hymn in Revelation 15 is general.

The hymn in Revelation 15 must also be read and understood in its context — it is apparently the culmination of a long series of «doxologies» which punctuate the book[69].

- In 1:4-8, John unites in the same praise God and Christ who has «redeemed» us by his blood and has made us «a kingdom of priests».
- In 4:11, it is the four animals and the twenty-four Elders who worship God as the Creator of the universe.
- In 5:9 these same characters first of all «sing a *new* hymn» to the Lamb who has redeemed people of every nation by his blood,
- the canticle is repeated in echo at v. 12 by the multitude of angels;
- finally, in v. 13, all living creation unite in the same praise of the Lord God and the Lamb.

69 The eight doxologies of Revelation have been studied in great detail by VANNI U., *La struttura*, 149-167.

• In ch. 7 the angels, Elders and four animals join together with the large crowd of those from all the nations who have washed their robes in the Lamb's blood to praise God (12) and the Lamb (10); this is repeated in 11:15-18.

• In 14:3, a «*new* hymn» is mentioned again[70] which can only be learned by those who have been redeemed from the earth and who bear the Lamb's name and that of his Father on their forehead; however the words of this hymn are not given in ch. 14. It is possible that this is the hymn whose text is given in ch. 15, since the same people are singing, «those who had fought against the beast and won and against his statue and the number which is his name», that is, the martyrs.

Note a further important difference between the canticle in Revelation 15 and all those which precede it. The others are all sung either by the four animals and the twenty-four Elders, or by the multitude of angels, or by all of creation, or eventually the martyrs. The hymn of Rev 15:3-4 is the only one in the whole book which is called «the hymn of the Lamb»[71]. In addition, if this really is the «new» song mentioned in 14:3, it is preceded by another «new song» in 5:8-14: this hymn is addressed in the first two parts (8-10; 11-12) to the Lamb, and gives what he has done as the reason for its praise — «You bought men for God of every race, language, people and nation and made them a line of kings and priests to serve our God and to rule the world» (9-10). So the content of this first «new song» explains the second by recalling the past. However, the final phrase is in the future, «[they will] rule the earth»[72], which heralds the center of the last part of the Lamb's hymn — «all the nations will come and adore you». Moses' hymn and the Lamb's hymn, therefore, are both situated at the same point, between an «already happened» and a «not yet».

The «not yet» is announced as having happened in the final canticle of the book (19:1-8) — «this is the time for the marriage feast of the Lamb. His bride is ready». And Revelation ends with the description of the Lamb's bride, the heavenly Jerusalem (21:9ff), whose Temple is the Lord himself as the Lamb.

70 See ALONSO MARINO P.J., *El Cántico Nuevo en el Apocalipsis*.

71 According to the start of ch. 14, the hymn seems to be sung by those who are «with him» (that is, the Lamb), accompanied by heavenly harps. The one who «teaches» the martyrs the canticle is not identified in the text; but as the start of ch. 15 calls the hymn «the hymn of the Lamb», it is not impossible to think that it is the Lamb who teaches the faithful.

72 Even if we prefer the variant where the verb is in the present, the broad sense of the text does not change substantially.

The hymn of Revelation 15, therefore, appears to be a re-working of all the earlier ones in the book of Revelation, and a preview of those which follow it. It is located at the same logical point in time as the Exodus 15 canticle. The two expressions of the introductory phrase (3ab), «the song of Moses» and «the song of the Lamb» do not refer to two different canticles — the new canticle is broadly the same as the earlier one, or, to use the common New Testament expression, it «accomplishes it»[73].

> The author calls this *the hymn of Moses and of the Lamb*, that is — Moses' hymn, which is also the Lamb's hymn, to show the indissoluble unity of the two covenants, through which redemption has been accomplished. He means that this canticle celebrates the whole of the work of salvation as God prepared it through Moses, accomplished by Christ[74].

This is an apocalyptic or eschatological accomplishment — the major difference, in fact, between the «new canticle» and that of Exodus is the absence of enemies, now included in «all the nations» whom the Lamb, through his Pasch, has reconciled in praise to the one God, and who «will come to prostrate themselves» before the Lord to recognize him as their king. This universal gathering is accomplished through the blood of the Lamb, but has not yet taken place — it is heralded, in the future, for the end of history[75].

INTERPRETATION

The king who judges

«The Lord reigns for ever and ever!». He is the only ruler of the universe and of history, and no-one in heaven or on earth is like him. He orders all the world's elements, the sea obeys his breath, the earth obeys his right hand, he unfurls fire

73 Having indicated the relationship between the two canticles, S. GAROFALO wrote at the end of his work, «L'Epinicio di Mosè», 22: «Really, in its epic splendour and greatness, Moses' magnificent poetic piece is worthy of immortality, and this immortality».

74 BONNET L., *Apocalypse*, 414. See too VANNI U., *La struttura*, 160, n. 26.

75 «Since the beginning of the Christian era, the Song of the Sea of Exodus 15 has played an important role in Jewish liturgy and theology. The text was read on the last day of Passover in ancient synagogues, accompanied by homiletic elaboration and eschatological sermons. The oldest rabbinical texts available consider the "Song of the Sea" to be part of an ongoing song which will end in the "new hymn" which will be sung at the opening of the Messianic era» (LEVINE E., «*Neofiti* 1», 304; references in the notes).

from the sky. His rule extends over all peoples, he throws the Egyptians into the sea like a stone and petrifies the Philistines and Canaanites, Edomites and-Moabites; he makes the rebels among his own people be swallowed by the earth and consumed by fire, and guides his faithful to the place he has chosen for them. No god in the heavens and no king on earth can resist him. All who fight his will — Pharaoh, who did not want to hear his word passed on by his servant; Korah's sons who stood up to Moses against his decrees; all those, in fact, who take themselves to be gods — are treated as vain idols of stone, without strength or voice, ruined in the sea or fixed in their speechlessness.

The king who saves

On the other hand, on the sea-shore, Moses and the children of Israel intone a long canticle in praise of the God of their salvation. Joyfully, they recognize all that comes from him — he alone has redeemed them from their slavery, he alone destroyed those hunting them down. In the shrine which they acknowledge will be given to them by God, like the land, they will be able to continue to praise the name of the one who alone has made the rebels disappear, the one who alone led his faithful through so many dangers, who alone will continue to guide them until the journey's end. Their hymn is not only a song of praise and thanksgiving for God's past actions, it is also at the same time an act of faith in his love and in his faithfulness which will not stop guiding them. «The Lord reigns for ever and ever!».

From «I» to «you»

The Song of the See immediately begins *fortissimo*, but also, as it were, in a minor key. The joy is such that «I», each of the children of Israel as well as all the people together, cannot resist expressing themselves with the spontaneity of the first person (1-5). Of course, the singer only has the Lord's name in his mouth, the name of the God who has saved him by snatching him from the enemy, but the words are addressed to a third party, and speak about God in the third person, just as though what was being recounted was in the past, and as though the person one was speaking about was absent. Then, suddenly, the second person singular erupts into the center of the first part (6) — now the song is addressed to the Lord himself, and will be almost until the end. Only the final acclamation — «the Lord reigns for ever and ever» — returns to the third person. The faith of the children of Israel is shown when they proclaim God's marvels, and is revealed even more brilliantly when it is addressed to the Lord: they would not do this were they not certain of being heard by him.

Strange questions

The double question asked at the very center of the Song of the Sea might seem simply to be a rhetorical question, which obviously does not require any answer, as it is anticipated — after what has just been proclaimed it is only too obvious that no one could be like the Lord! Henri Plantier explains the role in the argument of this question very clearly, and he has no hesitation in describing it as a «proof» or «demonstration»:

> *There are some questions which are worth more than any proof.* Moses' is one such — one feels so deeply that this defeat of the Egyptians is a wonder which God alone can be the author of, that one would be embarrassed to honor any man for it, however strong; and only ask if anything can compare to the arm which caused it, *which has shown* that this arm is unrivalled[76].

However, it is also possible to understand that this is the reader — or, rather, the auditor — who unites his voice to Moses' and the voice of all the community of the children of Israel, who is invited to answer the question in the depth of his heart, that is, to allow himself to become involved in the song's logic, to take part in the dance. However, thinking that the double question is really addressed to God and that he is invited to provide his own answer, is not forbidden.

The Lord's answer

The central question is odd, but it is much more surprising that the Song of the Sea does not limit itself to celebrating the miracles which God has just achieved in saving his people from slavery in Egypt. How is it that the whole of the second side praises the Lord for works, which he has not yet accomplished? How can we justify the fact that the punishment of Korah's sons, the terrors which paralyze the nations, the crossing of the Jordan, the settlement of the Promised Land, even the building of the shrine on the holy mountain, should all be narrated as though it has already taken place, just like the crossing of the sea? And

76 PLANTIER H., *Études littéraires sur les poètes bibliques*, I, 502 (my emphasis).

suppose, simply, as a poetic fiction, this was the Lord's answer to the double question which had just been asked?

A question of faith and hope

As we have seen, faith is at stake in the crossing of the sea. Logically, it would be difficult for it to be otherwise in the Song of the Sea which immediately follows. The narrative had finished on the positive outcome of the test, which the children of Israel, led by Moses, had been submitted to — «they believed in the Lord». This faith is then shown in the exultation of a hymn which is swiftly addressed to God himself. In the whole of the first part of the canticle, the people acknowledge that their God had guided events, when he drew their enemy into such a well-disguised trap that it appeared to have been made for Israel, when he led his people deep into the sea to make the Egyptian armies perish there. The certainty of having been saved by God, when only Moses' hand, not God, had been seen, is called faith. When, after the question addressed to the same Lord, the same certainty no longer looks to the past, but contemplates the future, this is called hope. «For we must be content to hope that we shall be saved — our salvation is not in sight, we should not have to be hoping for it if it were — but, as I say, we must hope to be saved since we are not saved yet — it is something we must wait for with patience» (Rom 8:24-25).

Part Two

The law of freedom

«The Decalogue» is one of the few titles which does not come from modern editions of the Bible[1]. «The Ten Words», in Greek, the «Deca-logos», is the original name, in the Scriptures themselves[2], of the famous Exodus passage and its twin in the book of Deuteronomy[3]. Despite, or perhaps because of, its venerable age, this description raises problems. We need only ask a number of people, even those with a good knowledge of the Bible, to list the commandments — even if more than a couple come up with the same list, this will only be after quite some hesitation and correction.

This is why most translations feel the need to supply the division of the Decalogue into the Ten Commandments as a note. As we might expect, earliest Christian tradition is divided on this matter between the Eastern tradition, following the Greek Fathers, and the Western tradition following St Augustine[4]. The number «ten», rather than indicating the number of different commandments of the Decalogue, could symbolize the total, just as, in the first creation narrative in Gen 1:1—2:4a, the world was made in ten words[5].

Scripture also uses another name, with a different number — «the two tablets»[6]. The two titles, «*ten* words» and «*two* tablets», have imposed a division into two on the text, while from a literary point of view, the text is organized in mirror fashion, focused on the only two positive commandments, which deal

1 This part returns to an article which appeared in Italian: «I due decaloghi, legge di libertà» in *Gr.* 81 (2000) 659-692; in French: «Les deux Décalogues, loi de liberté» in *StRh* 8 (11.04.2002; last updated 27.09.2005); and in English: «Two Decalogues, Law of Freedom» in *StRh* 16, (02.11.2004). An early version of this article appeared in 1984, «Les dix commandements, loi de liberté; analyse rhétorique d'Ex 20,2-17 et de Dt 5,6-21» in *MUSJ* 50 (1984) 405-421 (+7 plates inset). The analysis here is clearly improved, thanks in particular to comments and suggestions from Pietro BOVATI and to his study of the Decalogue in *Giustizia e ingiustizia nell'Antico Testamento*, 75-142 (henceforth Bovati). I also acknowledge WÉNIN A., «Le Décalogue. Approche contextuelle, théologie et anthropologie», 9-43 (see too his «Le Décalogue, révélation de Dieu et chemin de bonheur?»); and M. BALMARY's, *La Divine Origine*; ID., *Abel ou la traversée de l'Éden.*

2 Exod 34:28; Deut 4:13; 10:4.

3 Modern exegesis tends to attribute the Exodus version to the Priestly school and the Deuteronomy version to the Deuteronomic school, in which case the Exodus version would be most recent.

4 The difference depends on the identification of the first commandment (2-3 for the Jews and the Greek Fathers, whom the Orthodox and Reformed Churches follow, or 3-6 for the Latin Fathers, most of the Syriac tradition, Catholics and Lutherans) and, similarly, the last commandment (17ab for the former, 17b for the latter); see Bovati, 83, n. 34

5 See FRAENKEL A.A., «'Assarah Maamaroth — 'Assarah Dibberot»; see Bovati, 83-84.

6 Exod 31:18; 32:15; Deut 4:13; 5:22; 9:9-11.15.17; 1Kgs 8:9; 2Chr 5:10. P. Bovati (pp. 81-83) thinks that this number does not indicate the text's division into two parts, as all the iconography suggests, but the number of copies of the same text, one copy for each of the two parties who have concluded the agreement, as was usual when treaties were made at the time, and as still happens today for all written contracts.

with the sanctification of the Sabbath day, on the one hand, and the honor due to father and mother, on the other.

What we usually refer to as «*the* Decalogue», in the singular, in fact appears in two forms which are both very similar and very different. The most visible difference is at the heart of the two texts — the motive given for the commandment to observe the Sabbath is not at all the same in the two Decalogues. In Exodus 20, humanity is invited to «remember the Sabbath day and keep it holy»,

> For in six days YHWH made the heavens, and the earth, and the sea, and all that are in them, and he rested the seventh day. Therefore YHWH blessed the day of Sabbath and consecrated it (Exod 20:11).

In the Decalogue in Deuteronomy 5, humanity is invited to «observe the Sabbath day and keep it holy»,

> You will remember that you were servant in the land of Egypt and YHWH your God brought you with mighty hand and extended arm. Therefore I commanded you YHWH your God of doing the day of Sabbath (Deut 5:15).

In one case, the reason for the command is the Lord's rest on the seventh day of the first week, and in the other, it is the leaving of Egypt and slavery there. Here, then, is a question. One of the basic rules for interpretation requires that «when two related units appear opposed to one another in every sense, seek what is alike»[7]. We must therefore ask questions about the relationship, which links the two motives.

The fact that not one, but two Decalogues exist is a further enigma. Without claiming to resolve it, we will risk offering an interpretation.

7 *Traité*, 561.

Chapter 3

The Decalogue in Exodus

Exod 20:2-17

Exod 20:2-17

2 I am the Lord *your God who brought you from the land of Egypt, from the house of servants: 3 shall not exist for you other gods before me. 4 You shall not make for you sculpture or any representation, of what is in the heavens above, and of what is on the earth under, and of what is in the waters under the earth; 5 you shall not prostrate before them and you shall not be servants to them; because I am the* Lord *your God, the jealous God, who punishes the iniquity of the fathers on sons on third and on fourth generations for those who hate me, 6 and who does mercy to thousand generations for those who love me and observe my commandments. 7 You shall not pronounce the name of the* Lord *your God in vain: because the* Lord *does not hold innocent one who pronounces his name in vain. 8 Remember of the day of Sabbath to consecrate it. 9 Six days you will serve and you will do all your work, 10 and the seventh day is Sabbath to the* Lord *your God: you shall not do any work, you, and your son and your daughter, your servant and your handmaid, and your livestock and your guest who is at your door. 11 Because in six days the* Lord *made the heavens, and the earth, and the sea and all that are in them and he rested the seventh day. Therefore the* Lord *blessed the day of Sabbath and consecrated it. 12 Honor your father and your mother, so that your days are prolonged on the land that the* Lord *your God gives you. 13 You shall not kill. 14 You shall not commit adultery. 15 You shall not steal. 16 You shall not testimony against your neighbor falsely. 17 You shall not desire the house of your neighbor. You shall not covet the wife of your neighbor, and his servant and his handmaid, and his ox and his ass, and all that is to your neighbor.*

Exod 20:2-17 is a passage made up of four parts organized in mirror formation (see «The passage as a whole», p. 124). The first part (2-7) deals with duties to God, and the last part (13-17) with duties to one's neighbor. All the commandments in these two parts are expressed as negative orders. The two central parts (8-11; 12) are distinguished from the other two parts by the fact that they alone have the only two positive commandments — they begin with «Remember…»[1] (8) and «Honor…» (12).

1 In certain contexts an infinitive in Hebrew can have the meaning of an imperative. This infinitive is followed by two futures with the meaning of an imperative, which are also positive — «you will serve and you will do» (9).

A. THE FIRST PART (EXOD 20:2-7)

COMPOSITION

+ 2 I (am)		YHWH		your God	
	. who brought you	from the land	of Egypt,		
	.	from the house	of the *SERVANTS*:		
= 3 SHALL NOT EXIST			*for you*	*other gods*	before me.
= 4	You SHALL NOT	*MAKE*	*for you*	*sculpture*	
= or			any	*representation*,	
	. of what is in	the heavens	above,		
	. and of what is on	the earth	under,		
	. and of what is in	the waters	under the earth;		
= 5	You SHALL NOT prostrate		before	*them*	
= and You SHALL NOT BE *SERVANTS*			to	*them*:	
+ BECAUSE I (am)		YHWH		your God,	
+	(I am)	a God		jealous,	
	: who visits	the iniquity		of fathers	on sons
	- on *third*	and on *fourth* (generations)		for those who hate me,	
	: 6 and *DOES*	mercy		to *thousand* (generations)	
	- for those who love me			and observe my commandments.	
= 7 You SHALL NOT pronounce the name of			YHWH	your God	*in vain*:
+ BECAUSE does NOT hold-innocent			YHWH	one who pronounces his name	*in vain*.

The first part has two short sub-parts (2-3 and 7) which frame a more developed sub-part (4-6). While in the first sub-part the commandment (3) is preceded by the reason for it (2), this is reversed in the other two sub-parts where the commandment (4-5b and 7a) is followed by its reason (5c-6 and 7b) both introduced by «because».

The first sub-part (2-3)

This is made up of two segments. The first is a tri-member (2abc) in ABB' form. The first member is the titulature, or what the speaker says about his name and rank (2a); the two members which follow explain what he has done for those he is addressing (2bc).

The second segment is a unimember — the commandment is a result of the action carried out on behalf of the person to whom it is given (3).

The outer members match one another. The name of «YHWH» could be translated as «the Existing one», as it is in the Septuagint, to show its lexical relationship to the verb «there will not exist» «other gods» in 3, opposed to «your God» in 2a; «before me», at the end of 3, matches «Me» at the start of 2. We should also note that the second person singular pronoun is repeated three times (2b.3, translated by the pronominal adjective «your» in 2a).

The second sub-part (4-6)

This part has of two pieces. The first (4-5b) is made up of two bimembers (4ab; 5ab), which frame a trimember (4cde). At the outer parts, the prohibition is repeated twice. The central trimember lists the three parts of the cosmos — the earth (singular) between the «heavens» and the «waters» (plural)[2]. Note that the last term is broadened with the addition of «of the earth». The exhaustive list of elements emphasizes the absolutist nature of the commandment.

The second piece (5c-6) is made up of three bimember segments. The first one (5cd) is the titulature which begins with the same «I am» as 2a, but another description of God is added — «a jealous God». The second (5ef) and third (6ab) segments parallel one another:

visiting	the iniquity	*on third and on fourth* (generations)[3]	FOR THOSE WHO HATE ME
doing	mercy	*to thousand* (generations)	FOR THOSE WHO LOVE ME.

These two segments explain the title of the «jealous God» with which the first segment ends (5d). Note the repetition of the verb «do» at the start of the outer segments (4a and 6a).

The third sub-part (7)

This sub-part only has one bimember segment. The commandment (7a) is followed by the reason for it (7b). The same syntagma, «pronounce the name» is repeated in both members. The two occurrences of «in vain» act as final terms.

2 In Hebrew, both these words only exist in the plural form.
3 The Jerusalem Bible translates this as «I punish the fathers' faults in the sons, the grandsons and the great-grandsons»; this paraphrase makes the meaning clear.

The links between the sub-parts

+ 2 I (am)	Yhwh		your God	
. who brought you	from the land	of Egypt,		
.	from the house	of the *SERVANTS*:		
= 3 SHALL NOT EXIST		*for you*	*other gods*	before me.
= 4 You SHALL NOT	*MAKE*	*for you*	*sculpture*	
= or		any	*representation*,	
. of what is in	the heavens	above,		
. and of what is on	the earth	under,		
. and of what is in	the waters	under the earth;		
= 5 You SHALL NOT prostrate		before	*them*	
= and You SHALL NOT BE *SERVANTS*		to	*them*:	
+ BECAUSE I (am)	Yhwh		your God,	
+ (I am)	a God		jealous,	
: who visits	the iniquity		of fathers	on sons
- on *third*	and on *fourth* (generations)		for those who hate me,	
: 6 and *DOES*	mercy		to *thousand* (generations)	
- for those who love me			and observe my commandments.	
= 7 You SHALL NOT pronounce the name of		Yhwh	your God	*in vain*:
+ BECAUSE does NOT hold-innocent		Yhwh	one who pronounces his name	*in vain*.

In addition to what we have already said about the logical movement found in each sub-part between the commandment and the reason for the commandment, we should note:

- the repetition of «Yhwh your God» at the start of the outer sub-parts (2a and 7a), as well as at the start of the second piece of the central sub-part (5c);
- «other gods» at the end of the first sub-part (3) and «sculpture»/«representation» at the start of the second sub-part take on the role of median terms. The repetition of «for you» (3 and 4a) fulfils the same role, the more so as these are the only occurrences of this syntagma in the whole part;
- «servants» in 2c is taken up by «you will not be servants» in 5b;
- the past being recalled in the center of the first sub-part (2bc) is linked to the preview of the future at the end of the second sub-part (5ef-6); the mention of God's saving acts corresponds to the «historical prologue» of covenantal texts, while the threats correspond to the «curses and blessings» of the same texts[4];

4 See BEAUCAMP P., «Propositions sur l'alliance comme structure centrale».

• finally, note the link between the «other gods» at the end of the first sub-part (3; «sculpture» in 4a) and the two occurrences of «in vain» at the end of both members of the last sub-part (7a.7b) — idols are vanity (Jer 18:15: «My people have forgotten me! They burn their incense to *a Nothing*!»).

BIBLICAL CONTEXT

Like «the heavens», «the earth» and «the waters» (4cde), the verb «to make» (which can also be translated as «to do»), with which v. 4 begins refers to the first creation narrative — God «made» the firmament on the second day (Gen 1:7), the lights on the fourth day (1:16), and animals living on the earth on the sixth day (1:25). At the end of the sixth day, having crowned his work by creating man and woman, «God saw all he had made, and indeed it was very good» (1:31)[5]. The verb «to be» is used for light — «God said, "*Let there be* light", and there *was* light» (1:3). With the firmament the two verbs are linked: «God said, "*Let there be* a vault...". And God *made* the vault...» (Gen 1:6-7) It is this same verb «to be», translated by «to exist», which is used just before the verb «to make»/«to do» in the Decalogue — «There will not exist for you other Gods before me» (Exod 20:3).

INTERPRETATION

«I the Lord your God who brought you from...» (First Commandment)

None of the three commandments which we can see in this first part (3.4-5b.7a) is an impersonal law, like those we might find in a penal code, where they begin abruptly with «To ... is forbidden». Before giving any commandment, the speaker introduces himself — «I, the Lord» (2a); but he is not content with introducing himself with his name, he also identifies the person he is addressing — «I, the Lord *your* God»[6]. The «Ten Words» are, first of all, words from an «I» to a «You». However, as often happens between people, it is not enough for the one introducing himself to give his name to be recognized. He must recall the circumstances of the previous meeting, to bring his own unique face back to the other person's memory. The liberation from slavery in Egypt worked by the Lord on behalf of the person he is talking to identifies both himself and his in-

5 See p. 258.

6 Personal pronouns in Hebrew go to the ends of the clause — «*I*, Yhwh, the God of *you*».

terlocutor — in just one Hebrew word, *hôṣētîkā*, «I have brought you out» (2b), the first and second person pronouns (*tî* + *kā*) are brought together. The whole history of the relationship between God and the children of Israel is reduced to the leaving of Egypt — this is not one event among many others, or even the first, it is the founding event, the birth by which God's fatherhood and the filiation of his chosen people are recognized. Only the reference to the origins can be the basis of the law's expression.

«I, the Lord your God, a jealous God...» (the first commandment with the other two)

The reminder of origins is not limited to the «historical» event of the leaving of Egypt. The mention of «in heaven or on earth beneath or in the waters under the earth» (4cde) refers — albeit indirectly — to the original beginning, to the event which it is impossible to describe except with the language of «myth», to the creation which the reader knows was entirely the Lord's work. However, it should be recognized that the Lord is not introducing himself as Creator, and he is not giving his law in this capacity, but as the Lord who has intervened in history. At what could be identified as the Second Commandment (4-6), the speaker repeats the same formula he began with — «I, the Lord your God» (5c). This time, however, it is not to recall benefits in the past, but to look towards a future left to humanity's choosing. Making the sins of the fathers fall on their descendents to the third and fourth generation is probably a way of making it understood that this address is not given to an individual and that the present generation's responsibility involves the future of those generations to come. The huge gulf between the three and four generations, who take on the curse, and the thousandth generation who benefit from the blessing, shows the extent to which God's mercy prevails over his punishment. The Lord God of Israel thus paints himself as the absolute master of history, the savior of the past from the beginning (2-3) and the supreme judge of the future (4-6).

«You shall not...» (Second Commandment)

«Listen, Israel: Yhwh our God is the one Yhwh. You shall love Yhwh your God with all your heart, with all your soul, with all your strength» (Deut 6:4-5). The whole and total nature of love, emphasized three times in this phrase in Deuteronomy, expresses nothing more than that of the first part of the Decalogue — «everything» for the Lord, that is, nothing for anyone else (3). What the accumulation of these three «all»s expresses in a positive way (Deut 6:4) is impressed here by the insistent reiteration of five negative commands (3.4a.5a.5b.7a). Everything is focused on the repeated prohibition of idolatry (4-5b), which is another way of proclaiming the Lord's absolute uniqueness. In fact, after a brief general commandment (3) forbidding Israel from having any other god except their Lord, the central sub-part forbids them at length from «making» idols, representations or images of any of the world's elements. «To make» a god of what is in the heavens, on the earth or in the seas would be to overturn the order of creation, to instill confusion between the Creator and one of his creatures — this would be «hatred» (5f). Making a god means denying oneself as a creature. In addition to not «loving» the Lord their God and not «observing his commandments» (6), to make a god is to arrogate to oneself God's own place, to play at being God. This initial interpretation of the central sub-part needs to be completed or corrected, however, by another one. The Second Commandment (4-6) can be understood, not simply as an amplified repetition of the First (2-3), but as another commandment — what is forbidden is making a «statue» or some other representation of the Lord God of Israel, which is exactly what the children of Israel asked Aaron for and received when they made the Golden Calf, which was not another god — in effect, they were saying, «Here is your God, Israel, who brought you out of the land of Egypt» (Exod 32:2).

«You shall not bow down» (still the Second Commandment)

Having arrived as free men in Egypt, presented to Pharaoh by their brother Joseph, his governor (Gen 46-47), Jacob's children end up being reduced to hard labor by the Egyptians (Exod 1). «The land of Egypt» was to become «the house of slavery» for the children of Israel, until the day when Yhwh, having revealed his name to his servant Moses (Exod 3:14) brought Israel out of slavery. Then Moses and the Israelites intoned the hymn to Yhwh which ended with these words, «Who among the gods is your like, Yhwh? Who is your like, majestic in holiness, terrible in deeds of prowess, worker of wonders?» (Exod 15:11; see p. 86). After this, hardly had the covenant on Mt Sinai been concluded than the people were prostrating themselves before the Golden Calf (Exod 32). Idolatry and any representation, even of Yhwh, is slavery[7]. It is a return to the land of Egypt,

7 Verse 5b is usually translated with an active verb «You shall not bow down». In fact, it is a passive (*hofal*; lit. «You will not be bowed down to them»).

a denial of the liberation carried out by the Lord. Israel is not called to «bow down» (5b), but to «love» the Lord (6b) by keeping his commandments. Obedience is not the servile attitude of one who is forced to carry it out, but the fruit of a free choice by one who knows that he has been saved from slavery.

«You shall not pronounce the Name in vain»

The commandment to adore the one God to the exclusion of all others has its corollary—if one is not to acknowledge the existence of other gods before Yhwh (3), it is also imperative not to treat the only Existing One «in vain» (7), that is, as though he did not exist, not to pronounce his name, not to bear witness by swearing oaths in his name, as though he were nothing more than vain idols and their empty images (4ab). God's punishment which will come down on the perjurer (7b) will not be in vain, and the guilty party will receive proof of both his sin and of the existence of the one he has offended in this way.

B. THE SECOND PART (EXOD 20:8-11)

COMPOSITION

This part has two sub-parts—the commandment (8-10), and the reason given for the commandment (11).

* 8 Remember		of the DAY OF SABBATH	to CONSECRATE IT.
+ 9 *Six*		*DAYS*	you ***will serve***
+ and **you**	will do	*all your work,*	
– 10 AND THE SEVENTH		DAY	is Sabbath to YHWH your God:
– **you**	*shall not do*	*any work,*	you,
		: and your son	and your daughter,
		: and your ***servant***	and your handmaid,
		: and your livestock	and your guest **who is at your door**.
+ 11 Because	*in six*	*DAYS*	YHWH made
		. the heavens	and the earth
		. the sea	and all **that are in them**
– and he	*rested*		THE SEVENTH DAY.
* Therefore YHWH blessed		the DAY OF SABBATH	and CONSECRATED IT.

The first sub-part (8-10)

This has three pieces. The first piece (8) is made up of a single unimember segment, later developed at length. The other two pieces (9 and 10) oppose what should be done on six days of the week to what should not be done on the Sabbath day. While the second piece (9) has only one bimember segment, the third (10) is made up of a bimember (10ab), followed by a trimember (10cde), which list in pairs all those, in addition to «you» in 10b, who are not to work on the Sabbath. We should note the words with the same root, «you will serve» in 9a and «your servant» in 10d (in Hebrew, «female servant» has another root).

The second sub-part (11)

This sub-part is made up of two pieces. The first piece (11a-e) includes a trimember (11abc — what God made «in six days»), opposed by a unimember (11d — what he did «on the seventh day»). This piece is constructed concentrically — temporal adverbs at the outer parts, then the verbs, and finally the list in the center. The last piece (11e) is a unimember which brings the sub-part to a conclusion.

The links between the two sub-parts

The outer segments parallel one another and are the inclusio (8 and 11e). The first tells humanity what he is to do, and the other what God has done — humanity is invited to do what God has done — the «consecration» of the «Sabbath day».

The first piece of the second sub-part (11a-d) corresponds to vv. 9-10 of the first sub-part:

- the opposition between «six days» (9a) and «the seventh day» (10a) is repeated in 11a and 11d;
- the clauses in 9-10 are doubled compared to clauses 11a-d — two syntagmas, opposed by negation, «you shall/you shall not» + «all (your) work» are added to «you will serve» (9a) and «is Sabbath for the Lord your God» (10a)[8];
- 9-10 is a parallel construction; 11a-d a concentric construction;
- at the end of the first sub-part (10cde), and in the middle of the second (11bc) are two lists in three tenses, the first more developed than the second. Each ends with a similar expansion, «who is at your door» and «[all] that are in them», emphasizing their symmetry. These two lists have the same exhaustive nature.

8 «All» in 9c and «not any» in 10c translate the same Hebrew word, *kol*.

BIBLICAL CONTEXT

The Lord's rest

The reason for the commandment (11) refers to the conclusion of the first creation narrative. Note the many lexical repetitions in italics:

> [1] Thus the heaven and the earth and their entire host are completed. [2] Then God, in the *seventh day* brought to end *the work* that he *did* and *ceased* (*šbt*) in the *seventh day* from each of *his work*. [3] God *blessed* the *seventh day* and *consecrated it*, because in it he had *ceased from every work* that he had done creating (Gen 2:1-3).

Divine resemblance

The reason for the commandment to rest on the Sabbath is God's action — in other words, in this commandment, humanity is called to imitate the Lord. In fact, still in the first creation narrative, man was made «in the image» of God. «And God said: "Let us make man in our image, in our resemblance". God created man in his image; in the image of God he created him; male and female he created them» (Gen 1:26-27).

We should not gloss over the difference between these two expressions: «in our image and in our resemblance» is God's plan, and «in his image» is its realization. «The image» is given, but «the resemblance» is left to humanity's initiative, a vocation to be lived out[9].

INTERPRETATION

The commandment to work

It is true that this part deals above all with the consecration of the Sabbath — this is in fact how the text begins — «Remember the day of the Sabbath» (8a). However, after this initial general commandment, humanity is given the order to work for six days (9). Whoever has not first «done all his work» cannot respect the rest of the seventh day. Linked to the Lord's creative «doing» (11a), humanity's «doing» (9b) is presented as a collaboration in the work of creation — in fact, the same words, «to do work», describe God's work in the creation narrative, and humanity's work in the Decalogue. Created in the image of God (Gen 1:27), humanity is given the vocation of a son who does the same work as his father.

9 See BALMARY M., *La Divine Origine*, ch. IV, «Où Dieu ne fait que la moitié de son travail», 109-147 (quoting Origen and Basil of Caesarea, 113-116).

The consecration of the Sabbath

What humanity is commanded to do for the seventh day might seem to be totally negative — it is a «do not», which applies to all the people in the house and to all the animals. However, prior to the prohibition (10b-e), it is said that «the seventh day is a Sabbath for the Lord your God» (10a), as though the Sabbath, the «stopping of work», were for the Creator before being for the creatures. «Remember» (8) appears to be mostly aimed at recalling creation, humanity's ultimate origins and the origins of their work, that is, to acknowledge that life is not the fruit of humanity's work, but of the work of the One who gives it. This is remembering the Sabbath, «to consecrate it» (8), «for the Lord your God» (10a).

The Blessing of the Sabbath

But the Sabbath is not only consecrated to God, it is also a blessing for humanity. It is given for the master of the house, and for all those who are part of his household, even including the stranger who works for him. The blessing is in the freedom from slavery — on the seventh day not only are the «son and daughter» (10c) not to be treated as «servant and handmaid» (10d), like the «livestock» or the «guest» (10e), that is, under the slavery of the work they do on the days when they «serve» (9a), but on the contrary, the slave and the servant are to be considered as son and daughter. Consecration and blessing ensure that all, including animals, become affiliated to the head of the household, who acknowledges he is begotten by the Father in heaven.

c. THE THIRD PART (EXOD 20:12)

COMPOSITION

– [12] Honor	the FATHER	of **you**	and the mother	of **you**,
– so that	are prolonged		the days	of **you**,
– on the land	that YHWH THE GOD	of **you**	donates	to **you**.

This part is the size of a trimember segment. From the syntactical point of view, the main clause (12a), that is, the commandment, is followed by a final clause (12b) and by a complement of place («on the land») which is completed by a relative clause. The last two members are a double reference to the blessing on time (long life) and space (possession of the land); from this perspective the trimember can be described as ABB'. However, the outer members link parents and «YHWH» who «gives» the land to the child, which parents do when they pass on an inheritance. Note that the three members end with the pronominal suffix *-kâ* («you»), and that this pronoun is repeated twice more in the outer members.

INTERPRETATION

The life which is given to you

In its brevity, this commandment hides its two wonderful surprises. The first is that one would expect the second member to finish with a different pronoun — «so that their days are prolonged»; unconsciously, in fact, this is how we read it[10]. The honor due to father and mother, that is, caring for one's parents, might also be aimed at supporting them so that they might live as long as possible. This is the normal reaction, the dearest wish of children. The biblical text subverts this natural desire in a certain way — it does not deny it, of course, but the reason given for the commandment is different. The aim is not the parents' long life, but the children's. «The persecuting law of the Superego said, "Honor your father and mother so that *their* days may be lengthened". The prophetic law of revelation says, "Honor… so that *your* days may be lengthened"»[11]. Honoring the parents allows the children to live their own life, and it is precisely for this reason that children can honor them.

The land which is given to you

But there is a further surprise in the text. One might expect «on the land which your father and mother give you», that is, on the property which you have received or will receive as an inheritance from your parents. Honor would be due to father and mother because they give the children the possibility of living by working their own land[12]. On the contrary, the text says, «the land which *the Lord your God* has given you». The reason for the commandment to honor one's parents is that, with the inheritance which allows them to live as freemen, life it

10 See BALMARY M., *La Divine Origine*, 227-230; showing that Freud himself read this incorrectly.

11 BALMARY M., *La Divine Origine*, 228.

12 The term *ʾădāmâ* tends to indicate land which may be cultivated, while *ʾereṣ* means «country», as in v. 2, «the land of Egypt» (see JENNI E. and WESTERMANN C., *Dizionario teologico dell'Antico Testamento*, I, 49-52). «The fruit of the earth» is *pᵉrî hā-ʾădāmâ*; the syntagma *pᵉrî hā-ʾāres* occurs only four times in the Hebrew Bible, three times to describe the produce of the land of Canaan reported by the explorers sent by Moses (Num 13:20.26; Deut 1:25) and once to describe either the Messiah or the remnant of Israel (Isa 4:2). However the term *ʾădāmâ* is ambiguous and is sometimes used as a synonym for *ʾereṣ*, for example in Deut 26:15: «Look down from the dwelling place of your holiness, from heaven, and bless your people Israel and the soil (*ʾădāmâ*) you have given us as you swore to our fathers, a land (*ʾereṣ*) where milk and honey flow» (see too Deut 11:9.17), or replacing *ʾereṣ* (Deut 7:13; 11:21; 30:20).

self is passed down to the children like a gift from God. To honor father and mother as the Decalogue commands is for humanity to honor the ultimate origin of life and freedom. The vague and, as it were, rather empty, verb «to honor» can probably be opened up to give different particular meanings, according to the child's status: as a minor he is to obey his parents; as an adult, he must ensure that his elderly parents, unable to work, are cared for. Above all, the child is to respect those who have handed on life and, with the descent from Abraham, the faith and promises given to the children of Israel[13].

D. THE FOURTH PART (EXOD 20:13-17)

COMPOSITION

+	13	You	SHALL NOT **KILL**.		
–	14	You	SHALL NOT COMMIT ADULTERY.		
–	15	You	SHALL NOT STEAL.		
+	16	You	SHALL NOT **ANSWER**	against *your neighbor*	testimony of deception.
–	17	You	SHALL NOT DESIRE	the house	of *your neighbor*.
–		You	SHALL NOT COVET	the wife	of *your neighbor*,
			. and	his servant	and his handmaid,
			. and	his ox	and his ass,
			. and	all that is	to *your neighbor*.

This part is made up of two parallel sub-parts (13-15 and 16-17). The first has three similar unimember segments. Each segment is a commandment[14], which has only one term, a verb modified by the same negative and the same modalities of tense, person and number[15]. The second sub-part (16-17) includes two trimember segments (16b-17a and 17cde); «your neighbor» is repeated four times, in each member of the first segment (16.17a.17b), and at the end of the second trimember.

The first members (13 and 16) match to the extent that false witness in a court could lead to the death of a «neighbor». The link between the other members appears to be inverted — coveting a woman (17b) is clearly linked to the prohi-

13 See Bovati, 139-142.

14 The unusual translation of v. 14 seeks to follow the brevity of the original and to respect the rhythm (which the usual translation, «You shall not commit adultery» does not do).

15 Unimember segments are rare, but it is even rarer to encounter members with only one term. We could possibly have considered these three verses to be a trimember segment, but it is preferable to follow the Masoretic punctuation, especially given the parallelism between the first (13-15) and second (16-17) parts.

bition on adultery (14); coveting a house (17a) could correspond to the prohibition on theft (15). However, the fact that 17a and 17b begin with the same verb might allow us to think that the «house» does not mean the physical building, but the household, which also includes all the people living there as well as the objects in it.

+	13	You SHALL NOT **KILL.**
–	14	You SHALL NOT COMMIT ADULTERY.
–	15	You SHALL NOT STEAL.

+	16	You SHALL NOT **ANSWER**	against *your neighbor*	testimony of deception.
–	17	You SHALL NOT DESIRE	the house	of *your neighbor*.
–		You SHALL NOT COVET	the wife	of *your neighbor*,
		. and	his servant	and his handmaid,
		. and	his ox	and his ass,
		. and	all that is	to *your neighbor*.

BIBLICAL CONTEXT

The verb «to covet» (*ḥmd*), used twice (17a.17b) has the same root as the participle «enticing/desirable» (*neḥmād*), used first of all to describe the trees which God made grow in the garden (Gen 2:9: «*enticing* to look at and good to eat») and, above all, in the eyes of the woman tempted by the serpent, for the tree in the middle of the garden, the only one forbidden by God. «The woman saw that the tree was good to eat and pleasing to the eye and that it was *desirable* for the knowledge that it could give. So she took some of its fruit...» (Gen 3:6).

INTERPRETATION

The triple dimension of the neighbor

The other must be recognized for what he is, in his physical (13) and social (16) life, in his married (14) and family (17a) life, in his economic (15) and domestic (17c-e) life; in short, in what makes him a person like me, my «neighbor». The three repeated commandments keep in their sights the three basic characteristics of humanity according to the Bible — first of all the person, both physically (13) and socially (16), as spouse (14) and head of a family (17a), then in charge of the whole household, from his wife (17b) to his livestock (17d), via his servants (17c). The neighbor's life, family and property are sacred — anyone who touches them commits a serious wrong against him.

To deny the other is to deny oneself

Whoever kills another person denies it in himself; whoever lies by giving false witness against the other denies it before others (16); he behaves as though the other did not exist, or makes out that he no longer exists. Taking a neighbor's wife or stealing his property, even just coveting them, that is, daring to think that they might be taken, is to hold one's neighbor to be nothing, to act as though he doesn't count. Committing adultery (14) or stealing (15), even «wishing» to do so (17) is basically the same as suppressing someone by murdering them (13) or destroying them in the eyes of others by bearing false witness (16). This is all to deny the other is one's «neighbor»; it is also to deny oneself as a human being, that is, as the other's neighbor.

Covetousness, the root of sin (second sub-part)

On a first reading it might appear strange that false witness and covetousness are mentioned after murder, adultery and theft. One might rather expect the opposite, a movement in order of seriousness, from the desire to the action, from the venial to the mortal. The text's order as it is, is clearly not indifferent, and in any case not insignificant. In fact, it is not only killing, committing adultery and stealing which are not allowed. The prohibition extends to the root of evil, hoping to root it out — prior to the murder itself, the false word which wounds and can be followed by death; prior to adultery and theft, the covetousness which leads one to touch a neighbor's wife and property. It was covetousness of the eyes which led the first woman to touch the forbidden fruit, and we know what that led to.

E. THE PASSAGE AS A WHOLE (EXOD 20:2-17)

COMPOSITION

The links between the outer parts (2-7 and 13-17)

2 I (am) THE LORD **YOUR** GOD
who brought you from the land of Egypt, from the **house** of *SERVANTS*:
3 Shall ***not*** exist for you other gods before me.

4 You shall ***not*** make for you sculpture or any representation,
- of what (is) in the heavens above,
- and of what (is) on the earth under,
- and of what (is) in the waters under the earth.
5 You shall ***not*** prostrate before them and you shall ***not*** be *SERVANTS* to them*:*

because I (am) THE LORD **YOUR** GOD,
the God jealous,
who visits the iniquity of the fathers on sons on third and on fourth (generations)
for those who hate me,
6 and who does mercy to thousand (generations)
for those who love me and observe my commands.

7 You shall ***not*** pronounce the name of THE LORD **YOUR** GOD in vain,
because does ***not*** justify THE LORD one who pronounces *his* name in vain.

[...]

13 You shall ***not*** kill.
14 You shall ***not*** commit adultery.
15 You shall ***not*** steal.

16 You shall ***not*** testimony against **YOUR** NEIGHBOR falsely.
17 You shall ***not*** desire the **house** of **YOUR** NEIGHBOR.
You shall ***not*** covet the wife of **YOUR** NEIGHBOR,
: and *his SERVANT* and his *HANDMAID*,
: and *his* ox and *his* ass,
: and all that is to **YOUR** NEIGHBOR.

• Each part has six negative verbs (3.4a.5a.5a.7a.7b; 13.14.15.16.17a.17b; all with the same negative *lō'*); these are all imperatives, except the last one in the first part («not justify» in 7b).

• The commandment in 16 ends with a synonym («falsely») of the word which both members in 7 end with («in vain»).

• «House» is repeated in 2b and 17a, but these are two different houses — in the first part it is the «house of servants», and in the last part the «house of your neighbor».

• The name of the «Lord», mentioned four times in the first part, qualified as «*your* God» three times, does not reappear in the last part; however, the word «neighbor» is repeated in that part four times, each time qualified as «*your* neighbor». The third person singular pronoun suffix is only found at the end of 7b and 17cd (translated as «your»).

The Lord God seems to be totally absent from the last part. However, one might think that false witness, with which the second sub-part begins (16), puts the oath on the Lord's Name at stake[16]. The link established between the final terms of the two last members of the first part (7a.7b) and the final term of the first member of the second sub-part of the last part (16), with the synonyms «in vain» and «falsely» support this interpretation — these are the two commandments which put the word at stake.

Links between the central two parts (8-11 and 12)[17]

8 REMEMBER of the *day* of Sabbath to consecrate it.		
9 Six *days* you will serve and do your work,		
10 And the seventh *day* is Sabbath to		THE LORD YOUR GOD:
you shall not do any work, you,		
and	**YOUR SON**	and **YOUR DAUGHTER**,
	your servant	and your handmaid,
and	your livestock	and your guest who is at your door.
11 **Because** in six *days* the Lord made the heavens and the earth and the sea and all that are in them and he rested the seventh *day*.		
Therefore the Lord blessed the *day* of Sabbath and consecrated it.		

12 HONOR	**YOUR FATHER**	and **YOUR MOTHER**,
So that your *days* are prolonged,		
on the land that		THE LORD YOUR GOD donates to you.

• Both these parts begin with the only positive commandments in the passage[18] — «Remember» (8) and «Honor» (12a).

• The name of the «Lord your God» appears once in each of the two parts (10a and 12c).

• «Day», which appears six times in the second part (8.9.10a.11a, 11c.11d), is repeated in the plural once in the third part (12b).

16 See BOVATI P., *Ristabilire la giustizia*, 261-263, n. 62.

17 See TAPIERO M., «"Honore ton père et ta mere"», 289; FRAENKEL A.A., «Du père au Père», 305-307.

18 The Sabbath commandment also has a negative imperative (10b).

[8] REMEMBER of the *day* of Sabbath to consecrate it.

[9] Six *days* you will serve
and do your work,

[10] And the seventh *day* is Sabbath to		THE LORD YOUR GOD:
you shall not do any work, you,		
and	**YOUR SON**	and **YOUR DAUGHTER**,
	your servant	and your handmaid,
and	your livestock	and your guest who is at your door.

[11] **Because** in six *days* the Lord made the heavens and the earth and the sea
and all that are in them
and he rested the seventh *day*.

Therefore the Lord blessed the *day* of Sabbath and consecrated it.

[12] HONOR	**YOUR FATHER**	and **YOUR MOTHER**,
So that your *days* are prolonged,		
on the land that		THE LORD YOUR GOD donates to you.

• The first commandment is followed by the reason for it («because» at the start of 11), a reason which goes back to the beginning; the second is followed by its consequence («so that» at the start of 12b), a consequence which is in the present in 12c and the future in 12b.

• «Son» and «daughter» (10c) belong to the same semantic field as «father» and «mother» (12a). The former are first-degree descendents and the latter first-degree ancestors. In Hebrew, all four terms have the same suffix pronoun in the second person masculine (-*kā*; «of you»), translated by the pronominal adjective «your». The complementarity of the sexes is found in each of these pairs, in the same order, just as it is in the pair «servant and handmaid», parallel to «son and daughter»).

The two commandments thus match one another — the commandment of the Sabbath is addressed to man as a father, and the next one addressed to him as a son. Both deal with internal family relations within the same place, the home.

The links between the four parts

2 I am THE LORD *YOUR* GOD
who brought you from the land of Egypt, from the house of *SERVANTS*:
3 Shall not exist for you other gods before me.

4 You shall not make for you sculpture or any representation,
• of what is in **the heavens** above,
• of what is on **the earth** under,
• of what is in **the waters** under the earth,
5 you shall not prostrate before them and you shall not be *SERVANTS* to them;
Because I am THE LORD *YOUR* GOD, the *jealous* God,
who punishes the iniquity of the **FATHERS** on **SONS**, on third and on fourth (generations)
for those who hate me,
6 and who does mercy to thousand (generations)
for those who *love me* and observe my commands.

7 You shall not pronounce the Name of THE LORD *YOUR* GOD ***in vain***,
Because THE LORD does not hold innocent one who pronounces *his* Name ***in vain***.

---

8 *Remember* of the day of Sabbath to consecrate it.
9 Six days you *WILL SERVE* and you will *do* all your work,
10 and the seventh day is Sabbath to THE LORD *YOUR* GOD:
you shall not *do any* work, you,
– and *YOUR* **SON** and *YOUR* **DAUGHTER**,
– *YOUR SERVANT* and *YOUR HANDMAID*,
– and *YOUR* livestock and *YOUR* guest who is at your door.
11 Because in six days THE LORD *made*
• **the heavens,**
• and **the earth,**
• and **the sea** and *all* that are in them
and he rested the seventh day.
Therefore THE LORD blessed the day of Sabbath and consecrated it.

---

12 *Honor* *YOUR* **FATHER** and *YOUR* **MOTHER,**
so that your days are prolonged
on the land THE LORD *YOUR* GOD donates to you.

---

13 You shall not kill. 14 You shall not *commit adultery*. 15 You shall not steal.

16 You shall not testimony against *YOUR* NEIGHBOR ***falsely***.
17 You shall not desire the house of *YOUR* NEIGHBOR.
You shall not covet the wife of *YOUR* NEIGHBOR,
– and *his SERVANT* and *his HANDMAID*,
– and *his* ox and *his* ass,
– and *all* that is to *YOUR* NEIGHBOR.

While the symbolic location of the first part (2-7) seems to be the Temple, the home of the worship of the Lord and the invocation of his Name, the location of the two central parts (8-12) is the home, the place where the children, servants, domestic animals and foreign employees are all gathered around father and mother. The location of the last part (13-17) is outside: «the "gate" (that is

2 I am THE LORD *YOUR* GOD
who brought you from the land of Egypt, from the house of *SERVANTS*:
3 Shall not exist for you other gods before me.

4 You shall not make for you sculpture or any representation,
• of what is in **the heavens** above,
• of what is on **the earth** under,
• of what is in **the waters** under the earth,
5 you shall not prostrate before them and you shall not be *SERVANTS* to them;
Because I am THE LORD *YOUR* GOD, the *jealous* God,
who punishes the iniquity of the **FATHERS** on **SONS**, on third and on fourth (generations)
for those who hate me,
6 and who does mercy to thousand (generations)
for those who *love me* and observe my commands.

7 You shall not pronounce the Name of THE LORD *YOUR* GOD ***in vain***,
Because THE LORD does not hold innocent one who pronounces *his* Name ***in vain***.

8 *Remember* of the day of Sabbath to consecrate it.
9 Six days you *WILL SERVE* and you will *do* all your work,
10 and the seventh day is Sabbath to THE LORD *YOUR* GOD:
you shall not *do any* work, you,
– and *YOUR* **SON** and *YOUR* **DAUGHTER**,
– *YOUR SERVANT* and *YOUR HANDMAID*,
– and *YOUR* livestock and *YOUR* guest who is at your door.
11 Because in six days THE LORD *made*
• **the heavens**,
• and **the earth**,
• and **the sea** and *all* that are in them
and he rested the seventh day.
Therefore THE LORD blessed the day of Sabbath and consecrated it.

12 *Honor* *YOUR* **FATHER** and *YOUR* **MOTHER**,
so that your days are prolonged
on the land THE LORD *YOUR* GOD donates to you.

13 You shall not kill. 14 You shall not *commit adultery*. 15 You shall not steal.

16 You shall not testimony against *YOUR* NEIGHBOR ***falsely***.
17 You shall not desire the house of *YOUR* NEIGHBOR.
You shall not covet the wife of *YOUR* NEIGHBOR,
– and *his SERVANT* and *his HANDMAID*,
– and *his* ox and *his* ass,
– and *all* that is to *YOUR* NEIGHBOR.

the central square) of the city could be considered, if not the exclusive location, at least one of the typical places of these public relationships»[19].

The Sabbath commandment is joined to the commandments about God which come before it, for «the Sabbath is for the Lord your God» (10a); the commandment to honor father and mother (12) begins the list of commandments

19 Bovati, 131.

about the neighbor (13-17), which follow it and which «father and mother» are part of, in a very special way.

There are particularly close links between the first and second parts. It is only here that God's original action on Israel's behalf is mentioned (2b), and then his action on behalf of all creation (11a-d). It is only here that the list of the «heavens» and the «earth» and the «waters» or the «sea» (4.11) are repeated, and only here that the verb «to do» is used, both for humanity (4a.9.10b; although note that 4a and 10b have negative imperatives) and for God (6a and 11a).

The terms «fathers» and «sons» in the first part (5c) are repeated, in the singular, in the second part («son» in 10c) and in the third part («father» in 12a).

The two lists of three terms in 10cd, e and 11bcd in the center are echoed, the latter in the heart of the first part (4bcd) and the first at the end of the fourth part (17cde). The mixing of these elements (A/BA'/B') seems to mark the unity of the whole better.

Words with the root *'bd* are found in the first two and in the fourth parts—«servants» and «bow down» in 2b and 5a; «serve» and «servant» in 9a, 10d; «servants» once again in 17c (accompanied, as in 10d, by «handmaid»).

The Hebrew word *kol*, translated by «not one» or by «all», is repeated in 4a in the first part, in 9a, 10b and 11d in the second part and, finally, at the end of the last part in 17e.

While «your» is only used of God in the first part («the Lord *your* God» in 2a, 5b and 7a) and is only used of the neighbor in the last part («*your*» neighbor in 16, 17a, 17b and 17e), in the two central parts it not only describes God («the Lord *your* God» in 10a and 12c) but also the six terms of the list in 10cde («*your* son and *your* daughter, *your* servant and *your* handmaid, *your* livestock and *your* guest») and of the parental couple («*your* father and *your* mother») in 12a.

The adjective «jealous» (5b), the two verbs «to love» (6b) and «to commit adultery» (14) and the syntagma «covet your neighbor's wife» (17b) belong to the same semantic field of marital and extra-martial relationships. We might also view the «and» which acts as a conjunction between «your father *and* your mother» (12a) as another, discreet, expression of the same type of relationship.

BIBLICAL CONTEXT

«Each of you must respect his father and mother and you must keep my Sabbaths»

The central chapter of the «law of holiness» (Lev 19:3) begins thus. The fact that these two commandments are joined together is an external confirmation of the Decalogue's composition, where the same elements are juxtaposed, the other way around, at the center of the whole. The link between these two commandments is surprising. What do a practice which is particular to the people of Israel, and a point of natural law which seems to belong to all nations have in common?

INTERPRETATION

The interpretation offered here will be developed from the center of the text, or from the whole formed by the second and third parts (8-12).

Uniqueness

Like the Lord God, father and mother are unique. A man can have many sons and daughters (10c), he may rule over a great number of servants and handmaids (10d), possess huge flocks and welcome many strangers to his doors (10e), but he will only ever have one father and one mother (12a). The relationship with those who brought him into the world is very special. The couple who begat him will never be replaced by brothers, sisters, wives, sons and daughters, however many of each there may be. Of all the family relationships, however strong, the link with father and mother is the only one which cannot be multiplied, just as God cannot be multiplied. The uniqueness of father and mother is an image and symbol of the divine uniqueness. The Lord God has created everything, and it is from him alone, to the exclusion of all others, that we owe our existence (11a). Our fathers and mothers, created in the image of God, are the route through which life is transmitted to us. In honoring them, we acknowledge in them the God's gift which has made us exist on earth (12bc).

Inheritance

Glorifying the Lord in one's father and mother, man acknowledges himself to be an heir. Everything that he is and that he has, servants and handmaids, cattle and donkeys (10de), the earth which feeds him (12c), all this has been left to him by his parents, and it has been «given» to him by God through them (12c). He holds his days (12b) and his land (12c) from Another; in sacrificing the seventh day (10a), which is also a gift from God, he acknowledges that even the work which he is given to do on the six days reserved for work (9), in the image of God who made heavens and earth and the sea and all that they contain (11a-d). Everything is a gift — what he is, what he has, what he does. His life and happiness are linked to this joyful admission. To deny the gift would be, in the same way, to refuse it — logically, this would be to shorten his days (12b) and suddenly to leave this earth (12c).

Filiation

Man is an heir even through his descendants. The children he produces on earth are the most wonderful gift, which God can give him. This is why sterility is the supreme curse in the Bible — because the supreme blessing, of becoming like God, a father and mother, is removed from the person. One can only be a true son, a full heir to God the Father, when one has also had children oneself. The man with no descendents, who has no fruit in flesh or in spirit, is not really a man. The two central commandments of the Decalogue define my existence in this double temporal dimension, in its double ontological truth. I am a son or daughter, and a father or mother; I beget and am begotten. Here is the fundamental dimension of my being. The Sabbath commandment is aimed at me as a father, who is to free my children from the slavery of work; the following commandment addresses me as a child, who is to honor my father and mother for the freedom which they have given me to leave them in order to become, in my turn, a father or mother.

Freedom

Man created by God is a free subject. The Sabbath is given to him to acknowledge and practice this freedom, himself first, by freeing himself from the slavery of daily work; and at the same time his son and daughter, his servants and his handmaids. He must not treat his son and daughter as slaves; on the contrary, he is to treat his servants as children. Sanctifying the Sabbath day is considering the son's freedom to be holy, sacred, not to be touched by anyone. The child's freedom is for all — the child that I am, even as my children, servants and employees, even the strangers, representing all humanity, are children. The father's and mother's freedom is to recognize that their son and daughter are free, that they are heirs, like them. It is to pass on the narrative of the gift which was made to them when God brought them out of the land of Egypt, from the house of slavery, along with the land which they received. Glorifying one's father and mother is to honor in them those who have received from God even more than those who give.

«The God of you», «the neighbor of you»

«The neighbor» exists (13-17), just as «God» does (2-7). Both have a proper name which is to be respected and honored. «Pronouncing the Name of the Lord your God in vain» (7) and «testifying falsely against your neighbor» (16) indicate treating them as though they did not exist. Behaving in this way would deny that the Lord is my God, that the neighbor is my neighbor; it would be to state that they don't count, that they are nothing *to me*, and thus to treat myself as not existing. To deny the other's name, that is, their person, is to refuse the other as a relationship which makes me exist as a person. It is not only the Lord my God who makes me exist, but also my neighbor. The «I» can only subsist next to a «you», in relationship with him.

«The house of servants»

The founding, creating act of the Lord is of bringing Israel out of the house of slavery. «The Lord» thus defines himself as the one who historically brought the children of Israel «out of the land of Egypt», but he is also the one who calls humanity each day to leave «the house of servants» (2b). Even more, he is the one who calls us to imitate him, freeing others from slavery. The father who reduces his daughter and son to slavery even during the Sabbath, who does not free his servant and handmaid, makes them live — if such is living — in a «house of servants». On the other hand, the one who does not treat his son as a slave, but treats his slave as a child, bringing him out of Egypt, imitating the Lord's behavior, gives them life. The man who «covets another's house», who steals his servant and handmaid, his cattle and ass, who takes his wife, shuts all of them up in a «house of servants». Deprived of «all which is his», the neighbor will soon be reduced to slavery himself. And lastly, the man who reduces the other to slavery also shows himself, more than his victim, to be a slave of his «covetousness» (17ab) — he kills the other, and kills himself.

Child not slave

Along with the land (12), only the child can receive the Law, the Law distilled here in the Ten Words. Land is not passed on to the slave, and neither is the Law, for then it would be coercion by power. The Law is what one accepts freely, the very substance of freedom. It could not be given in Egypt to those who were simply a bunch of slaves, oppressed by their masters, but in the desert, following the liberation achieved by the mighty hand of the Lord (2), to those who had become a people, the actors of their own history. The Law consecrates freedom at the same time as it founds it. The Lord's «mercy» will rest on the links between father and son until the thousandth generation for those who love him and observe his commandments (6). Love is the other name for the freedom given by the Law.

Jealousy, love, adultery

The Lord describes himself as a «jealous God» (5b). This adjective is surprising, and so needs to be interpreted. As is always the case, it can be understood negatively or positively. It would be negative if we understood that God does not want man to take what he owns. In the text, only God's Name is «his» — nothing else, not «what is in the heavens above, nor what is on the earth, nor what is in the waters under the earth» (4bcd) is said to belong to God, and, even more so, to humanity! If God has brought them out of the house of slavery, it is certainly not to bow down before him. God is jealous of humanity's freedom. His deepest wish is that humanity bow down to no one, not even an image of him (4a.5a). Love is not slavery, but free belonging in which each respects the otherness of the other. The idolater wants to own he who is totally Other as a thing. The adulterer does not respect the Other's identity, nor what it is his. Both deny the other and themselves. The truly free child is the one to whom the authority to honor in his parents, the conjunction «and» which both distinguishes and unites them, that is, the love which begat him.

The covenant

The Ten Words are not a Law above everything else. They are not a list of commands, imposed by a «boss» who will make humanity's debt weigh them down for ever. The gift of life and of freedom is not blackmail on God's part, in which humanity is indebted to the divinity. The commandments are a single word, which means commitment, promise, confidence. He who «gives his word» commits himself and at the same time trusts in the other, running the risk of being betrayed. Just as in love, like the signing of a marriage contract[20], in which the two contracting the marriage are equal[21], the Ten Words represent the pact God offers to his people, which will be concluded by the rite of the covenant (Exod 24). The gift of freedom presupposes that God has accepted the possibility of rejection, of being «hated» rather than «loved» (5-6)[22]. The punishment proposed for the one who betrays God's trust is not the vengeance of one who feels wounded by infidelity, but the remedy of the One who wishes to save life, a «visit» from the One who seeks to offer, alongside forgiveness, the restoration of the loving relationship[23].

20 On the marriage-type covenant concluded by the giving of the Decalogue, see MESSAS C., «Les Dix Paroles», 17.19.

21 Bovati, 135.

22 Bovati, 97-101.

23 Bovati, 119.121.

Chapter 4

The Decalogue in Deuteronomy

Deut 5:6-21

Deut 5:6-21

6 I am the Lord your God who brought you from the land of Egypt, from the house
of servants: 7 Shall not exist for you other gods before me. 8 You shall not do for
you idols or any representation, of what is in the heavens above, and of what is on the
earth under, and of what is in the waters under the earth, 9 you shall not prostrate
before them and you shall not be servants to them; because I am the Lord your God,
the jealous God, who punishes the iniquity of the fathers on sons, on third and on
fourth generations for those who hate me, 10 and who does mercy to thousand gen-
erations for those who love me and observe my commandments. 11 You shall not
pronounce the name of the Lord your God in vain, because the Lord does not hold
innocent one who pronounces his name in vain. 12 Observe the day of Sabbath to
consecrate it, according to what the Lord your God commanded you. 13 Six days
you will serve and will do all your work, 14 and the seventh day is Sabbath to the
Lord your God. You shall not do any work, you, neither your son nor your daugh-
ter, neither your servant nor your handmaid, neither your ox, nor your ass, all
your livestock, nor your guest who is at your doors, so that they rest your servant
and your handmaid, like you. 15 You will remember that servant you were in
land of Egypt and the Lord your God brought you from there with the mighty
hand and extended arm. Therefore the Lord your God commanded you of doing
the day of Sabbath. 16 Honor your father and your mother according to what the
Lord your God commanded you, so that your days are prolonged and so that
there is for you happiness, on the land that the Lord your God gives you. 17 You
shall not kill. 18 And you shall not commit adultery. 19 And you shall not steal.
20 And you shall not testimony against your neighbor in vain. 21 And you shall
not covet the wife of your neighbor. And you shall not desire the house of your
neighbor, his field and his servant and his handmaid, his ox and his ass, and all
that is to your neighbor.

Three books later, the Bible returns again to the Decalogue. According to the biblical account, forty years had passed, and the generation of those who had received the Exodus Decalogue had died. Before dying within sight of the Promised Land, Moses repeated the Ten Words to their children, who were preparing to enter the land which the Lord had promised to give them. In narrative terms, therefore, the first Decalogue is situated after the leaving of the land of Egypt and the crossing of the Red Sea, and the second before the crossing of the Jordan which enables the people to enter the Promised Land.

The overall composition of the second Decalogue is the same as the first (see «The passage as a whole», p. 142).

A. THE FIRST PART (DEUT 5:6-11)

+ [6] I (am)		YHWH		your God	
	. who brought you	from the land	of Egypt,		
	.	from the house	of the *SERVANTS*:		
= [7] SHALL NOT EXIST			*for you*	*other gods*	before me.
= [8]	You SHALL NOT	*MAKE*	*for you*	*sculpture*	
= or			any	*representation*,	
	. of what is in	the heavens	above,		
	. and of what is on	the earth	under,		
	. and of what is in	the waters	under the earth,		
= [9]	You SHALL NOT prostrate		before	*them*	
= and you SHALL NOT BE *SERVANTS*			to	*them*;	
+ BECAUSE I	(am)	YHWH		your God,	
+	(I am)	a God		jealous,	
	: who visits	the iniquity		of fathers	on sons
	- on *third*	and on *fourth* (generations)		for those who hate me,	
	: [10] and who *DOES*	mercy		to *thousand* (generations)	
	- for those who love me			and observe my commandments.	
= [11] You SHALL NOT pronounce the name of			YHWH	your God	*in vain*:
+ BECAUSE DOES NOT hold-innocent			YHWH	one who pronounces his name	*in vain*.

The first part of the Decalogue in Deuteronomy is absolutely identical to the Exodus Decalogue[1].

The difference between the two versions of the Decalogue is clearly marked in the central terms, even though they deal with the same commandments, which appear in the same order. This is further proof, if such were needed, that these two parts form units in themselves, clearly distinct from the two parts which frame them.

1 See p. 110.

B. THE SECOND PART (DEUT 5:12-15)

+ [12] *Observe*	THE DAY	OF SABBATH	to consecrate it,	
: according to what	*commanded you*		YHWH YOUR GOD.	
:: [13] Six	*DAYS*	*you will serve*		
:: and *YOU WILL DO*	***all***	*your work;*		
- [14] and the seventh	DAY	IS SABBATH to	YHWH YOUR GOD.	
– *YOU SHALL NOT DO*	***any***	*work,*		***you,***
.	and your son	and your daughter,		
.	and your servant	and your handmaid,		
.	and your ox	and your ass	and all your livestock,	
.	and your guest	who (is)	at your doors,	
= so that THEY REST	your servant	and your handmaid	like	***you.***
:: [15] And you will remember that	servant	you were	in the land of Egypt	
- and brought you	YHWH	YOUR GOD	from there	
- with hand	mighty	and arm	extended.	
: Therefore	*commanded you*		YHWH YOUR GOD	
+ of *DOING*	THE DAY	OF SABBATH.		

The Sabbath commandment in Deuteronomy (12-15) is quite different from the Exodus one, both in its composition and in the justification which is given: no longer creation, but the freedom from the land of Egypt. The concentric construction is more marked.

The first and last sub-parts (12 and 15de) mirror one another with «the day of the Sabbath», preceded by the verbs «to observe» and «to do» in the outer members (12a.15e), and «what has commanded you the Lord your God» in the second member of the first sub-part (12b) and then in the first member at the last sub-part (15d).

The central sub-part (13-15c) lays out exactly «what has commanded you the Lord your God», that is, what it means to «observe» (12) or «do» (15e) «the day of the Sabbath».

- The first piece has a single trimember AA'B segment (13-14a) in which the six days of work are opposed to the seventh day.
- The symmetric piece (15abc) is also a trimember, but this time it is ABB, with slavery opposed to freedom, so the six days of work during which one «serves» (13a) correspond to the time which the children of Israel spent as «servants» in

+ [12] *Observe*	THE DAY	OF SABBATH	to consecrate it,	
: according to what	*commanded you*		YHWH YOUR GOD.	
:: [13] Six	DAYS	*you will serve*		
:: and YOU WILL DO	***all***	*your work*;		
- [14] and the seventh	DAY	IS SABBATH to	YHWH YOUR GOD.	
– *YOU SHALL NOT DO*	***any***	*work*,		***you***,
	. and your son	and your daughter,		
	. and your *servant*	and your *handmaid*,		
	. and your ox	and your ass	and all your livestock,	
	. and your guest	who (is)	at your doors,	
= so that THEY REST	your *servant*	and your *handmaid*		like ***you***.
:: [15] And you will remember that *servant*		you were	in the land of Egypt	
- and brought you	YHWH	YOUR GOD	from there	
- with hand	mighty	and arm	extended.	
: Therefore	*commanded you*		YHWH YOUR GOD	
+ of *DOING*	THE DAY	OF SABBATH.		

the land of Egypt (15a), while the Sabbath (14a) corresponds to the freedom (15bc) brought about by «the Lord your God» (whose name is repeated in 15b as it is in 14a).

• The central piece (14b-g) is made up of a trimember (14bcd), a bimember, which completes the list (14ef), and a unimember (14g), in which the aim of stopping «work» is explained. Note the repetition of «servant and handmaid» (14d and 14g) and the pronoun «you» at the end of the outer members of the piece (14b and 14g).

+ [16] Honor	the father	of **you**	and the mother	of	**you**,
+ according to what	commanded	to **you**	YHWH THE GOD	of	**you**,
: *so that*	are prolonged		the days	of	**you**
: and *so that*	there is happiness			for	**you**,
: on the land that	YHWH THE GOD	of **you**	donates	to	**you**.

The final trimember (16cde) expresses the reason for the commandment (16ab), indicated by the repetition of the conjunction «so that» (16cd). Note the repetition of the syntagama «the Lord the God of you» in the final members (16b and 16e). Each member ends with the same pronominal suffix, «you», which also appears three other times (in 16a, 16b and 16e).

Compared to the Exodus version, the Deuteronomy version is expanded—there are two additional members inserted between the three members of segment as it appears in Exodus:

Exod 20.12	Deut 5.16
12 Honor your father and mother	16 Honor your father and your mother *according to what commanded you* *the Lord your God*
so that your days are prolonged	so that your days are prolonged *and so that you may be happy*
on the earth that the Lord your God donates to you.	on the earth that the Lord your God donates to you.

D. THE LAST PART (DEUT 5:17-21)

+	17		YOU	SHALL NOT	**KILL**		
::	18	and	YOU	SHALL NOT	*COMMIT ADULTERY*		
–	19	and	YOU	SHALL NOT	STEAL.		

+	20	And	YOU	SHALL NOT	**TESTIMONY**	against ***your neighbor***	in vain,
::	21	and	YOU	SHALL NOT	*COVET*	the wife	of ***your neighbor***,
–		and	YOU	SHALL NOT	DESIRE	the house	of ***your neighbor***,
					. his field	and his servant	and his handmaid,
					. his ox	and his ass	
					. and all that is		to ***your neighbor***.

This part is made up of two sub-parts. The first (17-19) is identical to Exod 20:13-15 (see p. 121), but the three commandments are now linked by two «and's», as though the three sins of murder, adultery and theft were interlinked[2].

The composition of the first segment of the second sub-part (20-21b) is almost the same as the composition of Exod 20:16-17b. The Deuteronomy version inverts the last two members, placing «the wife» before «the house», so that the parallelism with the three commandments in the first sub-part is more regular — not only does false witness correspond to murder, but «coveting the wife of your neighbor» corresponds to «commit[ing] adultery», and «desiring the house of your neighbor» to «steal[ing]». Note the addition of «field» in the last segment (21cde) and particularly the coordinating conjunctions which bring the terms together in sub-groups.

E. THE PASSAGE AS A WHOLE

COMPOSITION

Overall, the composition of the Decalogue in Deuteronomy is the same as in the Exodus version. The first part (6-11) is given to duties towards «the Lord *your* God», and the last part (17-21) to duties towards «*your* neighbor». In the center are the only two positive commandments, the consecration of the Sabbath (12-15) and the honor due to father and mother (16).

2 See BEAUCHAMP P., *D'une montagne à l'autre, la Loi de Dieu*, 43-47. The most well-known and emblematic account of this link is David, whose covetousness led him to commit adultery with Bathsheba, after which he followed the way of the liar and finally had her husband killed (see too the story of Naboth's vineyard in 1Kgs 21).

The links between the outer parts (Deut 5:6-11 and 13-17)

6 I am the LORD YOUR GOD
who brought you from the land of Egypt, from the house of *SERVANTS*:
7 Shall **not** exist for you other gods before me.

8 You shall **not** do for you idols or any image,
of what is in the heavens above,
and of what is on the earth under,
and of what is in the waters under the earth.
9 You shall **not** prostrate before them and you **shall not** be *SERVANTS* to them,
Because I am the LORD YOUR GOD, the God jealous,
who punishes the iniquity of the fathers on sons on third and fourth (generations)
for those who hate me,
10 and who does mercy as far as thousand (generations)
for those who love me and observe my commandments.

11 You shall **not** pronounce the Name of the LORD YOUR GOD **in vain**,
because the LORD does **not** hold innocent one who pronounces his Name **in vain**.

[...]

17 You shall **not** kill.
18 You shall **not** commit adultery.
19 You shall **not** steal.

---

20 You shall **not** testimony against YOUR NEIGHBOR **in vain**.
21 You shall **not** covet the wife of YOUR NEIGHBOR.
You shall **not** desire the house of YOUR NEIGHBOR,
. his field and his *SERVANT* and his *HANDMAID*,
. his ox and his ass,
. and all that is to YOUR NEIGHBOR.

These are the same as they were in Exodus (see p. 124). However, they are the more marked because of the repetition of «in vain» in 20, as in 11a and 11b; in Exodus, the synonyms «in vain» and «false», were used.

The links between the two central parts (Deut 5:12-16)

+ [12] *OBSERVE* the *day* of Sabbath to consecrate it,
:: **according to what commanded you** THE LORD YOUR GOD.

[13] Six *days* you will serve and will do all your work,
[14] and the seventh *day* is Sabbath to THE LORD YOUR GOD.

= You shall not do any work, you,
. and **YOUR SON** **AND YOUR DAUGHTER**,
. and your servant, and your handmaid,
. and your ox, and your ass, all your livestock,
. and your guest who is at your doors,
= so that they rest your servant and your handmaid like you.

[15] You will remember that you were servant in land of Egypt
and brought you from there THE LORD YOUR GOD
with mighty hand and extended arm.

So commanded you THE LORD YOUR GOD
of doing the *day* of Sabbath.

+ [16] *HONOR* **YOUR FATHER** **AND YOUR MOTHER**,
:: **according to what commanded you** THE LORD YOUR GOD,

so that your *days* are prolonged and so that there will be happiness for you,
on the earth that THE LORD YOUR GOD donates to you.

In addition to the links already demonstrated with the Exodus text (see p. 125), we noted above that the link between these two central commandments is more marked in Deuteronomy than in Exodus, so that the same clause is repeated in an identical place—«according to what has commanded you the Lord your God» (12b.16b). Here is confirmation that these two commandments are to be read together.

Note, too, that «the *land* of Egypt» in 15a corresponds to «the *earth* that the Lord your God donates to you» (16d), which link could lead us to interpret this «earth» as the land of Israel[3].

3 The term *'ădāmâ* is used with this meaning in, for example, Deut 30:20: «[19] I call heaven and earth to witness against you today: I set before you life or death, blessing or curse. Choose life, then, so that you and your descendents may live, [20] in the love of Yhwh your God, obeying his voice, clinging to him; for in this your life consists, and on this depends your long stay *in the land* which Yhwh swore to your fathers, Abraham, Isaac and Jacob, he would give them» (see too Deut 32:47; see p. 120, n. 10).

The links between the four parts (Deut 5:6-21)

6 I am THE LORD YOUR GOD
who **BROUGHT YOU** from **THE LAND OF EGYPT,** from the house of ***SERVANTS***:
7 Shall **not** exist for you other gods before me.
8 You shall **not** do for you idols or any image,
of what is in the heavens above,
and of what is on the earth under,
and of what is in the waters under the earth,
9 you shall **not** prostrate before them and you shall **not** be ***SERVANTS*** to them;
because I am THE LORD YOUR GOD, the jealous God,
who punishes the iniquity of the **FATHERS** on **SONS** three or four (times)
for those who hate me,
10 and who does mercy as far as thousand (times)
for those who love me and *OBSERVE* **MY COMMANDS.**
11 You shall **not** pronounce the name of THE LORD YOUR GOD in vain,
because the Lord does **not** hold innocent one who pronounces his name in vain.

---

12 *OBSERVE* the day of Sabbath to consecrate it,
According to what **COMMANDED YOU** THE LORD YOUR GOD.
13 Six days ***YOU WILL SERVE*** and will do all your work,
14 and the seventh day is Sabbath to THE LORD YOUR GOD.
= You shall not do any work, you,
. neither your **SON,** nor your **DAUGHTER,**
. neither your ***SERVANT,*** nor your ***HANDMAID,***
. neither your ox, nor your ass, all your livestock,
. nor your guest who is at your doors,
= so that they rest your ***SERVANT*** and your ***HANDMAID,*** like you.
15 You will remember that ***SERVANT*** you were in **LAND OF EGYPT**
and **BROUGHT YOU** with mighty hand and extended arm THE LORD YOUR GOD from there.
Therefore **COMMANDED YOU** THE LORD YOUR GOD
of doing the day of Sabbath.

---

16 *Honor* your **FATHER** and your **MOTHER,**
According to what **COMMANDED YOU** THE LORD YOUR GOD,
so that your days are prolonged and so that there is for you happiness,
on the land that THE LORD YOUR GOD gives you.

---

17 You shall **not** kill. 18 You shall **not** commit adultery. 19 You shall **not** steal.
20 You shall **not** testimony against YOUR NEIGHBOR in vain.
21 You shall **not** covet the wife of YOUR NEIGHBOR.
You shall **not** desire the house of YOUR NEIGHBOR,
. his field and his ***SERVANT*** and his ***HANDMAID,***
. his ox and his ass,
. and all that is to YOUR NEIGHBOR.

The link between the Sabbath commandment and the first part is established through the reminder of the leaving of Egypt (6b.15ab). The repetition of «your servant and your handmaid» at the end of 14 and of «servant» in 15a emphasize the importance of the theme of slavery (along with «serve», these words are repeated ten times). The verb and noun of the syntagma «those who observe my commandments» at the end of the central sub-part of the first part (10b) are repeated in the two central parts — «observe» at the start of the second part (12a) and «according to what commanded you» in 12b and 16b (and also in 15c)[4].

F. SYNOPTIC COMPARISON

Exod 20.8-17	Deut 5.12-21
8 ***Remember*** of the day of Sabbath to consecrate it. 9 Six days you will serve and you will do all your work, 10 and the seventh day is Sabbath to the LORD your God: you shall not do any work, you, and your son and your daughter, your servant and your handmaid, and your livestock and your guest who is at your doors. 11 BECAUSE IN SIX DAYS THE LORD MADE THE HEAVENS AND THE EARTH, AND THE SEA AND ALL THAT ARE IN THEM AND HE RESTED THE SEVENTH DAY. So the LORD blessed *the day of Sabbath* and consecrated it.	12 **Observe** the day of Sabbath to consecrate it, **according to what COMMANDED you the Lord your God**. 13 Six days you will serve and you will do all your work, 14 and the seventh day is Sabbath to the LORD your God. You shall not do any work, you, and your son and your daughter, **and** your servant and your handmaid, **and your ox and your ass** and **all** your livestock, and your guest who is at your doors, **so that they rest your servant and your handmaid like you.** 15 ***You will remember*** THAT SERVANT YOU WERE IN LAND OF EGYPT AND BROUGHT YOU FROM THERE THE LORD YOUR GOD WITH THE MIGHTY HAND AND EXTENDED ARM. Therefore **COMMANDED you the Lord your God**. of doing *the day of Sabbath*.
12 Honor your father and your mother, So that your days are prolonged on the land that the LORD your God gives you.	16 Honor your father and your mother, **according to what COMMANDED you the LORD your God**, so that your days are prolonged **and so that there is for you happiness**, on the land that the LORD your God gives you.
13 You shall not kill. 14 You shall not commit adultery. 15 You shall not steal. 16 You shall not testimony against your neighbor falsely. 17 You shall not desire *the house of your neighbor*. You shall not covet the wife of your neighbor, and his servant and his handmaid, and his ox and his ass, and all that is to your neighbor.	17 You shall not kill 18 **and** you shall not commit adultery 19 **and** you shall not steal. 20 **And** you shall not testimony against your neighbor in vain 21 **and** you shall not covet the wife of your neighbor **and** you shall not desire *the house of your neighbor*, **his field** and his servant and his handmaid, his ox and his ass, and all that is to your neighbor.

The first parts are identical (Exod 20:2-7; Deut 5:6-11). In the third part, the Deuteronomy version adds a member in v. 16 between the three members of its parallel passage in Exod 20:12. In the last part, the Deuteronomy version brings the commandments together (Deut 5:17-21), where the Exodus version juxtaposes them. In addition, the Deuteronomy text adds «his field» at the start of the list of prop-

4 The verb «remember» at the start of the Sabbath commandment in Exodus has not disappeared from the Deuteronomy version, but appears at the start of v. 15.

erty belonging to the neighbor: for in the desert where the first Decalogue is situated, no one owned a field, whereas at the point where the people were getting ready to enter the Promised Land to take possession of it, the addition of «field» was necessary.

The main difference between the two versions of the Decalogue is the reason given for the Sabbath commandment — liberation from slavery in Egypt in the second (Deut 5:15), imitating God, who rested on the seventh day of creation, in the first (Exod 20:11).

INTERPRETATION

Two of God's attitudes opposed

At first glance, the two reasons for the Sabbath rest do not appear to have much in common. What could there be in common between God's resting at the end of creation and the leaving of Egypt? The two points in time seem to be opposed to one another in every respect. To get his people out of the land of Egypt, God had acted — he had, as it were, got his hands dirty, or, as the sacred version would have it, he intervened «with mighty hand and outstretched arm» (Deut 5:15)[5]. On the last day of creation, on the contrary, he stopped all work, and did nothing — «On the seventh day God completed the work he had been doing. He rested (*šābat*) on the seventh day after all the work he had been doing» (Gen 2:2).

But it is still all about freedom

It is clear that the reason given by Deuteronomy puts freedom at stake — the freedom received by the children of Israel, held as slaves in Egypt (Deut 5:6); the freedom which the householder is invited to practice in his turn, first of all for himself, but also for all those who live under his roof (5:12-14). But it is not at all clear that the reason offered by the Exodus Decalogue is freedom. However, God's stopping for a whole day indicates that he does not occupy any of this time, but rather leaves it as a free space. He renounces the omnipotence, which could fill everything. In standing back, he shows that he is detached from his work, that he remains free in relation to it.

5 For example, Deut 4:34; 7:19; 11:2; 26:8; Ps 136:12.

By stopping, he in turn shows that he has mastered his own mastery by putting a limit on it. He shows that he is not a slave to his strength, nor to his work, to the extent that the text insinuates that there is an aspect, a danger even, of slavery in work (v. 9: «you will serve», *ta'abod*).

In brief, this is once again freedom — freedom towards oneself, one's own acts and one's own desire for power which usually becomes work, the desire to organize, to transform, to create, to produce[6].

In this sense, the two reasons complement one another. By taking his people out of Egypt, God conquers their freedom; by resting on the seventh day, he proves his own freedom. But this is not all. We can also see that, by stopping work on the seventh day, God leaves space for humanity, whom he has just called into existence and invited to resemble the divinity. The Sabbath is thus not only a demonstration of divine freedom, but also respect for human independence and freedom.

At this level, we can see there is a profound continuity between the two Sabbath texts of the Decalogue. Both mention freedom — the freedom taken from work so as not to become the slave of this master, and the freedom one offers to others so as not to be a despotic master, a kind of domestic Pharaoh. Both also mention power — the power which one limits to continue to master it, and the power one puts at the service of the freedom of others[7].

In this way, in each Decalogue the Sabbath commandment is God's invitation to humanity to do their own works, and to become his children.

Amen, amen, I say to you, the Son can do nothing of himself, if he may not see the Father doing; for whatever he does, these also does the Son likewise. Because the Father loves the Son, and shows him all that He himself does; and he will show him greater works than these, that you may be astonished (John 5:19-20).

6 Wénin A., «Le Décalogue, révélation de Dieu et chemin de bonheur», 176 (online version, 23).

7 Wénin A., «Le Décalogue, révélation de Dieu et chemin de bonheur», 179 (online version, 24); see too Id., *L'Homme biblique*, 125-126.

Chapter 5

Why are there two Decalogues?

The Decalogue in Exodus and the one in Deuteronomy are very similar and quite different. Their similarity might lead us to think that these are not two different texts, but two versions of the same text. The Bible calls both the «Ten Words»[1] or the «Two Tablets»[2]. We might wonder why such a fundamental text has been handed down in two different versions.

It is possible to look for this explanation in their origins, that is, by trying to trace the text's history[3]. There is no shortage of hypotheses, either about the primitive form of the text, or about the relative dating of the two versions[4], or about their *Sitz im Leben*, the occasion which brought them into being, but there is not one which seems most obvious. Whatever the case, the text's genesis cannot explain why the Torah kept both texts — it offers neither the cause nor the consequence.

We can examine the fruits, rather than the roots, in order to reflect on the effects of the repetition of this text. But before looking at this angle, we must first of all note that the double version of the Decalogue is far from being the only case of «doublets» in the Bible.

> The duplicated passages («doublets»), the repetitions and discrepancies ... strike the reader from the opening pages of Genesis onwards: two stories about the creation, 1-2:4a and 2:4b-3:24, two genealogies of Cain/Kenan, 4:17s and 5:12-17, two interwoven accounts of the Flood, ch. 6-8. In the stories of the patriarchs, there are two accounts of the covenant with Abraham, Gen 15 and 17; two dismissals of Hagar, 16 and 21; three versions of the misfortunes of a patriarch's wife in a foreign country, 12:10-20; 20; 26:1-11; two interwoven stories about Joseph and his brothers in the concluding chapters of Genesis. There are, furthermore, two accounts of the calling of Moses, Exod 3:1-4:17 and 6:2-7:7, two water miracles at Meribah, Exod 17:1-7 and Num 20:1-13; two texts of the Decalogue [...] many other examples could be quoted[5].

There is even a whole book of the Torah, the final one, which repeats what has already been previously written, to the extent that the Greek version of the Septuagint called it the *Deutero-nomos*, «the second law». Paul Beauchamp

1 See p. 105, n. 2.
2 See p. 105, n. 6.
3 See p. 33 and p. 105, n. 3; see too WÉNIN A., «Le Décalogue», 9-10, and particularly Bovati, 76-78 (with bibliography).
4 See Bovati, 76, n. 9.
5 *New Jerusalem Bible* (1994), «Introduction to the Pentateuch», 8.

has called this phenomenon, which he notes not only in the Pentateuch, with Deuteronomy, but also in the Prophets, with Deutero-Isaiah, and in other writings, which he calls Deutero-Sophia, «deuterosis»[6].

We find the same phenomenon in the New Testament with, among others, the double version of Jesus' infancy narratives in both Matthew and Luke, and the two versions of the Our Father. The fact that the Gospel is presented in four similar, yet different, ways is probably the most notable illustration of this.

The great law of binarity

In fact, what historical criticism calls «doublets» demonstrates the most fundamental law of biblical rhetoric, the law of «binarity»[7]. This is what Marc-Alain Ouaknine and Dory Rotnemer illustrate with a story which is close to their heart, as they quote it at the start of the introduction and repeat it three times, each time «in a different version»[8]. The third version is:

— What is the definition of a Jew?
— Someone who, when you tell him a story, always knows a different version!

Already, at the most basic level of the composition of texts, the «parallelism of members» — synonymous, antithetical, synthetical — is a characteristic of all poetic texts, including the prophetic oracles, but also of many «prose» texts. For example, Psalm 44 is made up of twenty-eight bimember segments in most of which the second member says the same thing as the first, but «is another version», with other words or from another point of view.

6 See BEAUCHAMP P., *L'Un et l'Autre Testament*, I, ch. IV, «Le Livre», 136-199; for a brief and straightforward introduction to deuterosis see BOVATI P., «Deuterosi e compimento»; see too *Traité*, 20-21.

7 «Repetition» may be preferable to «binarity», for the former term includes multiple repetitions. However, it can imply simple repetition between the repetitions, which in fact rarely happens. On binarity at the different levels of organization of the text see *Traité*, 15-21.

8 *La Bible de l'humour juif*, I, 15.22.29; see too 89.180.198. I could not resist quoting this story «a second time» (see my *Mort et ressuscité selon les Écritures*, 10).

1 To the choir master. By the sons of Korah. An instruction.

2 God, with our ears we have heard,	our fathers have recounted to us,
That which you did in their days	in the early days, 3 you, your hand:
The nations you dispossessed to plant them,	you destroyed the people to set them free.
4 Not with the sword they conquered the land	and their arm did not save them,
But your right hand and your arm	and the light of your face, for you love them.
5 You are my King, God,	who decides the salvation of Jacob,
6 In you our adversaries we push down	in your name we tread down our aggressors.
7 Not in my bow did I trust	and my sword did not save me,
8 But you saved us from our adversaries	and our enemies you confused.
9 In God we glory every day	and your name for ever we celebrate.
10 Yet, you rejected us and abased us	and you no longer go out with our armies;
11 You make us retreat the adversary	and our enemies stripped us.
12 You handed us like sheep for slaughter	and among the nations you scattered us;
13 You sold your people for nothing	and you have not gained by their price.
14 You have made us a reproach for our neighbors,	scorn and reproach of those around us;
15 You have made us a laughing stock among people,	a shaking head among the nations.
16 Every day my disgrace is before me	and the shame covers my face;
17 For the voices of insult and of revilers,	for the face of enemy and one who avenges.
18 Al this comes to us without forgetting,	without having betrayed your covenant,
19 Our heart has not turned back	nor turned aside our steps from your way.
20 But you have smitten us in the place of jackals	you covered us over with darkness.
21 If we have forgotten the name of our God	and spread our hands towards a foreign god,
22 Maybe would God not have discovered this,	he who knows the secrets of the heart?
23 For you we are killed every day,	we are treated as sheep for slaughter.
24 Rise up, why do you sleep, Adonai?	Awake, do not cast us out for ever!
25 Why do you hide your face,	do you forget our misery and oppression?
26 For our soul is bowed to the dust,	our body is cleaved to the earth.
27 Arise, come to our help	and redeem us because of your mercy.

Here is a text teeming with «doublets», and in a systematic way. No one would dare to offer a historical explanation for this, where the first members would be attributed to one source and the second to another! Rather than turning to the origins of those texts characterized by binarity, which it is impossible to grasp with any reasonable certainty, it would be better to stick to the final redaction, which is much more sure ground; it is these effects or functions of duplication which we will examine. We may note several.

The function of emphasis

The first function of binarity is emphasis, or, if we prefer, redundancy. Napoleon is said to have said, «Repetition is the strongest figure of rhetoric», or, «according to another version», «The most useful figure of rhetoric is repetition». Every teacher knows that it is not enough to say or explain something only once. It might have been badly explained, one or other pupil might have been distracted, or might not have heard, or not have understood. The teacher must therefore say the same thing at least twice; but the second time, he will not simply repeat what he has already said — he will use other words, expand what he said, or summarize it.

The «model» for this first function of binarity is clearly illustrated in the story of Joseph, Jacob's son. Pharaoh had had two dreams, being awake between them.

> 1 It came to pass Pharaoh had a dream: he was standing by the Nile 2 and it come up
> from the Nile seven cows of fair appearance, and fat in flesh, and they fed among the
> reeds. 3 But behold, seven other cows came up after them out of the Nile, bad in ap-
> pearance and thin in flesh, and they stood beside the other cows on the bank of the
> Nile. 4 And the cows of bad appearance and thin in flesh ate up the seven fat cows and
> of fair appearance. And Pharaoh awoke. 5 And he fell asleep again and had a second
> dream: seven ears of grain came up on a single stalk, fat and good. 6 But behold, seven
> thin ears and blasted by the east wind sprouted up after them. 7 And the seven thin
> ears swallowed up the seven fat and full ears. And Pharaoh woke up: and behold, it
> was a dream! (Gen 41).

Joseph's wisdom is revealed in his ability to interpret Pharaoh's dreams. The first stage in the process was to understand that the two dreams, one after the other, were in fact two versions of the same dream:

> 25 Joseph said to Pharaoh: « *The dream of Pharaoh is one*: that which God is about to do,
> he indicated it to Pharaoh. 26 The seven good cows are seven years and the seven good
> ears of grain are seven years, the dream is one. 27 And the seven thin and bad cows that
> came after them, are seven years and the seven empty ears, blasted with an east wind, are
> seven years: seven years of famine. 28 It is the thing that I told Pharaoh; that God is about
> to do, that he manifested to Pharaoh: 29 behold, seven years are coming, in which there

will be great abundance in the land of Egypt, 30 then seven years of famine will arise and
all the abundance in the land of Egypt will be forgotten and the famine will consume
the land. 31 It will be forgotten that there was abundance in the land because of famine
afterwards, because it is very grievous. 32 *And the fact that the dream of Pharaoh is repeated twice, signifies that this thing is decided by God and God is hastening to do it*».

Joseph's final sentence clearly indicates the function of emphasis that he recognizes in the repetition of the dream.

The function of totalizing

Binarity does not only have a function of emphasis, but is also often used to indicate adding up. Its simplest form is that of the merismus, joining together two components of a whole — «the heavens and the earth» is one way of describing the whole cosmos; «night and day» of describing how long something lasts. Ps 148 offers a simple example — framed by the same acclamation, the first part is about the heavens (1b-6), while the second deals with the earth (7-14d)[9].

9 See *Traité*, 270.

[1] PRAISE YAH!

+	**PRAISE**	**YHWH**	**FROM**	*THE HEAVENS*,
+	praise-him		in the heights!	
:: [2]	Praise-him	ALL	his angels,	
::	praise-him	ALL	his hosts!	
:: [3]	Praise-him	sun	and moon,	
::	praise-him	ALL stars	of light!	
– [4]	Praise-him	*HEAVENS*	of *HEAVENS*,	
–	and the waters	that are	above	*THE HEAVENS*!

+ [5]	**LET THEM PRAISE**	**THE NAME**	**OF YHWH**
:	**for** he	commanded	and they were created.
= [6]	And he set them up	FOREVER	and EVER;
=	a statute	he gave	and it shall not pass over.

+ [7]	**PRAISE**		**YHWH**	**FROM**	THE EARTH,
+	sea monsters		and ALL	deeps,	
. [8]	fire	and hail,	snow	and clouds,	
.	wind	of tempest	doing	his word,	
- [9]	mountains		and ALL	hills,	
-	tree	bearing fruits	and ALL	cedars,	
. [10]	wild animal		and ALL	cattle,	
.	creeping thing		and bird	flying,	
= [11]	kings	of THE EARTH	and ALL	*peoples*,	
=	princes		and ALL	judges of	THE EARTH,
:: [12]	young men		and also	virgins,	
::	old men		with	children!	

+ [13]	**LET THEM PRAISE**	**THE NAME**	**OF YHWH**,	
:	**for** sublime	his name	alone,	
:	his splendor	above THE EARTH	and	*THE HEAVENS*
= [14]	And he exalted	the horn	of *his people*,	
=	praise	for ALL	his faithful,	
	:	for the sons	of Israel,	
	:	*the people*	close to him.	

PRAISE YAH!

The following example is more complex (Luke 11:31-32)[10]:

+ 31	The queen	OF THE SOUTH	*will rise*	in the judgment	
–	with	the men of	this generation		
–	and will condemn		these;		
.	BECAUSE	she came from the ends of the earth			
:	to	*HEAR*	**THE WISDOM**	of	Salomon;
		=	AND BEHOLD, GREATER THAN	Salomon	IS HERE!

+ 32	The men	OF NINIVEH	*will arise*	in the judgment	
–	with		this generation		
–	and will condemn		this;		
:	BECAUSE	*THEY REPENTED* to	**THE PROCLAMATION**	of	Jonah;
		=	AND BEHOLD, GREATER THAN	Jonah	IS HERE!

The second piece (32) could appear to be simply a repetition of the first (31), a redundant, or even useless, «doublet». But to the undeniable function of emphasis we can add complementarity, increased at every opportunity:

- complementarity of gender between a woman («the queen») and «men» is one way of indicating all human beings;
- one might add that complementarity is also found between the one who rules («the queen») and those who are ruled over, «men», and this is another way of describing totality;
- geographical complementarity between the «South» and the north («Nineveh») which also indicates totality, as all the pagans will judge this generation of the children of Israel;
- there is also, particularly, chronological and necessary complementarity between «listen» and «convert»;
- there is further complementarity between the «wisdom» of the king («Solomon») and the «proclamation» of the prophet («Jonah»), which is one way of saying that Jesus is both king and prophet;
- and finally there is complementarity between the centripetal movement which leads the Queen of the South «from the ends of the earth» to Israel, and the centrifugal movement which brings Jonah of Israel to Nineveh.

10 See *Luc*, 530; *Traité*, 227.558.

«Poetic efficiency»

Binarity's effects are not only emphasis or totalization. There is also a further function, even more important, which has been called «poetic efficiency». The law of binarity allows a play on words.

> Thus, we can understand that it is the pressure of a law, at the risk of calling up a repulsive rigidity, which provides the indispensable conditions for it to be a play, that is freedom, on the works. This system of echoes always keeps, even in prose, poetical efficacy, and always directs the gaze towards a meaning which can only be «between the lines». This is true at the simplest level of the mere parallelism: «You will tread on the lion and the adder; the young lion and the serpent you will trample under foot» (Ps 91:13): this leads me to the *idea* of a threat, distinct from its materializations but inseparable from them. Energy is born out of the image, but it has to get free from it. This is probably why the biblical texts offer so much food for thought to the most demanding mind, without doing its thinking for him. They propel their reader towards the fearsome moment when he will have to do the interpretation by himself[11].

The meaning, that is, the author's presence, is not obvious to the reader — it is hidden and, at the same time, revealed «between the lines». This space calls the reader to risk interpretation, that is, not to fill in the gaps, but to dare to make themselves present with their own, personal words. A text's efficiency is measured by its ability to bring forth other texts, to make the reader feel called to write his or her own poem. Biblical binarity represents its openness, the essential condition of its fruitfulness. It defines a place, allowing a game, which is nothing more than freedom. Binarity's between-the-two allows the reader to breathe and to take the floor, in a way that the word becomes their own, with all that entails.

Theological function

Pushing the reflection further would risk offering not an «explanation» but a further «interpretation» of biblical doublets, a function we might call theological. It appears that we might say that binarity's main function is to avoid a text being considered to be absolute, to prevent its becoming idolized in some way. If there were only one text, only one Decalogue, or one Our Father, one might be tempted to worship it, like the Golden Calf. Once duplicated, both similar

11 BEAUCHAMP P., *L'Analyse rhétorique*, 13.

and different, they are like the cherubim on the ark of the covenant — facing one another symmetrically, their function is to mark the empty space which both separates and unites them, to indicate the location of the divine Presence:

> There I shall come to meet you; there, from above the throne of mercy, from between the two cherubs that are on the ark of the Testimony, I shall give you all my commands for the sons of Israel (Exod 25:22; see too Num 7:89).

Let us try to imagine how great would be the temptation to touch Jesus, to idolize his words, if we had not four, but only one, Gospel! Traditional iconography represents the evangelists with four different faces — the man for Matthew, the lion for Mark, the bull for Luke, and the eagle for John[12]. According to Ezekiel (Ezek 10:14), these are the four faces of the cherubim, which are not to be confused with the Presence they are the sign of — «The glory of Yhwh came out from the Temple threshold and paused over the cherubim» (Ezek 10:18). This is why the Church has always, with great determination, refused every attempt at reducing the four Gospels to a single text, both that of Marcion, who kept only the third Gospel and rejected the others, and that of Tatian, who composed the *Diatessaron*, a work combining the four Gospel rescensions into a single narrative. The fact that the canon kept four different Gospels leads the reader not to give in to the temptation to touch Jesus, as though he were a fixed statue. Difference calls us to follow a person, beyond each of the texts, to be seduced by him, as Jeremiah says (Jer 20:7). The Gospel is four-faced; Jesus is unique. The fact that the Decalogue has been handed down to us in two different forms leads us to listen to the one God beyond the texts.

The two cherubim and the ark of the covenant

The seven-branched candelabra is the symbol of concentric constructions, and we might suggest that the two cherubim of the ark of the covenant are doublets. Both are described in the same sequence which begins the description of the Temple God orders Moses to build after having given him the Decalogue (Exodus 20) and having made the covenant with the people (Exodus 24). This sequence (Exod 25:10-20), which describes four objects, is composed concentrically[13].

12 See BOGAERT P.-M., «Les Quatre Vivants, l'Évangile et les évangiles».

13 See PAXIMADI G., *E Io dimorerò in mezzo a loro*, 78; see too MEYNET R., «Es 25,10-40. A proposito del libro di G. Paximadi».

[10] **THEY SHALL MAKE AN ARK OF ACACIA WOOD.**
Two cubits and a half its length and a cubit and a half its breadth and a cubit and a half its height.
[11] **AND YOU SHALL OVERLAY IT WITH PURE GOLD;** inside and outside you shall plate it. **AND YOU SHALL MAKE A MOLDING OF GOLD AROUND IT.** — [12] And you shall cast for it *FOUR RINGS OF GOLD*, and you shall put them on ***its four feet***, and two rings on its first side and two rings on its second side. — [13] **AND YOU SHALL MAKE POLES OF ACACIA WOOD AND YOU SHALL OVERLAY THEM WITH GOLD.** [14] And you shall put the poles into the rings, on the side of the ark, ***to carry*** the ark ***with them***. [15] In the rings of the ark shall be the poles; they shall not be removed from it.
[16] AND YOU SHALL PUT INTO THE ARK THE TESTIMONY *WHICH I WILL GIVE YOU.*

[17] **YOU SHALL MAKE A PROPITIATORY OF PURE GOLD;**
Two cubits and a half its length and a cubit and a half its breadth.
[18] **And you shall make** two cherubim **OF GOLD. *Beaten work* shall you make them** at the two ends of the propitiatory.
[19] **And make one cherub at the one end and one cherub at the other end.** Of one piece with the propitiatory you shall make the cherubim on its two ends. [20] And the cherubim shall have their wings spread out above, covering the propitiatory with them; and their faces (are) one towards another, towards the propitiatory (are) the faces of the cherubim. [21] And you shall put the propitiatory on the ark above,
AND INTO THE ARK YOU SHALL PUT THE TESTIMONY *WHICH I WILL GIVE YOU.*

+ [22] And I will meet		*you* there,	and I WILL SPEAK *with you*
- from	**above**	the propitiatory,	
	BETWEEN	THE TWO CHERUBIM	
- that (are)	**above**	the ark of the Testimony,	
+ all that which	I COMMAND	*you*	*for the sons of Israel.*

[23] **YOU SHALL MAKE A TABLE OF ACACIA WOOD.**
Two cubits its length and a cubit its breadth and a cubit and a half its height.
[24] **AND YOU SHALL OVERLAY IT WITH PURE GOLD. AND YOU SHALL MAKE A MOLDING OF GOLD AROUND IT.** [25] And you shall make a frame of a handbreadth around it, and you shall make a molding of gold to its frame round about. — [26] And you shall for it *FOUR RINGS OF GOLD* and you shall put the rings on the four corners which are on ***its four feet.***
[27] Over against the frame shall the rings be as places for the poles to carry the table. — [28] **AND YOU SHALL MAKE THE POLES OF *ACACIA WOOD* AND YOU SHALL OVERLAY THEM WITH GOLD** and ***one shall carry with them*** the table.

[29] **And you shall make** its plates, its cups, its covers and its bowls by which they pour libations; of pure gold shall you make them.
[30] AND YOU SHALL PUT ON THE TABLE THE BREAD OF THE PRESENCE before me always.

[31] **YOU SHALL MAKE A CANDELABRA OF PURE GOLD.**
Beaten work* shall you make** the candelabra; its base and its branch, its calyxes, its buds and its flowers shall be of one piece with it. [32] And six branches shall come out it its sides. **Three branches of candelabra on its first side, and three branches of candelabra on its second side.** [33] **Three calyxes made like almonds in the one branch, with a bud and a flower, and three calyxes made like almond in the other branch, with a bud and a flower.** So for the six branches that are coming out from the candelabra. [34] And the candelabra shall be **FOUR** calyxes made like almonds, with their buds and flowers. [35] **And a bud under two branches of one piece with it, and a bud under the second pair of branches of one piece with it.** So for the six branches that are coming out from the candelabra. [36] Their buds and branches shall be of one piece with it. All of it shall be one ***beaten work **OF PURE GOLD.**

[37] **And you shall make** its lamps, seven; and one shall mount its lamps so that it may shed light on its front side.
[38] And its snuffers and its fire pans shall be of pure gold. 39 Of a talent of pure gold shall one make it with all these utensils.
[40] Notice and make them according to the pattern which was shown you on the mountain.

The first two objects have several things in common. The most obvious is that the throne of mercy is placed on top of the ark, as its lid, as said in the last verse of this pair of passages, v. 21. The same verse corresponds to the final verse of the passage which describes the ark (16), thus forming wonderful final terms. The last two passages are also paired. Among other links, they end in the same way, with the description of furnishings, the furnishing for the table in 29, and for the lamp-stand in 37-38. We also know that these two objects were placed in the first part of the Dwelling.

The most surprising thing for those who do not know the laws of biblical rhetoric is that the passages correspond remotely, the first with the fourth, that is, the ark with the table, and the second with the last, that is, the throne of mercy with the candelabra.

Note too that the candelabra and the two cherubim, as objects, are arranged symmetrically. The two cherubim face one another at either side of the throne of mercy, while on either side of the central stem of the candelabra, the other six branches correspond in pairs, symmetrically.

The second passage describes the throne of mercy and, in particular, the cherubim which are part of it (25:18-21). As already indicated, the end of the passage is clearly indicated by v. 21, which along with v. 16 acts as final terms. The following verse (22) is the sequence's center. The cherubim's value, therefore, is not so much in their shape or material, but rather in their position — on the one hand, they are facing one another across the throne of mercy, and on the other, the whole sequence is focused on their role, which can hardly fail to draw attention.

The ark, along with the throne of mercy, its lid, and the table as much as the candelabra are merely objects. But the ark, when finished with the throne of mercy, contains the «testimony», that is, the tablets of the Law, the Decalogue. These are the words spoken and written by the Lord himself on the stone — these are the divine words from the past, even though this past is presented as still recent. The words which describe the ark and its lid, the table and the seven-branched candelabra, and the cherubim, are spoken in the imperative by God to Moses. These are words in the present, the narrative's present.

Those, which appear at the center of the sequence, are the words which God foresees and promises to speak in the future. His word is not shut up in the ark, in the Decalogue. God has not spoken once and for all, in the past. His word will continue to be spoken to a «you», «between the two cherubim». The center of the central passage is the image of this place, hollowed out between the duplicate texts. This is the place of a divine word which makes itself present, each time a reader makes themselves present too, in order to receive it.

Part Three

Hymns to freedom

Since the second to third centuries BCE, Psalms 113 to 118 have formed a group of six psalms known as «the Hallel», which can be translated by the infinitive «to praise» or, probably better, the imperative «praise!» This group is also known as the «Egyptian Hallel», because it is sung during the Passover *Seder* when the liberation from slavery in the land of Egypt is celebrated, to distinguish it from the «Great Hallel», Psalm 136[1].

The Hallel was sung in the Temple on the fourteenth day of the month of Nisan, at the point when the lambs for the Passover meal were being sacrificed; it was sung again during the meal which followed on the night of the fifteenth, when the lamb was eaten by the family.

The Hallel psalms are still sung today in the synagogue on the great festivals of Sukkot (the Feast of Tents), Hannukah (the Dedication), the first day of Passover, and Shavuot (Pentecost). During the *Seder*, the family sing the first two Hallel psalms before the meal begins, when the second glass of wine has been poured; the last four psalms, followed by the Great Hallel, are sung after the meal, when the fourth and final glass of wine has been filled.

There is no doubt that these are the psalms which Jesus and his disciples sang during the Last Supper, which the Synoptic Gospels describe as a Passover meal. «After psalms had been sung they left for the Mount of Olives» (Matt 26:30; Mark 14:26).

The Great Hallel (Psalm 136) essentially celebrates the events of the Exodus. The whole of its lengthy central part (10-22) re-tells the story, from the death of the first-born sons to the crossing of the Sea of Reeds, in order to arrive, after crossing the wilderness, in the gifted Promised Land. This act is situated between the creation of the world (4-9) and the re-creation which is Israel's return from the Babylonian Exile (23-25). The Song of the Sea (Exodus 15) had already extended the account of the crossing of the sea by continuing it with what would follow, to the building of the Jerusalem Temple. In the same way, the Great Hallel widens the action by going back to the beginning of all and carrying on until the psalmist's present.

Of the six Hallel psalms, only Psalm 114 directly celebrates Exodus, starting with its very first words: «When Israel came out of Egypt, the House of Jacob from a foreign nation». Just as in the canticle in Exodus 15, this psalm is not restricted to the crossing of the sea recounted in Exodus 14. It in fact parallels the

1 See e.g., FINKELSTEIN L., «The Origin of the Hallel (Ps 113-118)».

sea, which drew back to allow the children of Israel across, and the Jordan which stopped flowing to yield a passage into the Promised Land. The whole of the forty years which separate the leaving of the land of slavery and the entry into the land given as inheritance to their children is thus covered by the eight verses of this brief psalm.

Unlike the one which follows it, the first Hallel psalm, Psalm 113, does not make any mention at all of Exodus. Its composition, however, refers discreetly, but effectively, to the Song of the Sea. It is in fact centered on a question, «Who is like Yhwh our God?», which cannot but recall the double central question of Exodus 15 — «Who is like you among the gods, o Yhwh? Who is like you, shining of holiness, terrible in praises, maker of miracles?» (Exod 15:11). The raising and exaltation of the weak and poor, the salvation of the barren woman, worked by the Lord (7-9), are thus placed on the same level as the original freedom from slavery in the land of Egypt.

The final Hallel psalm (Ps 118) does not recount any of the high points of the Exodus. This is the song of an individual, who invites all the children of Israel to join with him in celebrating the freedom and salvation, which the Lord has brought them. But the influence of the freedom from Egypt is such that the psalmist cannot help repeating some expressions from the Song of the Sea, such as, for example, «Yhwh is my strength and my son, he has been my savior» (Ps 118:14, just as in Exod 15:2).

The two psalms which are somehow central to the whole of the Hallel (Psalms 115 and 116) are marked by the presence of death, like Psalms 118. Unlike the idols of the nations, who are dead and bring death (Ps 115:4-8), the living God, who alone who can be relied on (9-11), is able to deliver those faithful to him. «You have rescued me from death» (Ps 116:8). Neither Psalm mentions the Exodus from Egypt. However, it was from death that the children of Israel were delivered, a death which did strike down their enemies (Exod 14:28.30). With enormous freedom of expression, the psalmists place themselves in the inheritance of their fathers when, each having escaped his own test, they proclaim that only the living can speak and sing: «The dead cannot praise Yhwh, they have gone down to silence; but we, the living, praise Yhwh, henceforth and evermore» (Ps 115:17-18). Everyone can proclaim his faith (10-11) and his love (1) along with the author of Psalm 116.

Even though it is the shortest psalm in the Psalter, Psalm 117 represents the perfection of freedom. The people who were once slaves and submitted need to be totally free of any resentment to invite «all the nations», including those from whom they have been freed, to praise the Lord their God. To crown it all, they, Egypt and Babylon, are called to glorify the God who deprived them of their slaves. By doing this, he will liberate them, too, from the slavery which they exercise over others. Victors and vanquished thus both find themselves free.

Chapter 6

Who is like Yhwh our God?

Ps 113

The composition of this psalm was examined at every level in *Traité*, 148-201.

Ps 113

[1] *Praise Yah!*

Praise, servants of Yhwh,
Praise, the name of Yhwh.

[2] *Let the name of Yhwh be blessed*
from now and unto the age;

[3] *from the rising of the sun unto its setting*
praised be the name of Yhwh!

[4] *Exalted above all the nations, Yhwh,*
above the heavens his glory.

[5] *Who is like Yhwh our God?*
He lifts up himself to seat

[6] *he humbles himself to see*
in heavens and upon the earth.

[7] *He raises from the dust the weak,*
from the dump he exalts the poor,

[8] *to seat him with princes,*
with the princes of his people;

[9] *he seats the barren of the house*
mother of sons joyous.

Praise Yah!

The first psalm of the paschal Hallel is brief. It has five parts (see «The psalm as a whole», p. 174). The outer parts are limited to the same, «Alleluia», translated literally as «Praise Yah!» Next there are two relatively developed parts (1b-4 and 5b-9b) which frame a short question (5a).

A. THE SECOND PART (1B-4)

COMPOSITION

+ [1b]	PRAISE,	servants	of YHWH,	
+	PRAISE	*the name*	of YHWH.	
– [2]	Let be	*the name*	of YHWH	*BLESSED*
		: from now	unto the age;	
		: [3] from the rising of the sun	unto its setting,	
–	PRAISED be	*the name*	of YHWH.	
+ [4]	*EXALTED*	above all the nations	YHWH,	
+		above the heavens	HIS GLORY.	

This part is made up of three pieces. The outer pieces (1bc and 4) each have a single bimember of parallel composition. The central piece (2-3) has two bimembers arranged in mirror formation.

God's name, «Yhwh», appears five times—as the final terms in the first piece (1bc), at the end of the outer members in the second (2a3b), at the end of the first member of the third piece (4a); at the end of 4b God's name is replaced by «his glory»[1]. The three occurrences of «praise(d)» (1b.1c.3b) are echoed by the synonymous «blessed» (2a) and «exalted» (4a). The two occurrences of «the name of Yhwh» (1c.2a) hold the first two pieces together.

INTERPRETATION

The «servants» at the start (1b) are, as it were, given more detail, or explained, in the following pieces—they are servants for ever (2b) and everywhere (3a), in all of time and space. The last piece (4) initially repeats the same idea: «all the nations» are those of the East and West (and also, surely, those of all time); then, at the end of the part, suddenly changing direction, «the heavens» (4b), not just the earth any more, are also «servants of Yhwh». In this way we understand that «his glory» will come to close the part: the invitation in the first piece, the desires which follow, are succeeded at the end by the stating of a reality which goes beyond all praise and whose acknowledgement is dazzlingly obvious.

1 The expressions «the glory of Yhwh» or «the glory of the God of Israel» are a respectful way of saying that the Lord himself has appeared (see Exod 40:34.35; Lev 9:23; Ezek 3:23; 10:4 JB).

B. THE PENULTIMATE PART (5B-9B)

COMPOSITION

+ 5b	He lifts up himself	***to*** SEAT		
+ 6	he humbles himself	***to*** see		
+	in the heavens	and upon the earth.		
– 7		He raises	from the dust	the weak
–		from the dump	he exalts	the poor,
: 8		***to*** **SEAT HIM**	with princes	
:		with the princes	of his people;	
– 9		**he SEATS**	the barren	of the house
:		mother	of sons	joyous.

This part has two pieces. The first (5b-6) is the length of a trimember segment, and the second has three bimembers[2]. The verses of the initial trimember seem to have the meaning that «He lifts himself up to sit *in the heavens* and he bends down to see *on the earth*». But as soon as the whole psalm is examined, it is clear that this position is not tenable.

The first segment of the second piece (7) is a bimember with six terms of the (ab) c / (b'a') c type. The second segment (8) is a bimember with four terms in which the two occurrences of «princes» are found as median terms. Syntactically linked to the first segment, this segment indicates the aim of the previous act[3]. The third segment is parallel to the first two. While the first member says that the Lord does for the «barren» what he did in the first segment for the «weak» and the «poor», the second member shows the result of the divine action — the «barren [woman]»[4] becomes the «mother» of «sons».

The clearest link between the two pieces is the triple occurrence of the verb «to be seated» (5b.8a.9a)[5]. The double movement of the raising up («raises» in 7a, «exalts» in 7b) and enthronement (8: «to seat with princes») of the second piece, joined with the conjunction «for» (8a), is found in the first piece under another

2 The unity of this part is also ensured by the fact that, apart from «he exalts» (7b), all the other verbs are participles which end with the suffix -*î* in an archaic form.

3 In the syntagma «his people», the third person pronoun normally refers to the nearest noun, which here is «the poor» (and «the weak»); however, it is still possible to understand these as the Lord's people.

4 «The barren of the house» could be understood as «without family», but also as «he seats, or establishes, in his own house the barren woman».

5 This hiphil, «make seated» is translated by «seat», and here it is transitive.

form — the same «for» (5b.6a) connects two opposing actions, the lifting up of the one who will sit as absolute ruler (5b) and the humbling to earth (6ab) of the one who is enthroned above the heavens themselves.

INTERPRETATION

God is at the same time above everything and close to the humblest (Isa 57:15). God's reign, affirmed at the beginning (5b-6) extends to the poor who share in it (7-8), as in an inheritance for the children given by God (9). The human vocation is to become a king, in the image of the Father. In this way the connection between «the heavens» and «the earth», which completes the first piece (6b), can be understood: humanity, which is of the earth, and particularly the person who is humbled, in «the dust» (7a) and «the dump» (7b), is exalted like God himself, and in a certain way comes to share in what can be called the heavenly nature. Heavens and earth are not only embraced by God's same glance, but the action of exaltation carries humanity from the earth towards the heavens.

C. THE PSALM AS A WHOLE

COMPOSITION

The outer parts have a single unimember segment. Next there are two more developed parts (1b-4 and 5b-9b). The first is a long invitation to praise; the other, which describes God's acts on behalf of the lowly, gives the reasons why the Lord is to be praised.

Between these two long parts, at the very heart, therefore, of the psalm, is a very short piece (5a), of a single unimember. Here the name «Yhwh», repeated five times in the previous part, and the shortened form, «Yah» of the outer parts, is repeated. The center is the only place where Yhwh is described as «our God». The central part is clearly distinguished from the four parts which surround it; it is in fact the only interrogative phrase in the whole passage, and is also the only one which has a first person pronominal adjective.

The last piece of the second part (4) and the start of the fourth part (5b-6) match one another: «the heavens and the earth» in 6b mirror «the heavens» in 4b and «the nations» in 4a. Additionally, «exalt» at the start of 4 and «he lifts up» at the start of 5b-6 are synonymous and act as initial terms. All these connections fulfill the function of distant median terms, via the central part (5a)[6]. We

6 Now we see why it is impossible to interpret vv. 5b-6 as linked. Verse 4 clearly states that the Lord is exalted «above the heavens».

[1] **PRAISE** YAH!

+ **PRAISE**, servants of YHWH,
+ **PRAISE** the name of YHWH.

– [2] Let the name of YHWH **be blessed**
. from now and unto the age;

. [3] from the rising of the sun unto its setting
– PRAISED BE the name of YHWH.

+ [4] EXALTED above all *THE NATIONS*, YHWH,
+ above THE HEAVENS his glory.

[5] Who is like YHWH our God?

+ HE LIFTS UP HIMSELF to *seat*
+ [6] he humbles himself to see
+ in THE HEAVBNS and upon *THE EARTH*.

– [7] He **raises** from the dust the weak,
– from the dump HE EXALTS the poor,

: [8] to *seat him* with princes,
: with the princes of his people;

– [9] he *seats* the barren of the house
: mother of sons joyous.

PRAISE YAH!

might ask whether «the earth» in 6b describes the land of Israel or the whole earth; the parallel with 4a clearly indicates that this is the whole of «all the nations», the more so given that nothing in the fourth part (7-9) which follows would enable the Lord's help to be restricted only to the children of Israel.

The list of all the words which indicate Yhwh's praise in the second part, «praise» (1b.1c), «blessed» (2a), «praised» (3b), «exalted» (4a), has its counterpart in the fourth part with a series of verbs where God is now the subject rather than the object, particularly «he exalts» (7b) which repeats 4a, but also «he lifts up» (7a).

BIBLICAL CONTEXT

The Song of the Sea (Exod 15)

Psalm 113 explicitly does not allude to the crossing of the sea. However, it is centered on a question which strongly resembles the question at the center of the canticle in Exodus 15 (see p. 72).

The Song of Hannah (1Sam 2:1-10)

The second piece of the penultimate part of the psalm recalls the central part of Hannah's song:

+ 4 The bow	of the ***MIGHTIES***	are broken,	the **FEEBLES**	gird on	strength.
+ 5 The ***SATIATED***	for bread	hire themselves,	the **HUNGRY**	become fat	with food.
+ The **BARREN**	bears	seven sons,	the ***ABOUNDING***	with sons	languishes.
6 THE LORD	puts to death	and gives life,	he brings down	to Sheol	and brings up.
7 THE LORD	dispossesses	and enriches,	he humbles		and exalts.
+ 8 He raises	from the dust	the ***POOR***	and from the dump	he exalts	the ***NEEDY***
+ to seat them with		the **NOBLES**	and a throne of glory	he makes them	to ***INHERIT***.

Verse 9 of the psalm matches the first member of 1Sam 2:5b; the earlier verses (Ps 113:7-8) refer to the last piece of the central part of Hannah's song (8)[7].

INTERPRETATION

Who is the psalm addressed to?

There is no question that whoever is speaking in this psalm is part of the people of Israel. It does not matter whether this is an individual or a group: at the heart of the poem, the speaker expresses himself in some way on behalf of all the chosen people, because in the specific name of the Lord, which has already been mentioned six times, he adds a seventh, with the apposition «our God». The problem, however, is identifying who the psalm is addressed to. Those who are addressed with imperatives at the beginning (1) and end (9c) are called «servants of Yhwh», from the second imperative (1b), but does this expression describe only the children of Israel, or all the nations? As «Yhwh» is the proper name of Israel's God, we might think, on hearing the first verse, that it is only addressed to the Israelites, priests or Levites, or even the whole of the people. However, vv. 3 and 4 indicate very clearly that the circle is quickly widened out, from East to West (3a), to «all the nations» (4a). If the first piece of the penultimate part (5b-6b) is in fact the introduction to the part, we must understand that «the weak» and «the poor» (7) along with «the barren [woman]» (9) do not only describe members of the chosen people, but all those «on earth» (6b), from «all the nations» (4a) who are unhappy. In this way those who are called to «praise» and «exalt» the Lord in the psalm's first verse are all

7 For an analysis of the whole of Hannah's song see *Luc*, 72-75. For the relationship between this psalm and Hannah's song see FREEDMAN D.N., «Ps 113 and the Song of Hanna»; HURVITZ A., «Originals and Imitations in Biblical Poetry: a Comparative Examination of 1 Sam 2:1-10 and Ps 113:5-9».

those he has saved, the men he has «lifted up» from humiliation, the women he has delivered from barrenness. The Lord, who is above «the heavens» (4b) is, at the same time, the one who «humbles himself» to «earth» (6) to «exalt» the poor (7b) as he himself is «exalted» (4a), who «seats» them (8a) as he himself «is seated» (5b), who makes princes of them (8) as he himself has his «glory» «above the heavens».

The central question

The central question (5a) appears to have a double role. It gushes up as a sort of admiring reaction to the burning invitation to praise, which precedes it (1b-4); it also triggers the list of reasons for praise which follow it (5b-9a). In reality, the penultimate part answers the question. What other god has done, or would do, what Yhwh has done for people? What god's total transcendence, as described at the end of the second part (4), consists in «humbling himself» to the «dust» and «dump», where «the poor» and «the weak» reside? Not only does the Lord humble himself to the lowest point; he does so to «exalt» the lowly (7) as he himself is «exalted» above all (4). So much so that the answer to the question, which seems to be obvious — «there is absolutely no one on earth or in heaven who can be like the Lord our God!» (see Ps 40:6; 86:8) — can be completed or even totally reversed: it is the poor and the barren one who are «like the Lord our God». Here is what is truly unbelievable. But this is really what humanity has been led to from its origins: «God created man in the image of himself, in the image of God he created him, male and female he created them» (Gen 1:27).

A possible inclusio

Ancient Greek translations rendered the vocative, translated here as «servants» (1b), as *paides*, which can mean both «servants» and «children». This is why the Vulgate translates it as *Laudate pueri Dominum*, which recalls Ps 8:2, «Above the heavens is your majesty chanted, by the mouths of children, babes in arms». It was from this perspective that the psalm was commented on by most of the Church Fathers[8]. In this reading, it is possible to see a link between the second word of the body of the poem and the penultimate, «son» (9b), which could be considered as a sort of inclusio. In this way a link could be established with the psalm's central question — those who are «like the Lord our God» are his children, those whom he has given to the barren wife, like a husband. The image is not un-

8 See Ravasi, III, 336-337.

heard of, if one recalls the prophetic texts in which Israel is described as a wife unable to have children, whom the Lord once again gives the ability to have children:

> 1 Shout for joy, O barren one, you who did not bear;
> Break into cries of joy, of clamors, you who did not bring forth,
> for more numerous are the sons of the desolate than the sons of the married one, says Yhwh. [...]
> 4 Do not fear, you shall not be put to shame again,
> Do not be confounded, you shall not be blush again;
> For you shall forget the shame of your youth,
> you shall no longer remember the dishonor of your widowhood.
> 5 Your creator is your spouse, Yhwh Sabaoth is his name,
> the Holy One of Israel is your redeemer, he is called God of all the earth.
> 6 Yes, like a woman forsaken and grieved in spirit, Yhwh has called you,
> as a wife of his youth who was repudiated, says your God.
> 7 For a brief moment I have forsaken you, commoved by a great compassion,
> I will gather you back to me.
> 8 In overflowing wrath, for a moment, I hid my face from you.
> In an everlasting love, I have taken pity on you, says Yhwh, your redeemer (Isa 54).

«Who is like Yhwh our God?»

To the Christian reader, the psalm's central question leads to an answer which, while it follows the ancient meaning, also leads to a new meaning. The link between the psalm and the Magnificat has been noted[9], to the extent that Ps 113 is known as «the Old Testament Magnificat»[10]. It seems that texts like 2Cor 8:9:

> For you know the grace of our Lord Jesus Christ, that for your sake he became poor, although he was rich, so that you might become rich by his poverty.

are closer to the movement of the psalm than the hymn in Philippians (Phil 2:6-11)[11]. Here, unlike in Philippians, there is no question of the humbling followed by the exaltation of one person — the one who humbles himself from the heavens does so to exalt the lowly.

9 See MINELLA M.J., «A Christian Looks at Psalm 113».
10 E.g., Ravasi, III, 336.
11 See e.g., Alonso Schoekel and Carniti, II, 538-539.

Chapter 7

«What happens to you, sea, that you fled?»

Ps 114

This psalm is the first example which Robert Lowth gives of «synonymous parallelism» in his nineteenth lesson (see LOWTH R., *Lectures on the Sacred Poetry of the Hebrews*, 205; *Traité*, 33). For the French translation of the analysis of the psalm by N.W. Lund see *Traité*, 104-105; my rewriting, *Ibid.*, 265.

Ps 114

1 *While came out Israel from Egypt,*
the house of Jacob from a people of foreign language,

2 *Judah became the sanctuary of Him,*
Israel dominion of Him.

3 *The sea saw and fled,*
The Jordan turned backward,

4 *the mountains skipped like rams,*
the hills like lambs of a flock.

5 *What happens to you, O sea, that you fled,*
Jordan, that you turned backward,

6 *mountains, that you skipped like rams,*
hills, like lambs of a flock?

7 *Before the Master, tremble, earth,*
before the God of Jacob,

8 *who changes the rock into a pool of waters,*
the flint into a fountain of waters.

This psalm (see «The psalm as a whole», p. 188) has two parts, each the length of a piece (1-2 and 7-8) framing a longer part, made up of two pieces which parallel one another (3-6).

COMPOSITION

+ [1] In the going out	of ISRAEL	from Egypt,	
+ the house	of Jacob	from a people	of foreign-language,
- [2] became	Judah	*the sanctuary* -of HIM,	
-	ISRAEL	*the dominion* -of HIM.	

The first part is the length of a piece, made up of two bimember segments, which constitute a single sentence. In the first segment, «in the going out» in the first member is not repeated in the second. However, the two terms «the house of Jacob» correspond to the term «Israel», and «Egypt» is qualified by the two terms «a people of foreign language». The two members of the second segment are parallel, with the second member saving on a verb by re-using «became». «Judah» and «Israel» are complementary, the first indicating the southern kingdom, and the second the northern kingdom. Judah is called the Lord's «sanctuary», while Israel is described as his «dominion», that is, his property.

The name Israel returns in the outer members from one segment to another; at the end of the four members, the two suffix pronouns translated by «of him» (2a, 2b) are opposed to «Egypt» and «people of foreign language» (1a, 1b).

BIBLICAL CONTEXT

Jacob - Israel

«Israel» is the other name of «Jacob» son of Isaac, the name which God gave him (Gen 35:10). Both became the names of the Hebrew people, the people of God. Beyond the link of identity — the two names described the same person and the same people — we should not ignore the relationship of, if not opposition, at least of complementarity — the initial chronological succession, because «Israel» is «Jacob's» second name, which he received long after his first name[1], but also a theological relationship, because while «Jacob» is, as it were, the natural, human name of Isaac's son, «Israel» is the name God gave him because of his mission and new existence, the new birth which this mission demonstrated.

1 This is also the usual order of the two names in the texts, in the Book of Psalms, Ps 14:7; 22:24; 53:7; 78:5.21.71; 105:10; 135:4; 147:19. Here, as in Ps 81:5 and 105:23, the order is reversed, perhaps because of the inclusio formed by the two occurrences of «Israel».

Judah and Israel

Although it was also called «the house of Jacob», Israel only came together as one people at the point where they left Egypt. Having crossed the Jordan, the twelve tribes which bore the names of the sons of Jacob-Israel divided up the land of Canaan among themselves. On Solomon's succession, the kingdom unified by David was divided into the kingdom of Israel in the north, and the kingdom of Judah in the south. The two occurrences of the name «Israel» (1a.2b) cannot, therefore, be describing the same situation. While Judah is called the Lord's «sanctuary», because it is there that the Jerusalem Temple, the one place of worship for the twelve tribes — all honor to our Lord — was to be found, the «Lord's dominion» extends over the whole of Israel, including Judah.

INTERPRETATION

The shorthand — only two verses to leap from Egypt to Mount Sion, to the Jerusalem Temple — is striking. The text does not say «after Israel had left Egypt»[2], but «When Israel went out of Egypt», as though the departure and arrival times had so shrunk that they were now the same; as though, in fact, it had not been necessary to complete all the long journey of the Exodus, and to wait for the next generation to reach the finish. As though, from the very moment of its freedom from slavery in Egypt, Israel's belonging was to God. This belonging is of another order, as it is no longer serving another people, being subservient to them, but being dedicated to the Lord's service, becoming his people, his dominion, on a land where the children of Israel, now become a people to themselves, can live free and independent.

2 As M. Dahood translates, commenting, «it was *after* the Exodus from Egypt that Palestine became the abode of Yhwh» (*Psalms 101-150*, 134).

B. THE SECOND PART (3-6)

COMPOSITION

=	3	The	SEA	saw	and *fled*,
=		the	Jordan	turned	backward,
:	4	the	*MOUNTAINS*	SKIPPED	like rams,
:		the	*hills*	like *lambs*	*of flock.*
=	5		What is-to-you,	SEA,	that *you fled*,
=			Jordan,	that you turn	backward,
:	6		*MOUNTAINS,*	that YOU SKIPPED	like rams,
:			*hills,*	like *lambs*	*of flock?*

This part has two parallel pieces (3-4; 5-6). The first is made up of two bimember segments with six terms in which, at the start of the members, the River Jordan is paralleled with the sea. «Saw» is not repeated in the second member, but the two terms, «turned back», which correspond to «fled» make up for its absence. At the start of the second segment members, «mountains» and «hills» are both high places; «skipped» is not repeated in the second member, but its absence is compensated for by the two terms «like lambs of flock», which corresponds to «rams». Note that logically the mountains are compared to rams, while the smaller hills are compared to the lambs. The two segments correspond to the extent that the difference between the high mountains and the low hills of the second segment is also found between the sea and the river in the first.

The second piece repeats, word for word, the terms in the first (apart from «saw» in 3a, replaced by the initial interrogative in the second piece). The parallelism of each piece is thus increased. Where the first piece was a quadruple statement, the second is a list of four questions. Each of the subjects of the members of the first piece become vocatives in the second.

BIBLICAL CONTEXT

Sea and river

The sea is the sea which drew back before the children of Israel when they came out of the land of Egypt (Exod 14). At the other end of the Exodus, the Jordan also drew back so that the people might cross dry-shod and enter the land of Canaan (Josh 3; see the summary of the Exodus in Josh 24:2-13, where the crossing of the Jordan is paralleled with the crossing of the sea).

Mountains and hills

«Mountains» and «hills» do not seem to be describing two different realities or events. The connection between the two terms is required by the parallelism with «sea» and «Jordan». It is not unusual for mountains and hills to be paralleled, for example:

> [2] It shall come to pass in the end of the days
> that the mountain of the house of Yhwh
> shall be established   on the top   of the mountains
> and shall be raised   above   the hills (Isa 2:2; see also 2:14)

Most commentators are of the opinion that vv. 4, 6 allude to the Sinai Theophany, when «the whole mountain shook violently» (Exod 19:18). However, the comparison with rams and skipping lambs leads the reader to joy rather than fear. It is true that in the oft-quoted Psalm 29, it is the Lord who «makes Lebanon leap like a calf, Sirion like a young wild bull» (6), this Lord who «shatters the cedars» (5) and whose voice «shakes the wilderness» (8). The verb used here, *rqd* suggests not just violence (as in Joel 2:5 et Nah 3:2, where it is fighting chariots which clatter at the charge), but also joy: Qo 3:4 where «dance» is opposed to «groan», 1Chr 15:29, where David dances in front of the Ark of the Covenant, Job 21:11, where children run and gambol like lambs. Note, too, that at the Sinai Theophany only one mountain shook, whereas here the plural is used, increased by the doubling of the terms «mountains» and «hills». The personification of the mountains is not isolated — in Isa 55:12 they «break into joyful cries», as the trees «clap their hands» like they do in Ps 98:8.

This is not, of course, to exclude a reference to Sinai, but that would suggest an interpretation of the earthquake in terms of joyful thanksgiving for the gift of the Torah. The psalm's construction suggests something else. If the first segment of the first part (1) speaks about the crossing of the sea, and the second segment (2) refers to Mount Sion, on which the sanctuary is built, the same alternating can be read in the two pieces of the central part — 3 and 5 describe the fear which the sea and the Jordan felt on seeing the Lord's work, while 4 and 6 report that the mountains and hills of Judah and all Israel leapt with joy because of the Lord's presence in his Temple[3]. This is how the Book of Wisdom understood it, in its version of the Exodus story:

3 So Deissler, II, 185-186; Gerstenberger, II, 283.

Like horses,	they were at pasture,
like lambs,	they skipped,
in praising you,	O Lord, their liberator (Wis 19:9).

INTERPRETATION

A somewhat enigmatic question

How astonishing that the elements, sea and river, mountains and hills, are apostrophized as though they were animated beings (5-6). It is true that, prior to being addressed, they had already been introduced as characters, fleeing or dancing (3-4). It is the more astonishing when we realize that this kind of question is very rare. Of course, sometimes a psalmist addresses creatures, but only to invite them to praise the Lord (Ps 98.148; Isa 49:12-13; [Greek] Dan 3:58-81); it is not to ask them questions. Elsewhere in the Psalter this only occurs in Ps 68:16: «Peaks of pride, have you the right to look down on a mountain where God has chosen to live?». It is all the more curious if, along with many other commentators, we see a hint of irony in the question asked of the sea and the Jordan.

c. THE THIRD PART (7-8)

COMPOSITION

–	[7] *Before*	the Master	tremble,	*earth*,
–	*before*	the God	of Jacob,	
+	[8] he who changes	the rock	into a pool	**of waters,**
+		the flint	into a fountain	**of waters.**

This part, the size of a piece, has two bimembers each of which has seven terms. Only the first members have verbs. In the first segment, «before» acts as an initial term; the two terms «the God of Jacob» correspond to the single term «Master» in the first member, compensating for the fact that the verb and the vocative «tremble, earth» have no equivalent in the second member[4]. The members of the second segment are parallel, but the initial verb has no equivalent in the second member; the two occurrences of «water» fulfill the role of final terms.

4 On Kraus' correction to the first member («before the Master of all the earth») see B. RENAUD's suggestive article, «Les deux lectures du Ps 114». It is preferable to follow the Masoretic Text (MT) which itself follows all the ancient versions.

The two segments form a single phrase. The second segment is a relative clause which describes «the Master», «the God of Jacob» in the first segment. At the end of the first member of the first segment, «earth» might seem to be opposed to the two occurrences of «water» at the end of the last two members of the second segment. However, *ʾereṣ* does not mean «ground», but «the country», or even «the whole earth», that is, «the world».

BIBLICAL CONTEXT

Water from the rock

If we reflect on the Exodus event, the water gushing from the rock refers to what happened in the desert when God, faced with the remonstrating thirsty people, gave his people water through the hand of Moses who struck the rock with his staff (Exod 17:1-7; Num 20:2-13; Deut 8:15 which uses the expression «the hardest rock», terms parallel to v. 8).

The theme and the vocabulary are repeated at the time of the Exile, when the prophets announce a new Exodus (Isa 35:6-7; 41:18-20; particularly 43:16-20 which parallels the two Exoduses) when the Lord will once again make water gush forth from the rock.

INTERPRETATION

A gift which gives rise to fear

The two segments oppose one another. It might seem strange that the gift of water makes the earth «tremble». This is probably why some have understood the verb in the first segment in a positive light, and therefore translate it by «dance». It is probably preferable to keep the better-attested meaning, «tremble», which implies fear. Whether we understand «earth» as the country to which Israel is exiled, or the whole world which will be as though it were petrified, there is no doubt that the gift of water is to do with the house of Jacob. What happened during the Exodus from the land of Egypt is about to be renewed according to the prophets' promise.

COMPOSITION

+ [1] While came out	Israel	*from Egypt,*	
+ the house	of JACOB	from a people	of foreign language,
– [2] BECAME	**Judah**	the sanctuary	of Him,
–	**Israel**	the dominion	of Him.

= [3] The	SEA	saw	and *fled,*
= the	Jordan	turned	backward,
: [4] the	*MOUNTAINS*	SKIPPED	like rams,
: the	*hills*	*like lambs*	of flock.
= [5]	What is-to-you,	SEA,	that you *fled,*
=	Jordan,	that you turned	backward,
: [6]	*MOUNTAINS,*	that YOU SKIPPED	like rams,
:	*hills,*	*like lambs*	of flock?

+ [7] Before	the Master,	tremble,	*earth,*
+ Before	the God	of JACOB,	
– [8] who CHANGES	**the rock**	into a pool	of waters,
–	**the flint**	into a fountain	of waters.

We will consider this psalm to be a concentric composition[5]. Pieces 3-4 and 5-6 are so parallel to one another that it would be very difficult not to consider them as forming a part.

Apart from segments 3 and 5, in which each member has a verb (two, in fact, in 3a), all the other segments have in common the fact that they do not have a verb in their second member.

The outer parts (1-2; 7-8) parallel one another. At the end of the first members, «earth» (7a) corresponds to «Egypt» (1a). The second segments begin with two verbs, «became» and «changes» (2a.8a), both indicating a transformation, which could lead us to think that «Judah» and «Israel» are paralleled with «rock» and «flint». The name «Jacob» returns in the second members (1b.7b). Finally, note that God's name only appears in the last part (7a.7b), while he was only mentioned by way of a pronoun in the first part, at the end of the members of the second segment (2a.2b).

5 «When the central part is in parallel composition, we still talk about concentric composition if the central part is no more developed than the sum of the two parts which frame it», *Traité*, 265.

«Tremble» in the last part (7a) recalls «flee» and «turn back» in the central part (3.5), all actions which are carried out when gripped by fear. Ancient versions understood the verb as describing the jolts and convulsions of a woman in labor[6]. Such a meaning could be related to the psalm's first word — «come out» is the verb used for birth (e.g., for the «coming out» of the twins Esau and Jacob in Gen 25:25-26).

The same complementarity which marks the two segments of the last piece between the fear which strikes one (7) and the joy which takes over another (8) is found in each of the four pieces of the psalm. We have already seen that it is fear which makes the sea and the Jordan roll back, while joy makes the mountains and hills leap. In the first part, too, the link between Egypt (1) and Israel (2) can be understood in this same way, since the former has to do without its slaves, who God now has a monopoly on.

While the first half of the psalm (first part and first piece of the second part) is narrative or descriptive, the second (second piece of the central part and last part) is discursive. It will have been noted that, once again, as in Exodus 14, Exodus 15 and Psalm 133, the text's only question is situated in the center, even though it only takes up the second half of the center.

INTERPRETATION

Like the Lord himself

As usual, it is the question which is the problem! And this is normal, because it is in a privileged position. Clearly, the psalmist is asking this question, while recalling history from the start of the psalm. But who addresses creatures in the Bible, ordering them, asking them questions, other than their Lord? «He says to the snow, "Fall on the earth", or tells the rain to pour down in torrents» (Job 37:6); he «spoke to the fish, which vomited Jonah on to the shore» (Jonah 2:11); he orders the sea «come thus far and no farther: here your proud waves shall break» (Job 38:11; see too Ps 104:7-9, and, especially, Genesis 1). The psalmist questions the sea and the Jordan, the mountains and hills intensely, not only as though he had been present when these fled and those exalted, but also as though it were he who had put the waters to flight and who had made the heights gambol with joy. He is crowned with God's very power, as described in the outside of Psalm 29 — «Pay tribute to Yhwh, you sons of God, tribute to Yhwh of glory

6 See e.g., Beaucamp, II, 205 (he translates this as «quiver»).

and power … Yhwh gives strength to his people, Yhwh blesses his people with peace» (Ps 29:1.11). This is how he can manage to question the earth and threaten it, as though he himself were its master. «Having become "sacred" (Jer 2:3), a "dominion" proper to their Lord, Judah and Israel make the world tremble (Hos 13:1) just as Yhwh himself does»[7].

A God who changes

The Lord is the God of Jacob, able to change flinty rocks into gushing springs. It is he who has brought his people out of the house of slavery, as he says at the start of the Decalogue (Exod 20:2; Deut 5:6), he who has made Judah «become» his sanctuary and Israel his dominion (2). He it was who changed Jacob's name to Israel (Gen 32:39); he turns the laws which rule the elements upside down, putting the sea to flight and making the Jordan turn back, making the immovable mountains dance. So why should we be surprised at a similar change in the very form of the psalm? The person who began by recounting and describing events in a way which we might say is objective, detached, even, suddenly transforms himself into an actor in history, questioning the elements as though they helped in their transformations, finally addressing the whole «earth» as his Master would, to predict what will surely happen. The psalmist himself does what he says, plays out what he describes, takes part in the dance. He identifies himself with the doer of the mighty deeds he reports. But he would probably never have managed to do this had not the Lord himself worked such a transformation in him, leading him to such a faith.

7 Beaucamp, II, 206.

Chapter 8

«Israel, trust in Yhwh!»

Ps 115

N.W. Lund has already worked on the composition of this psalm in *Chiasmus in the New Testament*, 104-107.

Ps 115

1 Not to us, Yhwh,
not to us,
but to your name give glory,
for your fidelity, for your loyalty.
2 Why should the nations say:
« Where is now their God? »
3 Our God is in the heavens,
all that he desires he makes.
4 Their idols are silver and gold,
made by hands of man.
5 They have a mouth and they do not speak,
they have two eyes and they do not see,
6 they have two ears and they do not hear;
They have a nose and they do not smell;
7 two hands and they do not touch,
two feet and they do not walk;
they do not mutter with their throat.
8 Like them, shall be those who make them,
all those who trust in them.
9 Israel, trust in Yhwh:
their help and their shield, is he.
10 House of Aaron, trust in Yhwh:
their help and their shield, is he.
11 Fearful of Yhwh, trust in Yhwh:
their help and their shield, is he.
12 Yhwh, remembering us, he will bless;
he will bless the house of Israel,
he will bless the house of Aaron,
13 he will bless the fearful of Yhwh,
the small with the great.
14 May Yhwh increase you,
you and your sons;

15 blessed be you by Yhwh
who has made heavens and earth.
16 The heavens are the heavens of Yhwh,
but the earth he has given to sons of Adam.
17 Not the dead may praise Yah,
and not all those going down to silence,
18 but we, we bless Yah,
from now on and for ever.

This psalm has four parts, arranged in mirror formation (see «The psalm as a whole», p. 204). The outer parts (1-3; 14-18) are slightly shorter than the other two (4-8; 9-13).

A. THE FIRST PART (1-3)

COMPOSITION

. 1 Not to us,	YHWH,	
. not to us,		
- but to **your name**	give	glory,
- for your FIDELITY,	for your LOYALTY.	
. 2 Why	should say	the nations:
. « Where-now (is)	THEIR GOD? »	
- 3 **Our God**	(is) in the heavens,	
- all that he DESIRES,	he DOES.	

The first part has two pieces, each made up of two bimember segments[1]. The two segments of the first piece (1), which form a single phrase, are opposed to one another, beginning «not to us» and «to your name». The last member gives the reason for the request (1d). In the second piece, the question asked by the nations in the first segment (2) is answered by the psalmist in the second segment (3). «Their God» and «Our God» act as «median terms».

1 We will see later that the symmetry with the final part leads to the way this first part is divided into segments.

«Their God», in the first segment of the second piece (2b) corresponds to «Yhwh» at the start of the first piece. The binary rhythm of the last member of the first piece (1d) seems to be repeated by the two verbs in the last member of the second piece (3b)[2].

BIBLICAL CONTEXT

Faithfulness and loyalty

The noun pair *ḥesed wᵉʾĕmet* is very difficult to translate. The French *Bible de Jérusalem* uses «love and truth», Dhorme, «grace and truth», Osty, «faithfulness and loyalty». English translations variously use «mercy and truth», «loving kindness and truth», «righteousness and truth», «kindness and faithfulness/truthfulness», using different noun pairs within the same translation according to context. The expression is part of the covenant vocabulary. In Gen 47:29, the dying Jacob makes his son Joseph promise to respect his last wish: «If I enjoy your favor, place your hand under my thigh and promise to be *kind and good* to me, do not bury me in Egypt». The spies sent to Jericho promise to deal in this way with the prostitute Rahab who has taken them in: «When Yhwh has given us the land, we will deal with you *kindly and faithfully*». (Josh 2:14). This commitment is clearly reciprocated: «All Yhwh's paths are *love and truth* for those who keep his covenant and his decrees» (Ps 25:10). In the Psalms, the expression is most often used for God (Ps 40:11-12; 86:15; 98:3; 138:2); in Proverbs, on the other hand, it is rather the attitude of the man the master is trying to train to be his disciple (Prov 3:3; 14:22; 16:6; 20:28).

«Where is their God?»

The same question appears twice in Ps 42:4.11, but the start of Psalm 115 has most affinity with Psalm 79. Having described the enemy's attacks on Israel, «insulted by our neighbors» (4), the psalmist pleads:

> 8 Do not remember for us the iniquities of forefathers,
> haste, come to meet us in your compassion,
> for we are brought low too much.

2 These four terms are not unrelated. The expression «to deal faithfully and kindly» is not unusual (Gen 24:49; 47:29; Josh 2:14; 2Sam 2:6); Hos 6:6 links «desire» and «faithfulness» — «I desire faithfulness, not sacrifice» (see too Jer 9:23: «For I am Yhwh, I *rule with kindness*, justice and integrity on earth; yes these are what *please* me»).

[9] Help us, God of our salvation,
in regard of *the glory of your name*;
deliver us and forgive our sins,
for the sake of your name.
[10] Why should the nations say:
«Where is their God?»

INTERPRETATION

God's honor

When the pagans mock Israel, it is really God's honor which is at stake — the people he belongs to are humiliated, crushed by another people, because God was unable to defend and protect them — as though he did not really exist, as though he were spineless. Yhwh's people take the ironical question they hear, not even addressed to them — as though they, too, no longer existed — as a profanation of the name of their God. This is why they call on the covenant through which the Lord committed himself to keeping «his fidelity and loyalty». They do not call on their own fidelity and loyalty, but only on that of the God of the covenant. It is probably worth emphasizing his merits as the Targum does when it glosses «Not because of us, *nor our justice*», inspired to an extent by Psalm 79.

Profession of faith

Israel replies to the mocking and self-important question asked by the pagan nations (2) with a profession of faith in God's omnipotence (3). If faith consists in trusting even when one cannot see, and even when the evidence seems to prove the opposite of what one affirms, the faith of the oppressed and defeated Israel is great. Appearances lead the pagans to derision, but do not stop the people of God from continuing to think that he can save them, because of the covenant, and the fidelity and loyalty that he promised them, which he can never forget without going back on everything he stands for.

B. THE SECOND PART (4-8)

COMPOSITION

This part has three pieces arranged concentrically. The outer pieces (4, 8), which are the size of a bimember, match one another in mirror fashion. The pronoun, which the last piece ends with, refers to the first word of the first piece. The two participles «made» and «make» have the same root. It is possible to see a link between «gold and silver» and «trust» if we understand that humanity trusts in the precious metals idols are made out of.

The central piece is much more developed, with three segments, two trimembers which frame a unimember (6b). The trimembers match one another in mirror fashion — before the traditional pairing of eyes and ears (5b-6a) and following the pairing of hands and feet (7ab) the outer members (5a.7c) match in mirror fashion — «throat» refers back to its synonym «mouth», «do not mutter» refers to its synonym «do not speak». The nose, a single body-part is found at the center (6b), just as the outer parts deal with similar body-parts.

+ [4] Their idols — silver — **and gold**
– MADE — by hands — of man.

- - - - - - - - - - - - - - - - - - - -

- [5] A MOUTH they have and they do not SPEAK,
: two EYES they have and they do not SEE,
: [6] two EARS they have and they do not HEAR;

a NOSE they have and they do not SMELL;

: [7] two HANDS - of them and they do not TOUCH,
: two FEET - of them and they do not WALK,
- they do not MUTTER with the THROAT - of them.

- - - - - - - - - - - - - - - - - - - -

– [8] Like them shall be those who MAKE them,
+ all those who **trust** in them.

BIBLICAL CONTEXT

The nothingness of idols

This is a commonplace of biblical criticism of gods made up by humanity, particularly in Deutero-Isaiah (Isa 44:9-20; see too 40:19-20; 41:6-7, 29; Jer 10:1-16; etc.).

Ps 135:15-18

A similar, but shorter text is in Psalm 135. Although different, the constructions are still regular, on condition, of course, that they are established in the knowledge of the laws of biblical rhetoric[3].

+ [15] The idols	of the nations	**silver**	**and gold,**
– MADE		by hands	of man.
- [16] A	MOUTH	they have	and they do not SPEAK,
:	two EYES	they have	and they do not SEE,
: [17]	two EARS	they have	and they do not GIVE EAR,
- Also	there is no	BREATH	in their MOUTH.
– [18] Like them		shall be	those who MAKE them,
+ all those who		**trust**	**in them.**

INTERPRETATION

A deafening powerlessness

The idols seem to be mistaken for the goldsmiths who have made them. The goldsmith has named his price — his god is not of wood or stone, but of the most precious metals. The idols lack no body parts; their creator has thought of everything[4]. And yet, despite the gleaming appearance of gold and silver, nothing works. These gods are unable to speak, and have nothing to say to humanity; they cannot see humanity's misery, nor hear their prayers; they are unable to smell the offerings, the perfumes and smoke of sacrifices, which are made to them; they are approached in vain, for they cannot touch those who hold them and, unable to move, their servants have to carry them on their shoulders (Isa 46:7). The glittering of the metal only sets off their nothingness.

3 This is why Beauchamp's opinion should be avoided: «Verse 7 [of Ps 115], whose construction stands out in contrast to the rest of the passage, seems to be secondary, particularly the third stich. It does not however appear in Ps 135:15-18 which repeats Ps 115:4-8 with some variants for v. 6b» (Beauchamp, II, 208; similarly Gerstenberger, II, 287). See too what a misunderstanding of biblical rhetoric can lead to in Jacquet, III, 275.

4 The seven members of the central piece seem to indicate totality (Alonso Schoekel and Carniti, II, 554).

In his image

The basic and fatal error of the idol-maker is his claim to the creator's place. He «makes», arrogating to himself the role of originator, when he should acknowledge that he owes his existence and life to another. He perverts the order of creation. It is therefore unavoidable that, in making god in his image, he becomes like him. Many translate the last verse as a wish — it seems that the prayer of the one praying is more of a statement. The idolater's future is no more than that of the inertia of lifeless metal.

c. THE THIRD PART (9-13)

COMPOSITION

This part has two complementary pieces. The first is made up of three segments which strongly parallel one another. The same invitation is given to three groups — the people of Israel as a whole, then the priests in particular. Most modern commentators do not think that those who «fear Yhwh» are the pagans who worship Israel's God, for this meaning of the expression is quite late (Acts 10:2.22; 13:16.26); but, rather a group of faithful in Israel[5].

The second piece repeats the same list of three groups in its central trimember (12bc-13a). It uses the three categories included in the «us» of the initial member (12a). At the outer parts are two unimember segments, both marked by binarity — two verbs at the start, two adjectives at the end. With the traditional merismus, «the small with the great», the last segment repeats the whole in another dimension, that of age or even dignity.

+ 9 ISRAEL,		trust	in YHWH,
:: their help		and their shield	is he.
+ 10 HOUSE	OF AARON,	trust	in YHWH,
:: their help		and their shield	is he.
+ 11 *THE FEARFUL*	*OF YHWH,*	trust	in YHWH,
:: their help		and their shield	is he.
:: 12 YHWH	remembering us,		he will bless:
+	he will bless	the house	of ISRAEL,
+	he will bless	THE HOUSE	OF AARON,
+ 13	he will bless	*THE FEARFUL*	*OF YHWH,*
::	the small (ones)		with the great.

5 See especially Gerstenberger, II, 288.

BIBLICAL CONTEXT

The first piece's tirade is repeated in Ps 118:2-4 (see p. 246). In Ps 135:19-20, a fourth category, that of the Levites, is added, alongside the priests, just as here the call to praise the Lord immediately follows the criticism of idolatry (Ps 135:15-18).

INTERPRETATION

A communicative faith

The person addressing Israel, its priests and faithful is a member of this people. He questions them as though giving a homily, to stimulate and encourage the congregation. In so doing, he does not put himself outside the group — he soon moves to «us», which includes himself. His words are an urgent appeal to place trust, faith and hope in the one who can «help», that is, the savior, who is able to protect them from the enemy's blows. A convinced believer, the psalmist wishes that all would share his faith, as though faith cannot be real, full and whole if it is not shared by all the people, all categories, from the smallest to the greatest.

Faith and blessing

Humanity's faith is answered by God's blessing. Faith is not belief in truths, but a relation founded on a covenant, which unites two beings. If the psalmist can state with great confidence that the Lord will bless him and all the people, it is because he has placed his trust in the God. He practices what he preaches, which, he believes, will lead to the belief of all.

D. The fourth part (14-18)

: 14 May add	YHWH	*to you*,	
= *to you*	and *to your* SONS;		
: 15 BLESSED	(be) *you*	of YHWH,	
= who has made	**HEAVENS**	and ***EARTH***.	
- 16 The **HEAVENS**	(are) the **HEAVENS**	of YHWH,	
- but the ***EARTH***	he has given	to SONS of Adam.	
– 17 Not	the dead	praise	YAH,
– and not	all those going down	to silence,	
+ 18	but *we*,	WE BLESS	YAH,
+	from now on	and unto the age.	

This part has three pieces. The first (14-15) uses «you», while the third (17-18) uses «we». The central piece, a single bimember segment (16) expresses a general truth.

The first piece has two bimembers, which are both wishes. The first segment mentions the fertility which the second segment defines as a «divine» blessing. The final member describes Yhwh as an all-powerful creator. The last piece also has two segments, which make up a single phrase. The «we» of the second segments is opposed here to the dead in the first segment. Given the context, the dead are described as those who are unable to «praise» God. The first members of each segment are parallel — «we» corresponds to «the dead», «we bless» to «they praise» and «Yah» is repeated at the end.

Between the two pieces, the two occurrences of «Yah» (17a.18a) match the two occurrences of «Yhwh», also in the first members of each segment (14a.15a). The «blessing» of «we» in 18a corresponds to God's blessing in 15a. The bipolar expression in 18b, «from now on and unto the age», matches the one in 15b, «heavens and earth».

The central piece (16) repeats «heavens and earth» from the previous member, as well as «sons» (16b) like at the end of the first segment (14b). Despite these links to the first piece, the central segment remains enigmatic, and we might wonder how it fits logically into the part[6].

BIBLICAL CONTEXT

Moses' blessing

At the start of Deuteronomy, Moses addresses the following words to the people: «Yhwh your God has multiplied you, till you are now like the stars of heaven in number. And Yhwh your God is going to increase you a thousand times more, and bless you as he promised» (Deut 1:10-11).

A mutual blessing

The final passage of Luke's Gospel reports how, at the point when Jesus was leaving his disciples to be borne up into heaven, he «blessed» them, as a father blesses his children in his dying moments. Jacob did this to his twelve sons (Gen 49), and Moses to the twelve tribes of Israel (Deut 33). Jesus' paternal blessing is matched by the blessing of his children who «were continually in the Temple praising God» (Luke 24:53)[7]. From the moment Jesus returned to «heaven», responsibility for what he had begun was «given» to his disciples, which is the subject of Luke's second book.

INTERPRETATION

Each in his own place

The central verse states a clear separation — the heavens are God's domain, earth humanity's. Of course, although the earth belongs to humanity, it is because God has «given» it to them. He has not entrusted it to them, lent it to them, in the expectation that they will return it to him when he is ready to take it back. God's gifts are not taken back; otherwise they would not be gifts[8]. Although the psalmist uses the expression «Sons of Adam», rather than one of the syn-

6 To consider the last two verses of the psalm as a later addition (Jacquet, III, 281, repeating Briggs) is to avoid the problem. When the text's logic evades us, it is better to acknowledge that we have not understood it.

7 See *Luc*, 952-953

8 See M. BALMARY's commentary on the parable of the talents in his *Abel ou la traversée de l'Éden*, 64-109 (summary in *Luc*, 720-725).

onyms translated by «men»[9] this can lead us to think of the divine filiation of humanity, to whom God gives the earth as an inheritance. Each is in his own place, independent, but not without a close relationship. Fusion or confusion do not allow everyone to be free — such a distinction is what makes a covenant possible, as it is, by definition, two free beings who choose to bind themselves together.

«On earth as in heaven»

In a covenant between heaven and earth, humanity's blessing (18) responds to God's (15). The gift of praise and blessing rises to heaven from those who have received this life, a life which God makes fruitful and multiplies through successive generations, and are not dumb like the dead. The gifts, clearly, are not symmetrical, for humanity is not his own originator — he holds everything from his Creator, his father. God, however, makes him as his equal, as it were, when he grants him to give of himself, even if only a word of acknowledgement. No more is needed for the covenant between heaven and earth to be concluded.

9 The JB translates this as «man», just as at the end of Psalm 9, where *ʾenôš*, is used twice, Ps 22:7, which uses *ʾîš*: «Here am I, now more worm than *man*» (see too Ps 1:1: «Happy the *man*»; Ps 25:12) or Ps 32:2 which uses *ʾādām* («Happy the man»).

E. THE PSALM AS A WHOLE

COMPOSITION

[1] **NOT** to us, Yhwh, **NOT** to us,
but to your name give glory, for your fidelity, for your loyalty.

[2] Why should the nations say: «Where is now their God?»
[3] Our God is in the **heavens**, all that he desires he MAKES.

[4] Their idols are silver and gold, MADE by hands of Adam.

[5] They have a mouth and ***THEY DO NOT SPEAK***,
they have two eyes and they do not see, [6] they have two ears and they do not hear;
they have a nose and they do not smell;
[7] two hands and they do not touch, two feet and they do not walk;
THEY DO NOT SPEAK with their throat.

[8] Like them shall be those who MAKE them, all those who *trust* in them.

[9] Israel, *trust* in Yhwh: their help and their shield is He.
[10] House of Aaron, *trust* in Yhwh: their help and their shield is He.
[11] Fearful of Yhwh, *trust* in Yhwh: their help and their shield is He.

[12] Yhwh remembering us, HE WILL BLESS;
HE WILL BLESS the house of Israel,
HE WILL BLESS the house of Aaron,
[13] HE WILL BLESS the fearful of Yhwh,
the small ones with the great.

[14] May increase you Yhwh, you and your *sons;*
[15] BLESS be you of Yhwh who has MADE **heavens** and earth.

[16] The **heavens** are the **heavens** of Yhwh, but the earth he has given to sons of Adam.

[17] **NOT** the dead **PRAISE** Yah, and **NOT** all those who go down to silence,
[18] but we, we **BLESS** Yah, from now on and for ever.

The outer parts have a number of points in common. The most noteworthy is that the first piece is composed following the same model as the last piece. They are also both built on an opposition, between «we» and the Lord at the start, and between the same «we» and «the dead» at the end. Two double negatives act as initial terms. The bipolar expressions in 1d and 18b act as final terms. The two occurrences of «Yah» in the last piece (17a.18a) correspond to «Yhwh» (1a) and «your name» (1c) in the first piece[10].

10 It is this parallelism between the two pieces which led us to consider that 1a and a1 form a bimember segment (see *Traité*, 137-138.145-147).

– 1	**NOT**	*TO US,*		YHWH,
–	**NOT**	*TO US,*		
	+ but TO YOUR NAME		give	glory,
	+ *FOR YOUR FIDELITY,*		*FOR YOUR LOYALTY.*	

[...]

– 17	**NOT**	*THE DEAD*	*praise*	YAH,
– et	**NOT**	*ALL THE GOING DOWN*	to silence,	
	+ 18 but *WE,*		*we bless*	YAH,
	+ *FROM NOW ON*		*AND FOR EVER.*	

The end of the first part (3) and the start of the last part (15) repeat the verb «to make», with the same subject. In addition, «the heavens are the heavens of Yhwh» (16) recalls «Our God is in the heavens» (3).

The central parts have no common lexicon, apart from the verb «to trust», which appears at the end of the second part (8) and three times at the start of the following part (9,10,11), thus acting as median terms. The five positive verbs which have Yhwh as their subject in the second piece of the third part (12-13) are opposed to the seven negative verbs which have the idols as their subject in the central piece of the second part (5-7).

The two occurrences of «to make» in 3 and 4 hold the first two parts together. It is also possible to see a link between «the small with the great» at the end of the third part (13b) and «you and your sons» at the start of the final part (14). The repetition of «to bless» in 15, referring to the four occurrences of the same verb in 12-13, is heavier.

While the first part uses «us», but an «us», which is placed in opposition to the nations, the second part, dealing with these nations' idols, which have just been discussed, is entirely in the third person plural. The last two parts are also marked by the movement from the second person plural (9-11; 14-15) to the first person plural (12-13; 17-18): this is no longer the pagans, at least, not directly, but the triple occurrence of «help and shield» at the start of the second side (9-11) implies divine protection against enemies.

The proper name «Yhwh», and its shortened form «Yah» are repeated twelve times in the psalm, only once in the first part (1a), not at all the second part, six times in the third part and five times in the final part.

BIBLICAL CONTEXT

Ezekiel 36, a different literary genre, seems not only to correspond to the situation in which the author of Psalm 115 finds himself, but also to the content of the Psalm.

INTERPRETATION

Who is speaking?

Here is someone who, from the very first words, uses the first person plural, never «I». He is not, therefore, talking on behalf of himself, but on behalf of the whole people. Even the words he speaks, as an almost sarcastic reply to the pagans (2), are the confession of faith of a group, the whole community whose God is Yhwh (3). Rather than being addressed to a specific hearer, his ironic criticism of the idols seems to be for no one in particular. It could be understood as a sort of settling of accounts — the pagans do not address the children of Israel directly to mock them (2), so the psalmist will respond in the same way. But after his diatribe, he turns to Israel in the second person plural. He does not put himself outside the group, but in a position of authority, at the head of the whole of the people. Having started by turning to the Lord to remind him of his covenant, he does not repeat his prayer even once, and does not speak to God again, even though only his name is on his lips, unless we understand the hopes which he utters at the end are a kind of prayer — «May Yhwh increase you», «blessed be you by Yhwh». Was this type of blessing reserved to the priest? His call to «trust» in the Lord probably makes him seem even more of a prophet. In the end it makes little difference, if we realize that it is the reader, every reader, whatever his or her responsibilities within the community of believers, who, by the very fact of repeating the words of the psalm, is called to fulfill the same role. The author's voice has been extinguished for a long time, yet his words are not dead, they are accepted, repeated like a flame, by those who have believed in them and have trusted in the Lord after him. The role the psalmist took on, of leading all the people in the conviction of his faith, is passed on to everyone who repeats his call.

Where are we?

There is no doubt that the situation in which these words were written was far from ideal. This is not saying much, since the nations mock Israel in a way which could not be more scornful, as one would to a crushed enemy. They ask where their God is, because he is no longer seen. If the psalmist replies that he is in the heavens, it is because he is no longer on earth, because his Temple is destroyed, his worship abolished, his people chased out from their land and scattered among other nations. The situation of the Exile strikes a chord with the themes the psalmist is dealing with[11]. Everything was destroyed: religious institutions with the Temple and worship, political institutions with the monarchy, economic institutions with the land — all was lost. It was the end for Israel, a journey through death, as prophesied by Amos[12]. This is clearly what is being discussed, for the psalmist ends his poem with a sudden burst of resistance to the definitive silence of death. Exegetes are far from being in agreement on the psalm's date. Several prefer to situate it after the return from the Exile, a period which we know was difficult and problematic. Whatever the historical origins of the text, and its is best to acknowledge that we know little about this, the only thing which really counts is that it can be applied to any distressing situation when faith is put to the test, and comes out victorious.

Death is not what we think

Israel was held to be dead, just as its God was, for the nations said that they did not know where he had gone. Appearances surely made them right. But this is not the psalmist's opinion — from his first words, he addresses his God, reminding him of his covenant and his faithfulness. He would not speak to him if he shared his enemies' viewpoint. He immediately counter-attacks — it is the gods of the nations who are dead. In vain are they furnished with all the organs of the living, for they are incapable of perceiving or doing anything. And furthermore, it is those who make them and put their trust in them who are dead. These dead cannot praise the Lord, since they go down to silence together. Those who are truly alive are those who do not seek their own glory, but God's glory, who put their trust in him alone, believing that this God, who seems to have abandoned them to death, is still able to bless them, to give them increased life, not only them, but their children too. This is why «from now», at the heart of the situation of death where they find themselves, they bless the Lord and will do so «for ever».

11 «During the time when Israel was deprived of land and Temple God — according to the traditional criteria — could not compete with other gods, for a god who had no land and could not be worshipped was not a god at all. It was during this time that the people learned to understand fully what was different and new about Israel's God: that in fact he was not just Israel's god, the god of one people and one land, but quite simply God, the God of the universe, to whom all lands, all heaven and earth belong...» (RATZINGER J. — Benedict XVI, *Jesus of Nazareth*, 347).

12 See particularly the central part of the book (Amos 5:1-7), which we entitled «Funeral lamentation over the virgin of Israel» (see *Amos*, 159-185).

Chapter 9

«I believe!»

Ps 116

Ps 116

[1] *I love because Yhwh attends to*
the cry of my supplications,

[2] *because he turned his ear to me,*
and in my days I will call.

[3] *Surrounded me the snares of death,*
and the straits of Sheol have found me;

distress and sorrow I find,
[4] *and I call the name of Yhwh:*

I pray, Yhwh,
deliver my soul!

[5] *Gracious is Yhwh and righteous,*
and our God has compassion;

[6] *Yhwh protects the simple:*
I was helpless and he saved me.

[7] *Return, my soul, to your rest,*
for Yhwh has done good for you.

[8] *for you has delivered my soul from death,*
my eyes from tears,
my feet from the wrong path:

[9] *I will walk before Yhwh*
in the lands of the living.

[10] *I trust because I speak:*
«I have been greatly humbled!»

[11] *I said in my terror:*
«Every man is a liar!»

[12] *What shall I return to Yhwh*
for all the good that he has done for me?

13 I will lift up the cup of salvation,
and I will call the name of Yhwh.

14 I will fulfill my vows unto Yhwh,
Now, before all his people!

15 Costly in the eyes of Yhwh
is the death of his faithful.

16 Now I pray, Yhwh,
I am your servant,

I am your servant son of your handmaid,
you have loosened my chains.

17 I will offer the sacrifice of thanksgiving,
and I will call the name of Yhwh.

18 I will fulfill my vows unto Yhwh,
now, before all his people,

19 in the courts of the house of Yhwh,
in your bosom, Jerusalem!

Praise Yah!

In the Septuagint, which the Vulgate followed, this psalm is divided in two. The link between the two psalms of the Greek translation was marked by the remarkable correspondence of their *incipit*s, «I love» (1) and «I believe» (10). After a brief introduction (1-2) the text has three other parts (see «The part as a whole», p. 221): two are long (3-9 and 12-19), framing a part which is clearly much shorter (10-11)[1]. The division between verses 9 and 10 corresponds to the division between Psalms 114 and 115 in the Septuagint. The last part (12-19) is the part whose composition is most certain — its very coherence is what marks the boundary with the previous part.

1 There is no unanimity on the composition of this poem. See AUFFRET P., «Essai sur la structure littéraire du Ps 116»; ID., «"Je marcherai à la face de Yahvé"»; BARRÉ M.L., «Psalm 116: Its Structure and Its Enigmas»; PRINSLOO W.S., «Psalm 116: Disconnected Text or symmetrical Whole?» It is hardly worth mentioning ALDEN R.L., «Chiastic Psalms (III)»

A. THE FIRST PART (1-2)

COMPOSITION

+ [1] I love	**because** Yhwh	*ATTENDS TO*
. the cry of	my supplications,	
+ [2] **because** *HE HAS TURNED*	*HIS EAR*	to me,
. and in my days	I will call on.	

This part is the size of a piece. Its two bimember segments, with the same 3+2 rhythm, parallel one another. Their first members even match — the first verb, «I love», is not repeated in 2a, because it governs two causal clauses which start with «because» (1a.2a). In the same way, «Yhwh», the subject, is not repeated, but the rhythm is compensated by the repetition of «attends/turns his ear to». The link between the second members is not as clear. However, it is possible to identify a semantic relationship between the noun «my supplications»[2] and the verb «I will call», which the segments end with.

BIBLICAL CONTEXT

The first verse recalls the start of Psalm 18, «I love you, Yhwh, my strength» (Ps 18:1), even though a synonymous verb is used, rather than the same one. Many psalms begin with a cry to listen, which is addressed to God (Psalms 4, 5, 17, 28, 54, 55, 61, etc.). Others, on the other hand, begin by praising the Lord because he has listened: «I thank you, Yhwh, with all my heart, because you have heard what I said» (Ps 138:1; see too Ps 40:65).

INTERPRETATION

The first verb, «I love», is surprising in its abruptness. It is perhaps particularly surprising because it has no grammatical object. There is no other psalm, which begins in this way. This is why several have changed its construction to remedy this irregularity: «I love the Lord, for he listens». The most obvious result of this correction is a flattening of the text.

In Hebrew poetry, it is very difficult to note the precise value of the verbal «tenses» — this is often a matter of interpretation. It is possible that the two segments are synonymous, but it is not impossible that they might be complemen-

2 A more literal translation of the second member would give «my voice, my supplications».

tary. With the verb «attends to» in the present, the first segment indicates a general and habitual truth. In the second, the psalmist relies on his past experience (2a) to affirm that he will continue to «call on» the Lord in the future.

B. THE SECOND PART (3-9)

COMPOSITION

+ 3 Have surrounded me	the snares	of **DEATH**,
+ and the *anguishes*	of **SHEOL**	have found me;
+ *anguish*	and affliction	I find
– 4 and the name	of YHWH	I call on:
– I pray,	YHWH,	
– **deliver**	*MY SOUL*!	
- 5 Gracious	is YHWH	and righteous,
- and our God	has compassion;	
- 6 Protector	of the simple	is YHWH:
- I was low	and me	**he has saved.**
– 7 Return,	*MY SOUL*,	to your rest,
:: *for* YHWH	has been tender	of you;
:: 8 *for* **you have delivered**	*MY SOUL*	from **DEATH**,
::	my eyes	from tears
::	my feet	from stumbling:
– 9 I will walk	in the sight	of YHWH
–	in the lands	of the **LIVING**.

The second part has three pieces. In the first piece (3-4) the psalmist reports the prayer, which he addressed to God in the time of anguish. The second piece (5-6) is a confession of faith in the divine mercy which saved him, after which (7-9), the one praying rediscovers peace and returns to his path in life.

The first piece (3-4) is made up of three bimember segments. The first segment (3ab) is of the A (b c) / (b'c') A type, with the verbs at the outside. Although the «snares» and «anguishes» are the subjects of the first segment and the psalmist is the object, the psalmist becomes the subject in the second segment (3c-4a). This has a parallel construction, with the objects at the start and the verbs at the end. The central segment makes the transition between the outer segments. Its first member (3c) is close to the second member of the initial segment (3b) since the same verb is repeated at the end, and the first words have the same roots[3]. The second member of the central segment (4a) introduces the words of the final segment (4bc), whose brevity in comparison to the two previous segments stands out.

The second piece (5-6) only has two bimember segments. The first is general and amasses three descriptions of the Lord. While the first two («gracious» and «righteous») are adjectives, the third is a participle (translated by the present, «has compassion»). The second segment also begins with a participle, but this time this verb has an object, «the simple». In the second member the general truth is applied to the psalmist's case.

The third piece (7-9) has three segments, two bimembers framing a trimember, which is distinct from the others by the fact that it is addressed to the Lord. The second member of the first segment (7b) is repeated and developed by the segment which follows (8abc); both begin with «for». The first member of the first segment (7a) is matched by the third segment (9) — the initial verbs are verbs of movement. «My soul» re-appears in the middle of the first two segments (7a.8a), while «living», at the end of the third segment (9b) is opposed to «death» at the start of the second segment (8a).

The name «Yhwh» appears twice in each piece (4a.4b; 5a.6a; 7b.9a). «Death» and «Sheol» at the start are matched at the end by «death» (8a) and «living» (9b). The two occurrences of «my soul» at the end of the first piece (4c) and the start of the third (7a) act as remote median terms. The request for «deliverance» in the first piece (4c) is granted in the other two pieces (6b; 8a).

3 In the original, *mᵉṣārê* and then *ṣārâ*, which I have translated into English using the same word, once singular, once plural.

«The snares of death»

The start of the part recalls Ps 18:5-7 (= 2Sam 22:5-7):

5 *Have surrounded me the cords of Death,*
the floods of Belial terrify me;
6 the cords of *Sheol* tighten me,
the snares of Death wait upon me.
7 In my *distress I call on Yhwh,*
to my God I cry for help;
he attends from his Temple *to my voice*
and my cry reach his ears.

Ps 116:3a takes up precisely the thread of Ps 18:5a. Both texts also share «Sheol», «anguish», «I called on Yhwh», as well as «he attends», «my voice», «ears», which are repeated in the introduction (Ps 116:1-2).

Both texts refer to Jonah's psalm (Jonah 2:3-10), particularly the first verses:

I called out of *my distress to Yhwh,*
and he has answered me;
from the midst of *Sheol* I cried for help
you have heard my voice.
You have cast me to the depths into the heart of the sea
and the flood *has surrounded me* (Jonah 2:3-4)[4].

«For you have saved my soul from death...»

Ps 116:8 closely re-works the final verse of Psalm 56:

For you save my soul from death
yea, *my feet from stumbling,*
that *I may walk before* God
in the light of *the living* (Ps 56:14).

4 See the rhetorical analysis of Jonah's psalm in LICHTERT C., «La prière de Jonas (Jonah 2)».

INTERPRETATION

The difficulty in the midst of which the psalmist found himself was nothing less than danger of death — bound up and almost paralyzed by terror, suffocated by anguish, there was nothing left to him but to cry out. The intensity of his prayer comes from its extreme brevity — above all, it is the name of the Lord which he invokes and whom he calls on to help him. It is his «soul»[5], that is, his life, which is at stake, and it is on this word that his prayer ends. All that remains of his life is focused on his «throat» which seeks to continue to breathe and resists death.

Hardly has the psalmist pronounced God's name than he is immediately answered; this is why the names of the «the Lord», «God», accompanied by his attributes, «gracious», «righteous», «has compassion», pour in a torrent from his mouth. This confession of faith by the psalmist finally becomes concrete in the acknowledgement of salvation which he has just experienced (6b), as though this were but one example or particular case of the Lord's goodness for all «the simple» who call on him (6a).

Once the storm has calmed down, the one who is praying returns to his rest in a sort of appeasing monologue (7); but this immediately cedes to a new prayer to the one who has freed him from the chains of death. This is still not a formal prayer of thanksgiving — these words still have the form of a narrative, which they have had since the start. However, this narrative can now pause to give details of the various aspects of the good deed of his liberation (8). Quite naturally, the part ends with an opening on the future — returned to the land of the living, the saved psalmist will never be able to forget his savior, in whose presence he will walk from now on.

5 The Hebrew word *nefeš* has the primary meaning of «breath», the breath of life, thus «life», which is often translated by «soul».

C. THE THIRD PART (10-11)

COMPOSITION

+ 10 I trust	because I SPEAK:	
: «I,	I have been humbled	greatly!»
+ 11 I	HAVE SAID	in my alarm:
: «Every man	is a liar!»	

This part is the size of a piece made up of two bimember segments. The first members, which include synonyms translated by «speak» and «said», both introduce statements. The isolated pronoun «I» is repeated at the start of 10b and 11a.

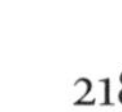

INTERPRETATION

As these two verses are the pivot around which the body of the psalm is arranged, they can clearly be interpreted in this context, as they will also enable us to understand the text as a whole.

The two declarations are complementary. The psalmist first acknowledges that he «is humble»[6], that is, unable to rely on his own strength. He then adds that he cannot put his trust in other men any more (11b), because they are liars. This is why he starts be stating that he «believes», which means, although the object is not expressed, that he believes, and puts his trust in God alone[7].

D. THE FOURTH PART (12-19)

COMPOSITION

The most noteworthy thing is the repetition of the three members of 13b-14 in 17-18; and we should add to this the fact that the first members of 13 and 17 match — in fact, in both cases, this is an offering presented by the same first person singular. The «cup of salvation» is a libation of wine, while the «sacrifice» (literally, «the throat-cutting») of the thanksgiving consists in shedding the blood of the sacrificed animal. Verses 13-14 and 17-18 match in parallel. The first segment (12) is a question which the following two segments answer, and together they form the first piece (12-14; note the repetition of «all» in 12b and 14b). The final segment (19) expands the previous member, «before all his people» (18b) by clari-

6 The verb «I am humble» has the same root as the adjective *ʿānî*, generally translated by «afflicted/ humble». The term is related to *ʿānāw* (pl. *ʿānāwîm*), used in the expression «Yhwh's poor».

7 This interpretation is close to that of BARRÉ M.L., «Psalm 116: Its Structure and Its Enigmas», 74-75.

fying where «his people» are to be found; along with the two previous segments, this final segment forms the final piece (17-19).

These pieces therefore match in mirror formation. The initial question (12) finds its answer not only in 13-14, but also in 17-18. The final segment (19) explains «all his people», not only those of the previous segment (18b), but also those of the end of the first piece (14b).

: 12 What shall I return	to **YHWH**	
: (for) all his tenderness	upon me?	
+ 13 THE CUP	OF SALVATION	I will lift up,
+ AND THE NAME	OF **YHWH**	I WILL CALL ON;
= 14 *MY VOWS*	*UNTO* **YHWH**	*I WILL FULFILL,*
= *NOW, BEFORE*	*ALL*	*HIS PEOPLE!*
- 15 Precious	in the eyes	of **YHWH**
- **the death** of	**his faithful.**	
:: 16 Ah now,	**YHWH,**	
:: for *I am*	**your servant,**	
- *I am*	**your servant**	**son of your handmaid,**
- you have opened	**my chains.**	
+ 17 To you I will sacrifice	THE SACRIFICE	OF THANKSGIVING,
+ AND THE NAME	OF **YHWH**	I WILL CALL ON;
= 18 *MY VOWS*	*UNTO* **YHWH**	*I WILL FULFILL,*
= *NOW, BEFORE*	*ALL*	*HIS PEOPLE,*
: 19 in the courts	of the house	of **YHWH,**
: in the midst of you,	Jerusalem!	

There remains a piece at the center (15-16) which is also made up of three bimembers. The central segment is the only one which has only two sets of two terms; the other two each have three sets of two terms. The third segment is linked to the previous one by the repetition of «I am your servant», the first two occurrences of which acted as median terms. The relationship to the first segment is not as clear, but «his faithful» (15b) heralds «your servant» (16b.16c). The «chains» at the end (16d) refer back to «death» at the start (15b).

BIBLICAL CONTEXT

The sacrifice of praise and the cup of salvation

Lev 7:11 spells out the ritual of this sacrifice, linked to the sacrifice of communion. There is no mention of the cup. This could indicate a libation poured on the sacrificial altar; but it is more likely that the cup of wine accompanies the ritual meal, during which the victim was eaten. A libation of wine is also provided for in the daily sacrifice of two lambs in Exod 29:38-42.

Since the psalm is part of the paschal Hallel, recited during the celebration of the Passover, we cannot but remember the four cups of wine from which all are to drink during the ritual meal. The verse of the cup (Ps 116:13) is recited just before the blessing over the wine in the fourth cup, following which the recitation of the Hallel psalms continues with Psalm 115. During Jesus' Seder meal, the cup became the sign of the new covenant in his blood (Luke 22:20; 1Cor 10:16; 11:25-29).

«Precious in the eyes of the Lord the death of his faithful»

The verb with the same root as the adjective used in the psalm, translated here by «precious» (15) means «to have worth», «to count». It is used in Isa 43:4, «Because *you are precious* in my eyes, because you are honored and I love you», as well as in Ps 72:14, «He will redeem their lives from exploitation and outrage, their lives *will be precious* in his sight».

INTERPRETATION

The question the psalmist begins with is clearly an rehtorical question, a way of once again proclaiming, this time «before all his people» that the Lord has filled him with his good things. It would be completely wrong to think that the one praying imagines that he can settle his account with God. What, in fact, could he give in compensation for the life which has been given back to him? The sacrifice he offers is not, of course, nothing, but it bears no relation to the gift which is received. It is symbolic of the joy felt and the acknowledgement which could not be complete if it were not shared by «all the people». The banquet which follows the sacrifice, sprinkled with the «cup of salvation», will be offered to all who are present who, having heard the story of God's works recounted, will share the thanksgiving of the one who has been released from his chains.

There is no banquet without wine, but there is no feast or rite of worship which is not accompanied by music and singing — songs in which the savior is acclaimed, in which one «calls on the name of the Lord» (13:17). We can easily imagine that the first psalm of the Hallel might be intoned at such an occasion — «You servants of Yhwh, praise, praise the name of Yhwh ...» (Ps 113:1). In reality the psalmist is already singing when he announces that he will invoke the Lord's name and fulfill his vows. The words of this song of thanksgiving are focused, as indeed they should be, on the very heart of the part (15-16) where they transform themselves into a prayer. However, before speaking about himself to God, the one praying cannot stop himself from speaking about God to those who are listening, to all the people, in a word of praise which celebrates his goodness to those confronted by death (15). In this way his cry of personal acknowledgement can well up (16) — the name of the Lord comes first, followed by the declaration of allegiance in which he is aware that God's love has gone before him, «from his mother's womb», as the prophets love to say. Finally, the good thing which his Master has achieved for him, freedom, is set out.

So the psalmist takes up what he has already said, but, as at the start of his prayer, he continues to address God. «I will offer the sacrifice of thanksgiving». Then having returned to a discourse in which, once again, he speaks about God to those who are invited to the feast, he once more returns to the second person when he addresses the holy city — «in your bosom, Jerusalem». This might imply that the psalmist is not there, even, that he is far away, in an exile which fans the desire for return[8].

E. THE PSALM AS A WHOLE

The first, introductory part (1-2) is matched by the final «Alleluia» (19b). The first part directly introduces the following part, which develops it, while, with its call to praise, the final part sums up and concludes the penultimate part.

The second and penultimate parts are almost the same length (the former has seventeen members, the latter eighteen). In the second part the psalmist reports how the Lord freed him from the danger of death he found himself in, while in the penultimate part he announces that he will offer a sacrifice of thanksgiving to the Lord. «Death», which appears twice in the outer pieces of the second part (3.8), is taken up again in the central piece of the matching part (15) — «the chains» from which the psalmist has been freed (16b) recall «the snares of death» (3). «I pray, Yhwh» appears in both 4b and 16a. Both occurrences of «and I will

8 So Alonso Schoekel and Carniti (II, 568) see the psalmist as the representative of the whole of the people of Israel.

call on the name of the Lord», in 13 and 17, repeat 4a (in Hebrew the imperfective is used); «[is] tender» appears in both 7 and 12. Finally, we can note the punning relationship between «on the land of the living» (9: *b^e'arṣôt haḥayyîm*) and «in the courts of the house of Yhwh» (19: *b^eḥaṣrôt bêt Yhwh*), both syntagmas acting as final terms[9].

---

1 I LOVE because Yhwh attends to	the cry of my SUPPLICATIONS,
2 because he turned his ear to me,	and in my days I WILL CALL ON.
3 Surround me THE SNARES of **DEATH**,	and the anguishes of Sheol have found me;
anguish and affliction I find,	4 AND I CALL ON THE NAME OF YHWH:
I pray, Yhwh,	deliver my soul!
- - -	- - -
5 GRACIOUS is Yhwh and righteous,	and our God has compassion;
6 Yhwh protects the simple:	I was low and he has saved me.
- - -	- - -
7 Return, my soul, to your rest,	for Yhwh **have been tender of you.**
8 for he has delivered my soul from **DEATH**,	my eyes from tears,
	My feet from stumbling:
9 I will walk in the sight of Yhwh	***on the lands of the living.***
10 I TRUST because I speak:	«I have been greatly humbled! »
11 I said in my alarm:	« Every man is a liar! »
12 What shall I return to Yhwh	for all **the tenderness he has done for me?**
13 I will lift up the cup of salvation,	AND I WILL CALL ON THE NAME OF YHWH.
14 I will fulfill my vows unto Yhwh,	now, before all his people!
- - -	- - -
15 Precious in the eyes of Yhwh	is **THE DEATH** of his faithful.
16 **I pray, Yhwh,**	I am your servant,
I am your servant son of your handmaid,	you have loosened MY CHAINS.
- - -	- - -
17 I will offer the sacrifice of thanksgiving,	AND I WILL CALL ON THE NAME OF YHWH.
18 I will fulfill my vows unto Yhwh,	now, before all his people,
19 ***in the courts of the house of Yhwh,***	in your bosom, Jerusalem!

Praise Yah!

In the introductory part (1), «supplications» (*taḥănûnāy*) finds an echo in «gracious» (*ḥannûn*; from the same root) in the center of the second part (5). In the last part, «Yah» refers back to the first occurrence of «Yhwh» in the first part (1), the seven names of God in the second part (4a.4b.5a.5b. 6.7.9) and to the eight occurrences of «Yhwh» in the penultimate part (once in each verse). The central part is the only one in which God's name does not appear.

9 See BARRÉ M.L., «Psalm 116: Its Structure and Its Enigmas», 67.

The central part begins with «I believe» (10), just as the psalm begins with «I love» (1). These verbs, whose objects are not expressed, are also followed by «because», and a verb in the imperfective («because he attends to», «because I speak»). Both occurrences of «I» (10.11) are in the center of the penultimate part, translated by «I am» (16a.16b). This part has no lexeme in common with the other parts of the psalm.

BIBLICAL CONTEXT

We noted above the link between the end of the second part and the end of Psalm 56 (see p. 216). We should add that the penultimate verse of Ps 56 is related to the penultimate part of Psalm 116.

> On me, O God, *my vows* to you,
> *I will fulfill the acts of thanksgiving* to you (Ps 56:13).

However, it is noteworthy that, despite these connections, Psalm 116 is distinguished from Psalm 56 and its parallel, Psalm 57 (and many others) by the fact that it does not mention human adversaries, and, therefore, does not ask God to punish them. The only «enemy» mentioned in Psalm 116 is «death». Neither is there even the briefest confession of sins in this psalm, any more than a protestation of innocence, as there is in Psalm 18, which has much in common with it.

INTERPRETATION

«I believe» and «I love»

The whole psalm is focused on the psalmist's confession of faith (10-11), which is in a single word: «I believe». It is a single verb which does not even need an object, as it is so obvious. The one praying has placed all his confidence in God; not in himself, because he has experiences of his extreme lowliness (10), not in anyone else, for it is clear that one cannot count on other people (11). Not having been able to rely on his own strength, nor to depend on another's help, he acknowledges that it is from God alone that he has received freedom, salvation and life. This is why, from the very first word of his song, he speaks of his love — «I love» (1) — another verb which does not need an object. With his love, his faith is expressed from the beginning — confessing, in fact, that God has listened to his supplications, he immediately draws the lesson from this when he undertakes to call on him all his days (2).

«The last of the enemies to be destroyed is death» (1Cor 15:26)

Beyond the difficulties, contradictions and anguishes of life, beyond all those who wish us ill and do us harm, humanity's only real adversary is none other than death, to such an extent that the psalmist mentions no other enemy than this one. We might think that he has seen it close-up, and it has only just failed to send him down to Sheol (3). But, looking closer at things, and taking the words literally, as they should be, it seems that the psalmist did not simply find himself in danger of death, but that he really had the experience of death, really went through it — «the snares of death surrounded me and the anguishes of Sheol found me» (3). The Lord has not freed him from even a serious danger, but from death itself (8). The historical situation which most resembles the psalmist's is that of the Exile. When Amos prophesies the fate of his people at the center of his book (5:1-17), he intones a funerary lamentation: «Listen to this oracle I speak against you, it is a *dirge*, House of Israel: She is down and will rise no more, the virgin of Israel. There she lies all alone on her own soil, with no one to lift her up» (Amos 5:1-2)[10]. Death, however, does not have the last word, and the Lord «will re-erect the tottering hut of David» (Amos 9:11)[11]. Another character, also representing the whole of his people, also went through death and was returned to life for the salvation of his people. Whoever is intoning Psalm 116 is the brother of the Servant of the Lord (Isa 52:13-53:12)[12]. And, of course, this is how he persistently refers to himself at the end of his song — «I am your servant, son of your handmaid, you have loosed my chains» (16). The strongest text for the return from death is Ezekiel 37.

10 See *Amos*, 159-185.

11 *Amos*, 355-363.

12 See MEYNET R., «Le quatrième chant du Serviteur».

Chapter 10

«Praise the Lord, all you peoples!»

Ps 117

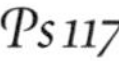

Ps 117

1 Praise Yhwh, all you peoples
glorify-him, all you nations;
2 for mighty to us (is) his faithfulness
and the steadfastness of Yhwh (is) forever.
Praise Yah!

Ps 117, with only two verses, is the shortest in the whole Psalter. It is so short that some believe that it is either the conclusion of the previous psalm, or the introduction to the following one[1].

COMPOSITION

+ 1	PRAISE	YHWH,	ALL THE PEOPLES
+	glorify-him,		ALL THE NATIONS;
:: 2	for mighty	TO US	**his faithfulness**
::	**and the steadfastness**	of YHWH	for the age.

The body of the psalm is the size of a single piece, followed by the final acclamation, «Alleluia», which, as in the previous psalm (see p. 222) and many others, is its conclusion. We will therefore treat the psalm as having two parts.

The first part has two bimember segments. The first segment (1) is parallel, with the second term of the first member, «Yhwh» becoming a pronoun in the second member. The second member (2a, b) is in mirror construction:

– 2 for MIGHTY
: *for us*
his faithfulness
and the steadfastness
: *of Yhwh*
– FOR THE AGE.

The predicates are outside[2], the subjects in the center. The intermediary terms first of all describe the beneficiaries («us»), and then the benefactor («Yhwh»).

1 For example, see Jacquet, II, 215.
2 See p. 195 for the noun pair «faithfulness and loyalty».

The two segments form a single phrase. Two juxtaposed main clauses (1a.1b) are followed by two nominal clauses introduced by «for» (2a.2b) which express the reason for the call to praise. The name «Yhwh» is repeated in the outer members. «For us», in 2b, describing Israel, corresponds to «all the peoples» and «all the nations» in 1a and 1b, probably describing other nations, but not excluding Israel.

+ 1	PRAISE	YHWH,	ALL THE PEOPLES
+	glorify-him,		ALL THE NATIONS;
:: 2	for mighty	TO US	**his faithfulness**
::	**and the steadfastness**	of YHWH	for the age.
=	PRAISE	YAH!	

When translated literally, the final Alleluia takes up the first two words of the first part, where the name of God has its complete form, «Yhwh».

BIBLICAL CONTEXT

«Where is their God»

When Israel was defeated, its enemies mocked it and its God (see p. 195). However, once it had been freed, and had recovered its land, its institutions and its Temple, it rediscovered its dignity before other peoples. Ezekiel 36 emphasizes the enemy's scoffing (2-6.15), but God promises to «sanctify his name» before the nations (21-23), and so «they shall know that I am Yhwh» (23.36). The conclusion of the book of Zephaniah opposes praise and disgrace:

18 I have removed from you, reproach,
so that you do not bear anymore disgrace.
19 Behold, I am dealing with all your oppressors.
At that time, I will save the lame, I will gather the outcasts,
and *I will set them for a praise and renowned by all (peoples of) the earth,*
when I bring about their restoration.
20 At that time, I will bring you in, at that time where I will gather you;
that time I will give you praise and renown among all the peoples of the earth,
when I bring about your restoration before your eyes, says Yhwh.

The peoples called to praise

Psalm 47 also invites the nations to praise the God of Israel: «Clap your hands, all you peoples, acclaim God with shouts of joy» (Ps 47:2). However, it celebrates the domination Israel exercises over its enemies: «He brings the peoples under our dominion, he puts nations under our feet» (v. 3). There is none of this in Psalm 117, even if we suppose that the Lord's salvation and protection for his people could not have been realized without their oppressors being pulled down.

The Passover celebration of 515

Ezra 6:19-22 reports how those who had returned from the Exile in Babylon, finally reunited with those who had remained, celebrated the Passover. This restored feast gives an idea of the context in which the psalm finds its meaning.

Romans 15

In the Epistle to the Romans, Paul quotes Psalm 117 and places it in its biblical context, assigning to it not only another quotation from the psalms, but also a quotation from the Torah, and another from the Prophets. All the Scriptures are therefore used to witness that Israel's vocation to bring the nations to glorify God is accomplished in Christ.

[5] **May the God of steadfastness and encouragement grant you** to have same mind to
one another, according to the example of Christ Jesus, [6] that with one heart and one
voice you may glorify the God and Father of our Lord Jesus Christ. [7] Welcome as well,
one another, as Christ has done for you, to the glory of God. [8] For I tell you that Christ
became a minister of the circumcised to show divine truth, in order to fulfill the promises given to the patriarchs, [9] and the nations might glorify God for his mercy.
As it is written:

> *«Therefore I will praise you among the nations*
> *and sing for the glory of your name»;* (Ps 18:50)

[10] and again it says:

> *«Rejoice, O Nations, with his people»;* (Deut 32:43)

[11] and again:

> *«All the Nations, praise the Lord,*
> *And let all the peoples exult him»* (Ps 117:1)

12 And again Isaiah says:

«There shall come, the root of Jesse,
he who raises up to rule the nations.
In him the nations shall hope» (Isa 11:10)

13 **May the God of hope fill you** with all joy and peace in your believing, so that you may abound in hope by the power of the Holy Spirit.

INTERPRETATION

Whoever is filled with intense joy cannot stop themselves from communicating it, and shouting it from the rooftops — everyone must know about the happiness which has come to them, and share their joy. However, in addition to this psychological aspect, what is at stake in these few words is nothing less than Israel's election and its relationship to other peoples. Since the beginning, and all through its history, relations between the chosen people and their neighbors have been problematic, often marked by violence. The worst was the slavery in the land of Egypt, but the Exile to Babylon was no less trying. In addition to the inevitable tensions which mark relationships between peoples, the fact that Israel always claimed to have been chosen by the God of the whole earth to receive his revelation managed to incite the jealousy of, and persecution by, other nations, so strong that they sought to suppress the Lord's favored one. Such is the story of Joseph, after the story of the first two brothers (Genesis 4), and also the story of the deportation to Babylon, to speak only of biblical times.

This psalm is so eirenic that we cannot avoid thinking that it is this call which will resound at the end of time, when Israel will be freed from the pride it can take in its election and when the nations will definitively have vanquished the jealousy which this particular gift, given to the one chosen before all others, gave rise to; when, in short, all will understand and accept that his choosing was for the joy of one and all.

Chapter 11

«The Lord's right hand is exalted!»

Ps 118

Ps 118

[1] *Give thanks to Yhwh, yes he is good;*
forever indeed his faithfulness!

[2] *Let now say Israel:*
forever indeed his faithfulness!

[3] *Let them say the House of Aaron:*
forever indeed his faithfulness!

[4] *Let them say those who fear Yhwh:*
forever indeed his faithfulness!

[5] *In my anguish I cried to Yah;*
he answered me by enlarging me Yah.

[6] *Yhwh is for me, I do not fear;*
What can do to me an Adam?

[7] *Yhwh is for me, among my helpers;*
and I shall look on my enemies.

[8] *It is good to take refuge in Yhwh*
rather than to trust in the Adam!

[9] *It is good to take refuge in Yhwh*
rather than to trust in princes!

[10] *All the nations encircled me;*
in the name of Yhwh indeed I cut them off!

[11] *They surrounded me and they encircled me;*
in the name of Yhwh indeed I cut them off!

[12] *They surrounded me like bees.*
They are extinguished like fire of thorns;
in the name of Yhwh indeed I cut them off!

[13] *You have pushed and pushed me to make me fall,*
but Yhwh has helped me.

14 My strength and my song is Yah
and he has been for me salvation.

15 Cry of joy and of salvation
in the tents of the just:

«The right hand of Yhwh has done might!
16 The right hand of Yhwh is exalted!
The right hand of Yhwh has done might!»

17 I shall not die, I shall live
and I shall recount the deeds of Yah.

18 He has chastened and chastened me Yah,
but unto death he has not given me over.

19 Open to me the gates of justice;
I shall come in and give thanks to Yah.

20 This is the gate of Yhwh;
the just shall come in.

21 «I give you thanks for you have answered me
and you have been for me salvation.»

22 The stone which the builders rejected
has become cornerstone.

23 From Yhwh, this has become;
it was wonderful in our eyes.

24 This is the day which Yhwh has made;
let us rejoice and be glad in it:

25 «Please, Yhwh, save us we pray!
Yhwh, make us victorious now!»

26 Blessed is he who comes in the name of Yhwh;
we bless you in the house of Yhwh.

27 He is God Yhwh
and he illuminates us.

Bind the festal sacrifice with cords
unto the horns of the altar.

28 *«My God you are and I give you thanks,*
my God, I exalt you.

[I give you thanks for you have answered me
and you have been for me salvation»].

29 *Give thanks to Yhwh, yes he is good;*
forever indeed his faithfulness!

Two identical, very short parts (1.29) frame three more developed parts (see «The psalm as a whole, p. 246»). The psalmist invites all Israel to join with him in thanksgiving (2-12); proclaims how God has saved him from death (13-18); and finally gives thanks in the Temple with everyone (19-28).

COMPOSITION

+ [2] *Let now say*	ISRAEL,	***indeed*** *forever*	*his faithfulness!*
+ [3] *Let them say*	the house of Aaron,	***indeed*** *forever*	*his faithfulness!*
+ [4] *Let them say*	those who fear Yhwh,	***indeed*** *forever*	*his faithfulness!*
= [5] In my anguish	I cried to **Yah**;	he answered me	by enlarging me **Yah**.
- [6] Yhwh is for me,	I do not fear;	what can do to me	THE ADAM?
- [7] Yhwh is for me,	among my helpers;	and I shall look on	*MY ENEMIES*.
- [8] *Better to take refuge in* **Yhwh**		*than to trust in*	THE ADAM!
- [9] *Better to take refuge in* **Yhwh**		*than to trust in*	*PRINCES*!
+ [10] ALL THE NATIONS	encircled me;	*in the name of* Yhwh	***indeed*** *I cut them off!*
+ [11] They surrounded me	yea, they encircled me;	*in the name of* Yhwh	***indeed*** *I cut them off!*
+ [12] They surrounded me	**like** bees.		
= They are extinguished	**like** fire of thorns;	*in the name of* Yhwh	***indeed*** *I cut them off!*

The first part is organized into three sub-parts. The central sub-part (6-9) has two pieces. The first is in the first person singular, and the second in the third person, expressing a general law. In the first piece (6-7), the first members of the two segments begin in the same way with «Yhwh is for me». The parallelism between the two bimembers of the second piece (8-9) is the more marked as only the last terms of each segment are not identical. The final terms of the four segments match one another: «the Adam» is repeated at the end of the first segments of each piece (6.8), and «the princes» in 9 are paralleled with the «enemies» in 7.

The other two sub-parts (2-5; 10-12) parallel one another. Each has two pieces, the first made up of three segments, and the second of a single segment (5.12b). In the first sub-part, the three bimembers of the first piece are almost identical; only the subjects of the first members are different («Israel», «the house of Aaron», «those who fear Yhwh»). In the same way, although less forced, the three segments of the first piece of the last sub-part (10-12a) parallel one another. The first members have the same subject, expressed at the start of the first segment, and repeat the same verb four times[1]. The second members of the first two bimembers are identical, but the third segment (12a) is a unimember. The second pieces of the

1 The two forms of the verb, normal (*sabbûnî*) and separated (*sᵉbābûnî*; see Joüon, § 82a), have been translated by the synonymous «encircled» and «surrounded», following the French *Le Psautier: version œcuménique, texte liturgique.*

outer sub-parts (5.12b) only have single bimembers. They both represent, each in their own way, the conclusion of the sub-part. Verse 5 expresses the reason why all Israel is to proclaim that the Lord's «faithfulness» is «forever» — it is because Yah has saved the psalmist from agony. In the same way, at the end of the last sub-part (12b), the enemies who surrounded the psalmist «*like* bees» were burned «*like* fire of thorns». The second member of the final bimember (12b) repeats those at the end of 10 and 11, expressing the successful outcome of the fighting. It is in giving victory over the nations (12b) that the Lord «has enlarged» (4) the psalmist. Note the triple repetition of *kî*, translated as «indeed» at the start (2.3.4) and the end (10.11.12b).

All «Israel» at the start of the first sub-part (2) — which includes «the house of Aaron» and «those who fear Yhwh» — is opposed by «all the [pagan] nations» at the start of the last sub-part (10). The name «Yah» comes in the first sub-part (5), the name «Yhwh» comes twice in the second sub-part (8-9), and three times in the third sub-part (10.11.12b).

The central sub-part begins with a question (6), which once again proves the law of the center[2]. It is distinguished from the other two sub-parts by being more like a personal meditation than a proclamation addressed to others. In fact, while the previous verse is in the past, as is the whole of the last sub-part, this is in the present (the first members of 6-7), and looks to the future (the second members of the same segments). In addition, the second piece (8-9) is made up of nominal phrases which express a general law.

BIBLICAL CONTEXT

«Indeed for ever his faithfulness»

This is also the second member of the twenty-six segments of Psalm 136, known as the «Great Hallel» (see p. 267).

«Like bees»

The same image is used at the start of Deuteronomy: «The Amorites, who live in that country of hills, came swarming out against you like bees, pursued you...» (Deut 1:44).

2 See *Traité*, 417-435.

«I cut them off»

The Hebrew text uses the *hiphil* (factitive) of the verb *mūl*, «to circumcise», its only appearance in the whole Bible. The Septuagint translates it by «I repulsed them», while the Syriac version and the Targum use «I exterminated them». This latter interpretation recalls that King Saul promised to give David his daughter if he brought him back the foreskins of a hundred Philistines; David brought back twice as many, removed from the bodies of the enemies of the King of Israel (1Sam 18)[3].

INTERPRETATION

Affairs of state

If the whole of Israel — priests and faithful — are invited to celebrate the Lord's faithfulness (2-4), it is because its fate was at stake: all the nations had joined forces to attack Israel from all sides (10-12a). It would be difficult for the speaker in the first person singular to be one particular person — it is hardly likely that «all the nations» would pursue an isolated individual, unless, of course, this was a person who presided over the destiny of the people as a whole. The «enemies» he «will look on», that is, whose defeat he will see (7) are the «princes» (9) of the nations which have attacked him. Having had the experience of being «enlarged» (5) by the Lord, this leader of the people can now state his faith in God before all, a trust which allows him to confront the future in all safety, «for the Lord's faithfulness is forever» (2-4).

B. THE THIRD PART (13-18)

COMPOSITION

This part has three pieces. The outer pieces are made up of two bimember segments which match one another in mirror fashion. The outer segments start with the same syntactical construction of insistence, «you have pushed and pushed me», «he has chastened and chastened me»[4]; the second members are opposed to the first members. The second and penultimate segments (14.17) match one another in mirror fashion. In the outer members, «my song» (14a) heralds «I shall recount» (17b). The members end with the name «Yah». «Salvation» in 14b matches «I shall live» in 17a. The central piece (15-16) has a bimember (15ab), which introduces the trimember acclamation 15c-16b. This trimember is in ABA' form.

3 See Ravasi, III, 412.425-426.
4 For the accusative of the internal object as a phenomenon of binarity, see *Traité*, 15.

+ 13 You HAVE PUSHED AND PUSHED ME to ***make me fall***, but YHWH has helped me.
= 14 My strength and MY SONG, YAH
:: and he has been for me **SALVATION.**

15 Cry of joy and of **SALVATION**
in the tents of the just:

« The right hand of YHWH	*HAS WORKED* might!
16 The right hand of YHWH	is exalted!
The right hand of YHWH	*HAS WORKED* might! »

:: 17 I shall not ***die***, I shall live
= and I SHALL RECOUNT the *DEEDS* of YAH.
+ 18 He HAS CHASTENED AND CHASTENED ME YAH, but to ***death*** he has not given me over.

The name «Yhwh» or «Yah» is repeated twice in each piece. The two occurrences of «salvation» act as median terms for the first two pieces (14b.15a). «The deeds» in 17b recalls the two occurrences of «has worked» in the central piece (15c.16b). «I shall not die» in 17 and «death» in 18 make an inclusio for the last piece. It is possible to see a link between these two words, which have the same root, and «fall» in 13, for this verb is often a metaphor for death[5]. While the outer pieces are spoken in the singular by the psalmist, the central piece reports the words of the just in the plural.

BIBLICAL CONTEXT

The Song of the Sea

There are obvious links to the Song of the Sea. Verse 14 repeats the start of Exod 15:2 word for word. In addition, the central acclamation recalls Exod 15:6, « *Your right hand*, Yhwh, shining with power, *your right hand*, Yhwh, shatters the enemy».

The Book of Immanuel

Verse 14 is also taken up in Isa 12:2, in the brief psalm which concludes the Book of Immanuel. This psalm comes after an oracle which announces the return of the deported, where the return from Exile is placed in parallel with the Exodus:

5 For example, in Amos 5:2, «She is down and will rise no more, the virgin of Israel» (see *Amos*, 160).

15 The Lord shall dry up the tongue of the sea of Egypt,
he shall wave his hand over the River,
with the scorching of his wind.
He will shatter it into seven streams,
so that one may cross in sandals.
16 And there shall be a highway for the remnants of his people,
that is left from Asshur,
as there was for Israel,
in the day of his coming up out of the land of Egypt (Isa 11:15-16).

INTERPRETATION

«You have pushed and pushed me»

In the current version of the Masoretic Text the psalmist unexpectedly addresses a second person, which is most surprising. The Septuagint and the Targum have a first person singular passive: «I have been pushed». Most French translations and commentaries prefer to use an impersonal formula, «Someone pushed me» (translator's note: the Douay-Rheims English translation uses «being pushed»); others opt for a third person plural, following the earlier verses; «they encircled me, they surrounded me» (10-12), «they pushed me» (13) (translator's note: the God's Word English translation uses «they pushed»[6]. In French, only the TOB keeps the second person singular, indicating the difficulty as a note: «Ambiguity, either God (Ibn Ezra) or the enemy (Rashi)». (Translator's note: the majority of English translations retain the second person singular, «you»). The former interpretation might be based on the composition of the part, since the last segment (18), which parallels the first, has God as the subject. It appears, however, to be difficult to allow that the aim of the Lord's punishment was to make the psalmist fall, that is, die. Rashi's interpretation takes account of the second member of the segment — it is difficult to think that the one praying would move so brusquely from the first to the third person: «Yhwh» cannot be at one and the same time both the one who kills and the one who helps. Rashi's interpretation is probably inferred from the previous verses — having spoken about his enemy in the third person plural, the psalmist apostrophizes him in the singular as though «all the nations» were only one man. It is therefore possible to understand that the first words of this part represent the sensational start of his victory song.

6 Ravasi, III, 408.

«He has chastened, chastened me»

It was surely the enemy who had decided to finish Israel off, to push him down in such a way that he would never rise up again (13). And yet, the psalmist's conviction is that, through this human persecution, God directed history. By declaring that it was his Lord who punished him severely, he acknowledges his sin. Although he does not make a confession of the failings of the covenant, which have led to such distress, this is because while all is joy at having been saved from death is not the right time.

«The Lord's right hand is exalted»

The ancient Greek and Syriac versions interpreted the central member of the acclamation of the just as «The Lord's right hand has exalted me». This is also Louis Jacquet's choice, who writes, «with the LXX and Syr., rather than "has raised" (MT and Jerome) because of the context of 17-18»[7]. It seems, for this very reason, «the context», that we should stick to the Masoretic Text; not simply the context of just two verses, but, rather, the extended context of the part (13-18) as a whole, as is appropriate. It is true that it is the psalmist speaking, who proclaims that he has been saved; but his song is Yah — everything, even punishment, comes from him, but above all salvation and life. The triple acclamation in the center, placed in the mouth of the assembly of the just, is purely for the Lord and his glory.

7 Jacquet, III, 307.

c. THE FOURTH PART (19-28)

COMPOSITION

+ 19 OPEN to me	*the gates*	of justice;	I shall *COME IN*	I GIVE THANKS to YAH.
+ 20 This is	*the gate*	of YHWH;	the just	shall *COME IN.*
: 21 I GIVE YOU THANKS		*for you have answered me;*	YOU HAVE BECOME FOR ME	**SALVATION.**

– 22 The stone which the builders rejected		HAS BECOME	head of a corner.
= 23 It is of YHWH	that this HAS BECOME;	it was wonderful	in our eyes.

24 This is	the day	YHWH has made;	25 « Please, YHWH,	**SAVE US** we pray!
let us	rejoice	and be glad in it:	Please, YHWH,	make us success now! »

– 26 Blessed	*WHO COMES*	in the name of YHWH;	we bless you	from the house	of YHWH.
= 27 GOD	(is) YHWH		and he	makes shines	for us.

+ BIND	the sacrifice	with cords	unto the horns	of the altar.
: 28 My GOD,	you,	and I GIVE YOU THANKS,	my GOD,	I exalt you.
: [I GIVE YOU THANKS		*for you have answered me;*	YOU HAVE BECOME FOR ME	**SALVATION.**]

The part is made up of three sub-parts. The outer sub-parts (19-21; 27b-28), which only have a single piece, are in the third first person singular; the central part (22-27a), which is three pieces, is in the first person plural.

The first sub-part (19-21) has three bimember segments. The first two repeat «gate(s)» in the first members and «to come» in the second members. In addition, the «just» of the second member of 20 matches «justice» in the first member of 19. «Give thanks» returns in the outer segments. The last sub-part (27b-28) is parallel to the first—like it, it begins with an imperative («bind», like «open» in 19). With the repetition of «I give thanks», 28 matches 21. The Septuagint repeats the last sub-part of the final segment of the former (21) at the end.

The central sub-part has three pieces. The first (22-23) is made up of two bimembers. The second segment, which repeats «has become», reveals the origins of the marvels mentioned in the first segment. In the same way, in the third piece the second segment (27a) emphasizes that the blessing is given «in the name of Yhwh». The two pieces therefore parallel one another. Their first segments match, for «he who comes» (26) is none other than the person introduced as the stone which has been rejected, but which has become the cornerstone (22). The second segments also match, firstly a confirmation of the origin of the blessing (23), which is then «shining for us» (27a). The central piece is a double acclamation (25) introduced by the proclamation and the two imperatives in 24.

The verb «to come», used twice at the start (19-20) is repeated in 26—the one who is blessed in the central sub-part is the one who says come from the first segment (19). The «salvation» which has gratified the psalmist (21, at the end of the sub-part) is repeated in its verbal form as a prayer in the center of the central sub-part (25a; also at the end of the last sub-part, if we keep the Septuagint's addition). The name of God appears twelve times in various forms.

BIBLICAL CONTEXT

Blessing and light

The blessing by the priests as it is given in Numbers 26 is presented as the light coming down from God to shed light on humanity:

24 The Lord bless you	and keep you!	
25 The Lord makes shine	his face upon you	and do favor to you!
26 The Lord lift up	his countenance upon you	and grant you peace!

Repetitions in the New Testament

It is the outer pieces of the central sub-part which are quoted and applied to Jesus. In the first two Gospels, it is Jesus who applies verses 22-23 to himself at the end of the parable of the murderous wicked husbandmen (Matt 21:42; Mark 12:10-11). In the parallel passage in Luke 20:17 he only takes up verse 22 of the psalm; Peter does the same thing his address to the Sanhedrin in Acts 4:11. The First Letter of Peter (2:4-8) first of all alludes to Ps 118:22 in v. 4, and then quotes it liberally in v. 7; it alternates these citations with two others taken from Isaiah, first of all Isa 28:16 in v. 6, and then Isa 8:14 in v. 8:

> 4 Come to him, *the living stone, rejected by men, but chosen and precious in the sight of God.* 5 You also, as living stones, let yourselves be built into a spiritual house, to be a holy priesthood, to offer spiritual sacrifices, acceptable to God through Jesus Christ.
> 6 For it says in the Scripture: *Behold, I lay in Zion a cornerstone, chosen, precious, and whoever believes in it shall not be put to shame.* 7 To you then, who are believing, he is precious, but for the unbelieving, *the stone which the builders rejected has become the cornerstone,* 8 a stone of stumbling and a rock that makes fall; they stumble because they disobey the Word (1Pet 2:4-8).

The blessing in v. 26 is also repeated for Jesus' entry into Jerusalem in Matt 21:9 and parallels (also Matt 23:39 and parallels).

«Bind the sacrifice with cords»

The second word of 27b, *ḥag*, means both «feast» and the dances which accompany the feast, particularly the ritual dances which consisted of going around the altar several times. This is why most translations and commentaries follow the Septuagint in translating it as «With branches in your hands, draw up in procession», often understanding the branches to be *lulabs*, those ritual branches which were waved during the festival of the tents.

However, the word *ḥag* is also used to describe the sacrifice at the feast (Exod 23:18; Mal 2:3). The primary meaning of the final word is «thing bound», that is, primarily, «cord», as in the story of Samson (Judg 16:11). Since it is a matter of going up to the altar, the most obvious thing is to think about the sacrifice of «thanksgiving» (*tôdâ*), which would take place there; it is the verb from the same root which is used three times (19.21.28a. [28b]). The sacrifice of thanksgiving was also mentioned in the same position in Ps 116 (v. 17, see p. 221).

INTERPRETATION

«Who comes»

The person who is coming to the Temple seems to be someone used to being in charge — he orders that the gates be opened to him (19), and then that the victim is brought to the altar (27b). He gives orders to others, in a regal manner. But he is not proceeding alone — «the just» will go through «the gates of justice» before him (19-20). They come together to place an act of justice, the sacrifice of thanksgiving which the one who acknowledges in this way the justice of the one who has saved him has decided to make, and all those who are with him too.

«We bless you»

By arriving in procession with others and giving orders, the sovereign comes not only to his Lord, but also to all those in the Temple who find themselves at his service. It is as though a choir were formed around the one who has come to celebrate the marvels of God. The «we» which resounds (22-27a) seems to spring from all mouths. All recognize that the Lord has completely reversed the situation. The image of the stone rejected which then becomes the cornerstone is wholly appropriate in this house of God, where they know what it means to build; it also chimes well with the building up of a people who acclaim the one whom the Lord has placed at their head against any attacks. This is why the traditional formula of welcome is first of all addressed in the singular to the one coming at the head of his people (26a), and then immediately extended to all his companions (26b). Everything converges in a unanimous acclamation of jubilation and joy (24), which curiously, however, repeats the terms of supplication (25). Celebrating salvation by asking the Lord for it is possibly another way of most solemnly implying that it could only come from him; it is also no doubt a way to ask him for it to continue in future.

D. THE PSALM AS A WHOLE

COMPOSITION

1 *GIVE THANKS* to YHWH, yes he is **good**; *indeed for ever his faithfulness!*

2 Let now say Israel: *indeed for ever his faithfulness!*
3 Let them say the house of Aaron: *indeed for ever his faithfulness!*
4 Let them say those who fear of YHWH: *indeed for ever his faithfulness!*

5 In my anguish I cried to YAH; HE HAS ANSWERED ME by enlarging me YAH.

6 YHWH is for me, I do not fear; what CAN DO to me an Adam?
7 YHWH is for me, among my HELPERS; and I shall look on my enemies.

8 It is **good** to take refuge in YHWH than to trust in the Adam!
9 It is **good** to take refuge in YHWH than to trust in princes!

10 All the nations encircled me; *in the name of* YHWH indeed I cut them off!
11 They surrounded me and the encircled me; *in the name of* YHWH indeed I cut them off!
12 They surrounded me like bees.

They are extinguished like fire of thorns; *in the name of* YHWH indeed I cut them off!

13 You have pushed me severely to make me fall, but YHWH has HELPED me.
14 My strength and my song, is YAH and he has been for me SALVATION.

15 Cry of joy and of SALVATION in the tents of THE JUST:
« The right hand of YHWH HAS DONE might!
16 The right hand of YHWH **is exalted!**
The right hand of YHWH HAS DONE might!»

17 I shall not die, I shall live and I shall recount the DEEDS of YAH.
18 He has chastened me severely YAH, but to death he has not given me over.

19 Open to me the gates of justice; I shall come in and *I GIVE THANKS* to YAH.
20 This is the gate of YHWH; the JUST shall come in.
21 «*I GIVE THANKS TO YOU* for YOU HAS ANSWERED ME and you have been for me SALVATION.»

22 The stone which the builders rejected has become head of a corner.
23 Of YHWH this has become; it was wonderful in our eyes.

24 This is the day that YHWH DONE; let us rejoice and be glad in it:
25 « Please, YHWH, SAVE us! Please, YHWH, make us victorious! »

26 Blessed is he who comes *in the name of* YHWH; we bless you from the house of YHWH.
27 He is God YHWH and he makes shine for us.

Bind the sacrifice with cords unto the horns of the altar.
28 « MY GOD are you and *I GIVE YOU THANKS*, MY GOD, **I exalt you.**
[*I GIVE YOU THANKS* for YOU HAS ANSWERED ME and you have been for me SALVATION. »]

29 *GIVE THANKS* to YHWH, yes he is **good**; *indeed for ever his faithfulness!*

The outer parts, the size of a single bimember segment, are identical (1.29). The second member of the first segment is repeated precisely in the second members of the next three segments (2.3.4). The verb «to give thanks», which the last segments begins with, recurs several times in the penultimate part (19.21.28a.[28b]); we might add that «good» is repeated twice in 8-9.

There are not many links between the second and penultimate parts. «He has answered me» at the end of the first sub-part of the second part (5) is taken up again in an analogous position in 21 (and 28b). The verb «to do» is repeated in the central sub-parts, with «Adam» as its subject the first time (6) and «Yhwh» the second time (24). «In the name of», which is repeated three times at the end of the second part, is used once in 26.

The two occurrences of the verb «to do» at the center of the central part (taken up by «the deeds» in 17) match the two occurrences of the same verb in the center of the second and penultimate parts (6.24). The verb «to help», which clarifies the meaning of «to do», is used at the start of the central part (13), but has already been used in the center of the second part (7). God's help is nothing other than salvation. «And he has been for me salvation», in 14, will be taken up again in 21 (and 28b). «Salvation», which is used twice in the central part (14.15), thus reappears in 21 but also, in its verbal form, in the center of the penultimate part (25). «The just» in 15b is repeated in 20 (preceded by «justice» in 19). «Exalted» at the center of the central acclamation (16a) is repeated at the end of the fourth part (28a), but this time the verb is no longer in the passive, but has the psalmist as its subject. The name «Yah» or «Yhwh», which reappears six times (13.14.15c. 16a.16b.17.18) in the central part, is used ten times in the second part and nine times in the penultimate part, not to mention «my God» in 27-28a, and finally, once each in each of the outer parts.

BIBLICAL CONTEXT

The Song of the Sea

Verse 14 repeats Exod 15:2a word for word (see p. 86); and in addition the second member of 14 is repeated in the second member of 21. We should add that 28 echoes Exod 15:2b, c, «*He is my God*, I praise him, the God of my father, *I exalt him*». The psalm's central acclamation recalls the center of the first part of the Song of the Sea: «Your right hand, Yhwh, shining with power, your right hand, Yhwh, shatters the enemy» (Exod 15:6).

We should also add that «faithfulness», repeated five times in the psalm, is also found in Exod 15:13; in particular «all the nations» in Ps 118:10 can be linked to the Egyptian «enemy» of Exod 15:6-9, and with «all the peoples» whom the children of Israel will have to confront later — the Philistines, Edomites, Moabites, Canaanites (Exod 15:14-15).

Isaiah 45

The key terms of the central part of the psalm, «to do», «salvation», «the just», echoed in other parts, are found in abundance in Isaiah 45, for example.

: [7] I form	the light	and create	the darkness,
: I **MAKE**	weal	and create	woe,
:: I am,	Yhwh,	who **MAKES**	all these things.
+ [8] Pour down,	O heavens,		from above,
and let clouds	rain down		*JUSTICE*,
+ let open	the earth and produce		SALVATION,
and let *JUSTICE*	spring up		together.
:: I am,	Yhwh,	who have created	it.

In the New Testament

Verse 6 of the psalm is quoted in Heb 13:6. In Eph 2:20, Christ is called the «cornerstone», as in Ps 118:23 (see too 1Cor 3:11). But it is vv. 22-23 above all which Jesus applies to himself at the conclusion of the wicked husbandmen (Matt 21:42; Mark 12:10; Luke 20:17 only quotes the first of these two verses). The start of v. 26 is repeated during Jesus' entry into Jerusalem (Matt 21:9 and parallels; see too Mattt 23:39 and parallels), accompanied by the acclamation «Hosanna» («save us!»), which is also found in Ps 118:25.

INTERPRETATION

The deeds of the Lord

At the heart of the psalm the triple acclamation of the just resounds — «The right hand of the Lord is exalted» for «it has done mighty things» (15-16). The «deeds» of God which the psalmist recounts (17) can be summarized in a single word, «salvation» (14.15.21.[28b]). It was a «help» (7.13.14) which delivered him from nothing less than the death (17-18) which «the Adam» (6-8), «the princes» (9) and «all the nations» (10) intended to inflict on him. Through this aid, God «has answered» his cry (5.21). All of this is because of «the faithfulness» (1-4.29) the God of the covenant has sworn to his people.

«It is right to give you thanks»

The salvation worked by the Lord is matched by the acclamations of the just (15ab). Here, justice is human doing — it is only just to «give thanks» to God for his work of salvation. However, it is possible that the «gates of justice» do not refer only to those which the just pass through; they are also doubtless primarily those where the justice which God demonstrates when he saves his people is acknowledged and proclaimed. In fact, from the following verse (20), «the gates of justice» (19) are called «the gate of Yhwh». If «the just shall come in», it is in this passing place and meeting point God's justice is joined to that of his faithful. As Isaiah says, justice is poured down from the heavens, but the earth also buds forth (Isa 45.8). This is what «giving thanks» means (1.19.21.28a.[28b].29): to show one's justice, by proclaiming God's justice.

Nehemiah and Jesus

If, as many say, the psalm was composed during the Exile or even, more probably, after the return from Exile, the person who is speaking in such regal terms certainly can not be a king, since Israel had lost its king. Some see this as Nehemiah[8], who triumphed over those who sought to prevent him from rebuilding the walls of Jerusalem (Neh 4). However, we are reduced to pure conjecture about the historical origin of the psalm and the identity of the psalmist. What we do know with certainty, however, is that this psalm ends the series of the Passover Hallel, and that it was and is still recited at the moment when the fourth cup in the Passover Seder is poured. This, therefore, was the final psalm which Jesus sang with his disciples before going to the garden of Gethsemane, where he was arrested. Just as the paschal meal in which he gave his body and blood prefigures and realizes the sacrifice which he would accomplish in his Passion, so the singing of Ps 118 can be read as an anticipation of his paschal mystery. And of course, this is how his disciples interpreted it from the very beginning. This is why this psalm became the perfect psalm of the new and eternal Passover in the Christian liturgy — «This is the day which was made by the Lord, let us rejoice and be glad».

8 Deissler, 199.

Chapter 12

«Yes, forever his faithfulness!»

Ps 136

Ps 136

[1] *Give thanks to Yhwh, for he is good,*
yes forever his faithfulness!

[2] *Give thanks to the God of gods,*
yes forever his faithfulness!

[3] *Give thanks to the Lord of lords,*
yes forever his faithfulness!

[4] *To him who made great wonders by himself,*
yes forever his faithfulness!

[5] *To him who made the heavens by understanding,*
yes forever his faithfulness!

[6] *To him who spread the earth over the water,*
yes forever his faithfulness!

[7] *To him who made great lights,*
yes forever his faithfulness!

[8] *the sun to rule over the day,*
yes forever his faithfulness!

[9] *the moon and stars to rule over the night,*
yes forever his faithfulness!

[10] *To him who smote Egypt in their first-born,*
Indeed forever his faithfulness!

[11] *and led Israel out from the midst of them,*
yes forever his faithfulness!

[12] *by strong hand and by stretched arm,*
yes forever his faithfulness!

[13] *To him who cut the sea of Reeds into parts,*
yes forever his faithfulness!

14 and led Israel pass through the midst of it,
yes forever his faithfulness!

15 and overthrew Pharaoh and his army in the sea of Reeds,
yes forever his faithfulness!

16 To him who led his people through the desert,
yes forever his faithfulness!

17 To him who smote great kings,
yes forever his faithfulness!

18 and slew famous kings,
yes forever his faithfulness!

19 Sihon, king of the Amorites,
yes forever his faithfulness!

20 and Og, king of Bashan,
yes forever his faithfulness!

21 And he gave their land for inheritance,
yes forever his faithfulness!

22 inheritance to Israel his servant,
yes forever his faithfulness!

23 He who in our lowliness remembered us,
yes forever his faithfulness!

24 and tore us away from our oppressors,
yes forever his faithfulness!

25 He who gives bread to all flesh,
yes forever his faithfulness!

26 Give thanks to the God of heavens,
yes forever his faithfulness!

Although it only uses the verb «to praise» (*hallēl*) once, Psalm 136 is known as «the great Hallel». It is made up of five parts organized concentrically (see «The psalm as a whole», p. 267).

A. THE FIRST PART (1-3)

COMPOSITION

+ [1] GIVE-THANKS	to Yhwh,	for (he is) good,	YES FOREVER HIS FAITHFULNESS!
:: [2] GIVE-THANKS	*to the God*	*of gods,*	YES FOREVER HIS FAITHFULNESS!
:: [3] GIVE-THANKS	*to the Lord*	*of lords,*	YES FOREVER HIS FAITHFULNESS!

The first part has three bimembers. The first members begin with the same imperative, «Give thanks», and the second members are identical. These three segments are in ABB'. In the second and third segments, the objects of the imperative («the God of gods», «the Lord of lords») share the same syntactical structure.

BIBLICAL CONTEXT

Jeremiah 33

With two short additions, we find verse 1 in an oracle in Jeremiah announcing the return from Exile:

> 10 Thus says Yhwh. In this place of which you say: «It is a waste, without man or beast,» in the cities of Judah and in the streets of Jerusalem that are desolate, without man or beasts, there shall be heard again
> 11 the cry of joy and of gladness, the voice of bridegroom and of the bride, the song of those who say, as they bring to the Temple of Yhwh the offerings of thanksgiving: «Give thanks to Yhwh *Sabaot* for he is good *Yhwh*, forever is his faithfulness!» For I will cause to return the captivity of the lands, as at first, says Yhwh (Jer 33:10-11).

Deuteronomy 10

The names give to God in the first part — «Yhwh» (1), «God of gods» (2), «Lord of lords» (3) — are also found in Deut 10:17. In the same way, «God of heavens» echoes Deut 10:14. After the incident of the golden calf, Moses received the Decalogue for the second time on the mountain, and placed the tablets with the law in the ark of the covenant. Then he said to the children of Israel:

> 12 And now, Israel, what does Yhwh, your God, ask of you except to fear Yhwh, your God, to follow his ways, to love Him, to serve Yhwh your God with all your heart and with all your soul,
> 13 to keep the commandment of Yhwh and His statutes which I am commanding you today for your good?
> 14 *Behold, to Yhwh your God belong heavens*

and the highest heavens, the earth and all that is on it. 15 Yet Yhwh was so delighted in
your fathers, to love them, and He chose among all the nations their descendants after
them, that's you, as it is today. 16 Circumcise your heart and do not be stubborn any
longer, 17 for *Yhwh your God is the God of gods and the Lord of lords* [...] 20 It is Yhwh
your God that you shall fear and you shall serve, cling to Him and swear by His name.
21 It is Him you shall praise and He is your God.

INTERPRETATION

«Yhwh» is the proper name of the God of Israel, and the psalmist invites us to give him thanks. But this god is not a particular divinity on the same level as the gods of the nations where the people of the one God have been scattered. Although they were humiliated and appeared to have been abandoned by a god who, in their oppressors' eyes, was unable to defend them and save them, the children of Israel remained convinced that their God was the «God of gods» and «Lord of lords». Despite all appearances to the contrary, they continued to believe that, «yes, forever [is] his faithfulness» to the covenant, which is what the rest of the psalm demonstrates.

C. THE SECOND PART (4-9)

COMPOSITION

+	4 TO-HIM-WHO-MADE	wonders	GREAT	by himself,	YES FOREVER HIS FAITHFULNESS!
::	5 TO-HIM-WHO-MADE	*the heavens*	by understanding,		YES FOREVER HIS FAITHFULNESS!
::	6 **To**-him-who-spread	*the earth*	over the water,		YES FOREVER HIS FAITHFULNESS!
–	7 TO-HIM-WHO-MADE	lights	GREAT,		YES FOREVER HIS FAITHFULNESS!
..	8 the sun		*to rule*	*over* the day,	YES FOREVER HIS FAITHFULNESS!
..	9 the moon	and stars	*to rule*	*over* the night,	YES FOREVER HIS FAITHFULNESS!

This part has two pieces, both made up of three bimembers. Each of these pieces is ABB'. In the first piece the last two segments, which parallel «the heavens» and «the earth» give details of the «wonders» the first segments mentions. In the second piece, the last two segments, which link the star which rules the day and those which rule the night, describe «the lights» of the first segment in more detail.

The second members of all six segments are identical. The verbs which the first segments of each piece begin with are the same and act as initial terms; both are followed by the same adjective, «great», which fulfils the same function.

«Wonders great»

This is the only appearance of this expression in the whole of the Hebrew Bible[1]. The second term is translated by an adjective, because of the parallelism with the first member of the second piece, «lights great» (7). However, it is also possible to understand these as two juxtaposed nouns («wonders greatness»), for each of the two terms is often used on its own, as in Exod 34:10, «In the presence of all your people I shall work such wonders as have never been worked in any land or in any nation». Mostly, «wonders» describe the saving acts of God rather than his work of creation, for example in the center of the Song of the Sea (Exod 15:11; see p. 86), in the psalms (Ps 40:6; 72:18; 75:2; 78:4.11; 86:10; 106:21-22; 107:8.15.21.24.31, etc.); only in Ps 96:3 does it appear to be linked to creation. The same goes for «great things» (Deut 10:21; Jer 33:3; Job 5:9; Ps 71:19; 106:21).

This is why some think that this expression not only introduces the second part which deals with creation, but all of God's works (4-25)[2]. However, it is possible to interpret «the great wonders» mentioned here within the context of one single creation, understood as God's victorious battle against the forces of chaos (Job 25-26; 38:8-11).

The fourth day

Of all the works of creation, the passage retains only the sun and moon, which separate day and night and govern time, the calendar and the years (Gen 1:14-19). «The stars» are added to the moon to rule the night, a role they do not have in Gen 1:16. This day takes on great importance in the first account of creation, for it is the one found at the center of the original week, linked to both the first day and the last, seventh day[3].

1 In Ps 131:1, the two words are joined together, but belong to two members of the same segment: «I am not concerned with *great affairs* / nor *marvels* beyond my scope». The expression «great wonders» is found twice in Dan 4:37a.37c (Septuagint).

2 For example, Ravasi, III, 738; Gerstenberger, II, 386.

3 See BEAUCHAMP P., *Création et Séparation*, 65-71.

«To make»

The text emphasizes God's «making» three times (4.5.7). Some feel this repetition is unbecoming[4], while others erase it in their translations[5]. The criteria of biblical and Semitic rhetoric are not those of classical Greco-Latin rhetoric. Rather than seeing this triple occurrence of the verb «to make» as a stylistic ignorance, it is worth pausing here to try to grasp, not the author's intention — which we will never reach — but at least the effect of this repetition on the reader. The effect of the emphasis is undeniable, and goes well with the general air of the psalm, in which there is no lack of repetition, if only with the acclamation which resounds at the end of each segment. The three «makes» draw more attention because far from being specific, as «to form», «to shape» and even «to create» would be, «to make» seems more general and vague. In fact, this is the verb which is used most often to describe God's work in the first creation account (Gen 1:1-2:4a), where it reappears eight times (1:7.16.25.26.31; 2:2[twice].3)[6], while «to create» is only used seven times (1:1.21.27[three times]; 2:3.4a). In addition, the verb «to make» is used in an intensive way to describe God's action on behalf of his people and humanity in general:

> For the priestly author, God does not have hands, but acts in the very center of things. At this time, the verb *'âśâh* had a further meaning which went way beyond the work of the craftsman — the prophets and psalms apply it many times to God's saving work[7].

Just as v. 4 can be considered as not only introducing this part but the body of the whole psalm, so the triple repetition of the verb «to make» somehow plays the title-role for all the «mighty acts» of God both in history and in creation[8].

4 Gerstenberger, II, 386, who thinks that the author could have been more varied, given the wealth of vocabulary for creation in Hebrew.

5 So Beaucamp, who translates them by «réaliser» [«to realise»], «œuvrer» [«to work»] and «faire» [«to do/make»]. He had already translated the three occurrences of «give thanks» (1-3) in a different way. «Note that the Hebrew verb, which we translate in three different ways in order to bring out all the nuances, is not a simple equivalent of our word «to praise» (II, 263).

6 The occurrences of the verb where God is the subject are not counted; there are also two occurrences where the subject is «the [fruit] trees bearing fruit» (Gen 1:11-12).

7 BEAUCHAMP P., *Création et séparation*, 87.

8 See, for example, Ps 118:15.16.17.24.

Creation and separation

While the verb «to separate» [«divide»], which reappears five times in the first creation account (1:3.6.7.14.17) is not used once in the part, the psalmist somehow retains from God's creating work the work of separation — of «heavens» and «earth» (5-6), «earth» and «waters» (6), «day» and «night» (8-9). So not just space is limited by the creator, but also time, which announces the next «historical» work of the savior.

Great things

With the word «make», the adjective «great», always in the plural, which describes God's works, marks the start of each of the two pieces of the part. This insistence leaves an impression; and the greatness of what is created reflects back on their author. In reality, «he alone» is great who was able to carry out such great things: «Can anyone measure the magnificence of Yhwh the great, and his inexpressible grandeur?» (Ps 145:3)[9].

9 The root *gdl* («great») appears four times in Ps 145:3-8; see R. MEYNET, «Le Ps 145», 216-217.

C. THE THIRD PART (10-22)

COMPOSITION

+ [10] TO-HIM-WHO-SMOTE	*Egypt*	*in their first-born,*	YES FOREVER HIS FAITHFULNESS!
:: [11] and-led-out	ISRAEL	*from the midst of them,*	YES FOREVER HIS FAITHFULNESS!
· [12] by hand	strong	and by arm stretched	YES FOREVER HIS FAITHFULNESS!
· [13] **To**-him-who-cut	the sea-of-Reeds	into parts,	YES FOREVER HIS FAITHFULNESS!
:: [14] and-led-pass	ISRAËL	*through the midst of it,*	YES FOREVER HIS FAITHFULNESS!
+ [15] and-overthrew	*Pharaoh*	*and his army* in the sea-of-Reeds,	YES FOREVER HIS FAITHFULNESS !
[16] **To**-him-who-led	HIS PEOPLE	through the desert,	YES FOREVER HIS FAITHFULNESS!
- [17] TO-HIM-WHO-SMOTE	*kings*	great,	YES FOREVER HIS FAITHFULNESS!
- [18] and-slew	*kings*	famous,	YES FOREVER HIS FAITHFULNESS!
· [19] Sihon,	*king*	of the Amorites,	YES FOREVER HIS FAITHFULNESS!
· [20] and Og,	*king*	of Bashân,	YES FOREVER HIS FAITHFULNESS!
= [21] And he gave	their land	for **inheritance**,	YES FOREVER HIS FAITHFULNESS!
= [22] **inheritance**	to ISRAEL	his servant,	YES FOREVER HIS FAITHFULNESS!

This part has three sub-parts, two made up of six segments which frame a part of a single segment (16). These three sub-parts match the three timescales of the Exodus — the leaving of Egypt (10-15), the crossing of the desert (16), and the gift of the land (17-22).

The first sub-part has two pieces made up of three bimembers. Each is a single phrase, beginning with a participle (10a.13a), continuing with a conjugated verb preceded by a coordinator (11a.14a). The third members are, in the first case, an object (12) and another phrase joined to the previous one in the second case (15). These two pieces match in mirror fashion, at least in their outer segments — «Pharaoh and his army» at the end corresponds to «Egypt in their first-born» at the start. The central members parallel one another term for term (11.14).

The last sub-part is made up of three pieces which each have two bimembers. The first two parallel one another, the second clarifying the name of two of the «great» and «famous» kings of the first piece. In the third piece, the kings whom he «smote» and «slew» are opposed to «Israel» to whom «their land» is given. Note the two occurrences of «inheritance» in the last piece, acting as median terms.

The outer sub-parts begin with the same «to-him-who-smote»[10], which indicates that their objects are linked. The four occurrences of «king(s)» (17-20) match the four symmetrical terms in the first piece: «Egypt in their first-born» (10) and «Pharaoh and his army» (15). The name «Israel» recurs at the center of both pieces of the first sub-part (11.14) and at the end of the last piece (22).

The whole part is focused on the very short sub-part where the crossing of the desert (16) is mentioned. «His people» matches the three occurrences of «Israel» in the other two sub-parts.

BIBLICAL CONTEXT

Leaving Egypt

The first sub-part summarizes the liberation from the land of Egypt. In the first piece (10-12) the ten plagues are reduced to the final plague, on the night of Passover (Exodus 11-13), which was the decisive one for leaving Egypt. The second piece (13-15) describes the crossing of the sea (Exodus 14).

The giving of the land

The final sub-part (17-22) summarizes all the battles Israel had to fight with different peoples in order to inherit their territory. The only ones quoted are the same as those in Ps 135. Sihon king of the Amorites, between Moab in the south and the Ammonites in the north, did not allow the children of Israel to pass through the country; they defied him (Num 21:13.21-32) and occupied his country. The same happened with Og, king of Bashan to the north of the Ammonites and Gilead (Num 21:33-35). These two were the first territories which the children of Israel conquered. Although they were situated to the east of the Jordan, these two regions, which Moses gave to the tribes of Gad and Reuben and the half-tribe of Manasseh (Numbers 32), are thus representative of the successive conquests of the land of Canaan (see too Deut 1:4-8; 2:24-36; 3:21).

Ps 135:10-12

The third sub-part (17-22) is also found almost word for word in the psalm which precedes it:

10 The two occurrences do not, therefore make an inclusio (see Ravasi, III, 732-733). In the same way, the two occurrences of «him-who-made» (4.7) are initial terms and not outer terms (or terms of inclusio); and the two occurrences of «give» in 21 and 25 do not make an inclusio.

[10] He smote many nations, and kill mighty kings,
[11] Sihon, king of the Amorites, and Og, king of Bashan,
and all the kingdoms of Canaan;
[12] and he gave their land for inheritance, inheritance to Israel his people.

Psalm 135 adds «all the kingdoms of Canaan» to Sihon and Og.

INTERPRETATION

The silence of the desert

The whole of the Exodus, the path which led the children of Israel from the leaving of Egypt to the entry into its own land is concentrated at the outsides. The forty years of wandering in the desert take up a single segment (16) whose function at first glance appears to be reduced to fastening the two ends of a chain. It is as if a veil were drawn over the long period during which the people, isolated in the middle of the desert, found themselves alone with their God, when the law of the Decalogue was given on Mount Sinai and the covenant concluded between the two parties of this unique agreement; as though the time in the desert has nothing to do with those who are called to «give thanks to the Lord of lords» (1-3), the «God of heavens» (26).

Israel and the others

God appears to be «the one who strikes» both Egypt and the kings of the Amorites and Bashan (10.17). This was the only means open to him of saving his people, freeing them from the slavery of the land of Egypt which sought to prevent them from giving birth, delivering his people from the hand of Sihon, who wished to forbid them from passing through his territory[11], and thus preventing them from reaching the Jordan and entering into the land which the Lord had sworn he would give them.

«My first-born son is Israel»

«Israel» is named three times, twice in the first sub-part and once in the third sub-part. At the center, however (16), it is called «his people», which draws our attention[12]. At the end of the part, Israel receives the land of its enemies from God «as

11 The same verb (*'br*, «pass through») is used in Num 21:22-23 and Ps 136:14.

12 Beaucamp thinks that «only v. 16 is foreign to the meaning of the whole, and can be considered to be secondary», which does not seem to be the case.

an inheritance» (21-22). This is a very obvious way of showing that Israel is the son of the Lord; it is also what God had described to Moses at the very beginning:

22 Then you shall say to Pharaoh: «Thus says Yhwh: *my son, my first-born son*, is Israel.
23 I have said to you: Let my son go, that he may serve me. Since you refuse to let him go,
behold, I myself will kill *your son, your first-born*» (Exod 4:22-23).

This is perhaps why the part begins with the mention of the Egyptians' «first-born sons», struck down in order to save the Lord's first-born son.

D. THE FOURTH PART (23-25)

COMPOSITION

– 23 He-who-in-OUR-lowliness	remembered	US,	YES FOREVER HIS FAITHFULNESS!
– 24 and-tore-US-away	from-oppressors-of-	US,	YES FOREVER HIS FAITHFULNESS!
+ 25 He-who-gives	bread	to *ALL FLESH*,	YES FOREVER HIS FAITHFULNESS!

The three bimember segments of this part can be considered as forming two pieces. While the first two deal with «us», that is, Israel, the third deals with «all flesh», that is, all the nations, the pagan nations as well as Israel.

This part is distinguished from the previous parts in several ways. It starts with the relative *šᵉ*, the only place it occurs in the psalm; it is the only part where the perfect is used; the only part where the first person plural is used; and, finally, the only part which is not preceded by the preposition *lᵉ*. In addition, the last verse is surprising in its openness to universality[13].

BIBLICAL CONTEXT

Freedom from Exile

The closeness of v. 24 to Lam 5:8 («Slaves rule us; no one rescues us from them») enables us to place the moment of its speaking at the time of the Exile, and even more probably after the return from Exile[14], for liberation is described as accomplished.

13 This is why some think these verses are «a later addition» (Alonso Schoekel and Carniti, II, 742-743).

14 Deissler, 272 who also makes a link with Isa 32:19 in which Jerusalem is said to be «low in a low place» (KJV), which is the same word as is used at the start of v. 23. According to Alonso Schoekel and Carniti, 743, these verses seem to refer to the time of the Judges. This would be possible were there no first-person plural with which the psalmist refers to the situation in which he and his community find themselves.

Those who devoured you

Israel's enemies are often presented as wild beasts which «devour» it: «To the east, Aram, to the west, the Philistines devour Israel with gaping jaw» (Isa 9:11).

14 Therefore, thus say Yhwh, the God of Sabaoth: Since you have spoken thus, behold, I myself will make my words a fire in your mouth, and this people wood that this fire shall devour. 15 I myself will bring against you from afar a nation, O house of Israel — oracle of Yhwh. It is a long-lived nation, it is a nation very ancient, a nation whose language you do not know, nor do you understand what they say. 16 Its quiver is as an open sepulcher; all of them are mighty ones.

17 It shall *devour* your harvest and your bread,
it shall *devour* your sons and your daughters,
it shall *devour* your flock and your herd,
it shall *devour* your vines and your fig trees;
it shall shatter down with the sword the fortified cities
in which you trust (Jer 5).

In Ps 27:12 we also read: «Do not deliver me to the will/desire[15] of my oppressors» (see too Ps 7:3-4; Zech 11:16). See too Ezek 35:12, where the Lord addresses the mountain of Seir as follows: «you will know that I, Yhwh, have overheard all the outrageous things you have said about the mountains of Israel, such as: They have been abandoned, they have been left for us to devour».

Torn from the lion's mouth

Isa 49:19 presents the liberation from Exile in this way — «For your desolate places and your ruins and your devastated country will now be too small for all your inhabitants, now that your *devourers* are far away». The prophet continues:

24 Can be *taken away* from a warrior his booty?
Can the captive of a tyrant be delivered?
25 But thus says Yhwh:
Even the captive of a mighty shall be *taken away*,
and the booty from a tyrant shall be delivered.
I myself will go to contend with those who contend with you,

15 Literally, «throat» (*nepeš*) which can also be translated by «mouth».

your children, I myself will save them.
26 To your oppressors I will make them *eat* their own flesh,
as with new wine, they shall be drunk with their own blood.
And *all flesh* shall know that I, Yhwh, am your Savior,
that I am your Redeemer, the Mighty one of Jacob (Isa 49:24-26).

Such language recalls that «David said to Saul, "Your servant used to look after the sheep for his father and whenever a lion or a bear came out and took a sheep from the flock, I used to follow him up and strike him down and *rescue* it from his mouth"» (1Sam 17:34-35), even though a different verb which is used (see too Ezek 34).

The gift of food

In the first account of creation, after the Lord had created humanity, he gave them «food», as he did to all living things (Gen 1:29-30). In Psalm 145, for example, the Lord is also good to all the children of Adam (9):

15 The eyes *of all* unto you, hope and you give them their food in its season.
16 You open your hand and satisfy the desire of *all* the living.

In v. 25 of Psalm 136, the word «food» is not used, as in Ps 145:15 (see too Ps 104.27, where the same word is translated differently: «All creatures depend on you to feed them throughout the year»), but the word for «bread». This word can describe food in general, but its primary meaning, as in English, is of a plant-based food made from grains, and wheat in particular. Recall that the food given by God in Genesis 1 to animals as well as to humans is exclusively vegetarian (see too Ps 104:14-15).

INTERPRETATION

An enigmatic verse

The final verse (25) is surprising and even disconcerting. To claim that the expression «all flesh» «is limited to all the Israelites»[16] is an unacceptable way out. Of course, we can see that the psalmist is trying to end his long list of God's wonders on a universal note in which some see the psalm's climax[17]. We, however,

16 Jacquet, III, 577.
17 Gerstenberger, II, 387.

will risk another kind of interpretation which seeks to take account of the striking contrast between the «we» of the first verses and the «all flesh» of the final verse. How can we justify moving so suddenly from a situation of oppression, into which God has to intervene in a brutal manner to wrest the weak from the hands of those who have crushed them, to the peacefulness of a situation where all conflict has disappeared and all share the same bread in peace?

An ironic verse

Of course, it could be not universalism, but a sort of biting, if veiled, irony. «All flesh» of course includes Israel, but also Israel's «enemies». If we take the composition of the part and its coherence seriously, «all flesh» firstly describes the two groups which have just been discussed. The Lord has «torn» his people from the grasp of their oppressors, from the mouth of those who devoured them. Man is not to be a wolf to man; he is not to feed himself on the «flesh» of another, but on the «bread» which God gives him.

E. THE LAST PART (26)

COMPOSITION

:: [26] GIVE-THANKS	TO THE GOD	of heavens,	YES FOREVER HIS FAITHFULNESS!

The last part is a single bimember segment.

BIBLICAL CONTEXT

«God of heavens»[18] appears only here in the whole Psalter[19]. Used in biblical texts particularly after the Exile[20], it is a title found in the religions of the surrounding peoples, and particularly the Aramaic world[21].

18 Doubtless it would have been preferable to translate this with the singular «God of heaven». However, we prefer to keep the plural form, not because the word only exists in this form in the Hebrew, but to maintain the relationship with the plurals in the first part, «God of gods» and «Lord of lords».

19 In the form *ʾelohê ha-ššāmāyim*, it is found nine times in the Bible, but only once in the form in Ps 136.26: *ʾel ha-ššāmāyim*.

20 For example, 2Chr 36:23; Ezra 1:2; Neh 1:4; 2:4; Dan 2:18; Jonah 1:9, but also Gen 24:7 (see for example Beaucamp, II, 262).

21 See VATTIONI F., «Aspetti del culto del Signore dei cieli».

COMPOSITION

[1] GIVE THANKS to Yhwh, yes he is good,	YES FOREVER HIS FAITHFULNESS!
[2] GIVE THANKS to the GOD of gods,	YES FOREVER HIS FAITHFULNESS!
[3] GIVE THANKS to the Lord of lords,	YES FOREVER HIS FAITHFULNESS!
[4] To him who made GREAT wonders by himself,	YES FOREVER HIS FAITHFULNESS!
[5] To him who made the HEAVENS by understanding,	YES FOREVER HIS FAITHFULNESS!
[6] To him who spread *THE LAND* over the water,	YES FOREVER HIS FAITHFULNESS!
[7] To him who made GREAT lights,	YES FOREVER HIS FAITHFULNESS!
[8] the sun to rule over the day,	YES FOREVER HIS FAITHFULNESS!
[9] the moon and stars to rule over the night,	YES FOREVER HIS FAITHFULNESS!
[10] To him who smote Egypt in their first-born,	YES FOREVER HIS FAITHFULNESS!
[11] and led-out Israel from the midst of them,	YES FOREVER HIS FAITHFULNESS!
[12] by strong hand and by stretched arm,	YES FOREVER HIS FAITHFULNESS!
[13] To him who cut the sea of Reeds into parts,	YES FOREVER HIS FAITHFULNESS!
[14] and led-pass Israel through the midst of it,	YES FOREVER HIS FAITHFULNESS!
[15] and overthrew Pharaoh and his army in the sea of Reeds,	YES FOREVER HIS FAITHFULNESS!
[16] To him who led his people through the desert,	YES FOREVER HIS FAITHFULNESS!
[17] To him who smote GREAT kings,	YES FOREVER HIS FAITHFULNESS!
[18] and slew famous kings,	YES FOREVER HIS FAITHFULNESS!
[19] Sihon, king of the Amorites,	YES FOREVER HIS FAITHFULNESS!
[20] and Og, king of Bashan,	YES FOREVER HIS FAITHFULNESS!
[21] And he ***gave*** *THEIR LAND* for inheritance,	YES FOREVER HIS FAITHFULNESS!
[22] inheritance to Israel his servant,	YES FOREVER HIS FAITHFULNESS!
[23] He who in our lowliness remembered us,	YES FOREVER HIS FAITHFULNESS!
[24] and tore us away from our oppressors,	YES FOREVER HIS FAITHFULNESS!
[25] He who ***gives*** bread to all flesh,	YES FOREVER HIS FAITHFULNESS!
[26] GIVE THANKS to the GOD of HEAVENS,	YES FOREVER HIS FAITHFULNESS!

The single segment of the final part (26) is similar to the last two segments of the first part, particularly the penultimate segment (2). Note that the first member of the psalm contains the only occurrence of «Yhwh». There are no formal links between the first members of the second part and of the penultimate part.

«Great» is repeated in 4, 7, and 17, and «land» in 21 and 6. Both occurrences of «give» act as final terms for the central part (21) and the next part (25). It goes without saying that the strongest link between the five parts of the psalm is the second members; this is unique not only in the Psalter, but in the whole of the Hebrew Bible[22].

BIBLICAL CONTEXT

The new creation

In addition to the links established at the level of the parts, we now need to draw out what the composition suggests the links are between the second and the penultimate parts. One celebrates the marvels of creation, the other the return from Exile when the psalmist moves to the «us» of the present. Now, these people are presented by their contemporary prophets as being a new creation:

[17] For behold, I am about to create new heavens and a new earth,
the things of the past shall not be remembered, it shall not come into mind.
[18] But be full of gladness and rejoice forever
of what I myself, am about to create:
for behold I shall create Jerusalem a rejoicing,
and her people a gladness (Isa 65:17-18; see too Isa 66:22)[23].

The link between these two parts is confirmed by the gift of food, which refers back to Gen 1:29-30. «All flesh» can thus be understood as describing not just the sons of Adam, but also animals[24].

We should not forget that the Exodus is already understood as creation:

22 A similar, although less regular phenomenon is found in the Song of the Three Young Men in the furnace (Dan 3:51-90 LXX).

23 See BEAUCHAMP P., *L'Un et l'Autre Testament*, I, 252-257.

24 «This psalm, before recalling the historical acts of salvation, begins by constructing a sort of cosmological plinth at the base of this memorial-column. Now the memorial, closely linked to Gen. 1, gives the main place to the celestial works... The ending (or the overhanging motif of the memorial-column) is as universalist as the start — «giving bread to all flesh» (v. 25). The theme — and its universalism — in contrast to the recollection of the acts of salvation, although it is announced by the acts which immediately preced the gift of the promised land (vv. 21, 22), matches Gen 1:29-30. The very last verse (v. 26) repeats the *hôdû* of vv. 1-3 to call for praise of the «God of heavens», which is suited to the initial cosmology» (BEAUCHAMP P., *Création et Séparation*, 352-353).

If the O.T. saw Exodus as the birth of Israel, the more recent books tend to present the event as a sort of new creation. This representation is the fruit of an on-going deepening, the past like the future more and more appearing as the uninterrupted work of the same Creator. The one whom the Exodus experience revealed as the Savior of Israel is revealed as the same God «who made heaven and earth», and the one who *makes* and will make history until its end[25].

«For ever [is] his faithfulness!»

We noted above the «faithfulness» (*ḥesed*) is part of the covenant language (see p. 195). The fact that faithfulness is «for ever» (usually translated as «eternal») fits the perspective of the new covenant very well.

INTERPRETATION

The new…

The psalm is based on the Exodus, from the leaving of Egypt until the entry into the land of Israel. This is what takes up most of the account. However, it ends in the present (23-25). This today, which the psalmist does not dwell on, is presented as a new Exodus, the recent «oppressors» resembling Pharaoh as much as Sihon and Og. The contemporary situation, paralleled with creation, is by that very fact equated to the new covenant of leaving Exile, such a new covenant that it is perceived and seen as a new creation.

… and eternal covenant

The insistent repetition of the acclamation which ends the twenty-six segments of the psalm could risk blunting the emphasis. The predicate is «for ever». There is no better way to link all the phases of history which link the present to the very beginning through the wonders of the Exodus. We know that one of the essential characteristics of the new covenant is that it is eternal, for ever and ever[26].

25 LE DÉAUT R., *La nuit pascale*, 88.

26 See BEAUCHAMP P., *L'un et l'autre Testament*, I, 263-264.270-274.

The universal covenant

The new, eternal covenant is therefore from the beginning, and is for the whole of humanity, all the sons of Adam. This does not erase the election of Israel — on the contrary, it implies that Israel's benefits and blessings are extended to «all flesh». When God separated day and night he distinguished between them but did not divide them. When he led the children of Israel out of slavery in Egypt and wrested them from the oppression of the Exile it was not to range them against one another. Only their shared dignity will allow them to recognize one another as a single flesh, fed by the same «God of heaven».

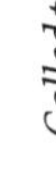

Epilogue

At various points, each of us has felt repulsed or, worse, crushed, by suddenly becoming aware that we are exploited by someone else, or that we are the victim of oppression. The experience of slavery is the more painful and frightening when it is not forced on us externally, but arises from within us. To discover that we are subject to ourselves and our own passions is no less distressing than seeing oneself subjected to others. At the very depths of our being, each of us has passionately desired to be free of what we perceive to be a real enslavement. We all gradually come to realize that this is the work of a whole lifetime. Those who see themselves as being in the biblical tradition believe that this is their essential vocation — in the words of Paul the apostle, who knew all about it, they know that they are «called to freedom» (Gal 5:13). Thus they discover that this freedom, which they lay claim to in their vows for themselves, is what they are also invited to work at achieving for and with others.

Israel's history begins with the freeing of the «house of slaves» from Egypt. It was by crossing the waters of the Red Sea that a people of exploited and oppressed immigrants, was finally born as a free people. Now they could start to speak, to address others and God in a song to celebrate the gift of freedom which had been given to them. This is why the account of the crossing of the Sea (Exodus 14) and the song of exultation which follow it (Exodus 15) gave rise in Israel to the greatest feast of the year, Passover, in which, down the centuries, and even today, all are invited to consider themselves as «having left Egypt, the house of slavery».

The God who shows himself in the Decalogue defines himself as a liberator: «I am the Lord your God who brought you out the house of Egypt, of the house of slavery». But this freedom would not be complete or real if did not become a gift offered by the person to his or her fellow creatures, starting with «his son and daughter». According to the positive double law of the Sabbath and the honoring of father and mother, on which the Decalogue is focused, man is invited not to reduce his son or daughter to slavery, but on the contrary, he is called to free his slave and servant, and even the immigrant working in his house, to treat them as his own children. In other words, it is suggested that he follows God's behavior, as a son would.

Hardly had they been saved from the hand of the Egyptians who pursued them as far as the sea to put them back under the yoke of slavery, than the children of Israel intoned the «Song of the Sea». In a single movement, they celebrated the freedom they had just received and the victories to come, which bring them to the Temple in Jerusalem, where they will be consecrated in praise to divine service. It is there, on Mount Sion that, responding to the Ten Words received on Mount Sinai, the children of Israel gradually composed the seven psalms of the «Passover praise» (Psalms 113-118), and the «Great Praise» (Psalm 136), which since then have been taken up into the family celebration of the Passover. So the words of God and man are exchanged in mutual freedom.

These were the three stages which this work set out to present, in a certain unity and coherence, bringing together the three very different literary genres of narrative, law and prayer. But it is very clear that the twelve texts commented on, even though they are the most basic, are far from covering the whole collection of those dealing with the same subject. They are all only drawn from the Old Testament. Now, we know that the themes of law and freedom are also very present in the New Testament — the title chosen for this work is taken from the Letter to the Galatians, in which Paul talks of nothing else.

Before concluding, we will return to the title of the central part of the book, «The Law of Freedom», which raises a question. At first sight, the two terms in this expression appear to contradict one another. The word «law» implies obligation and constraint, the exact opposite of freedom. «The ten commandments», as they are popularly known, are orders, most of which are framed negatively, that is, prohibitions. In neither of the two versions of the Decalogue are there fewer than twelve commandments! The others — the four in the Exodus text and the five in the Deuteronomy text — are no less orders for being framed positively.

The name «ten commandments» is of course useful, but it can lead to a false interpretation of the biblical text. The Hebrew title, followed by its Greek equivalent «Decalogue» is otherwise more faithful to both the spirit and the letter of the Bible. Here the text of Exodus 20 and Deuteronomy 5 is not called «the Ten Commandments», but «the Ten Words»[1], which is not at all the same thing. In Hebrew, *ʿăseret haddibb^{e}rôt* echoes *ʿăseret hammaʾămārôt*. The first expression describes «the Ten Words» of the covenant concluded at Sinai, and the second «the Ten Words» of creation, according to the account in Gen 1:1-2:4a. The two terms, *dibbēr* and *maʾămār* in the singular, are synonymous, and it would be very difficult to translate them any other way. If the account of creation ends on the Sabbath where God acts freely in renouncing his exercise of omnipotence, if he «masters his own mastery» to leave room for his other whom he also invites to

1 *ăseret hadd^{e}bārîm* (Exod 34:28; Deut 4:13; 10:4). The Hebrew of the Mishnah uses the form *dibb^{e}rôt*, plural of *dibbēr* in Jer 5:13 (where this noun describes God's word): «And the prophets? Nothing but wind; and the word (*hadibbēr*) is not in them», rather than *d^{e}bārîm*.

freedom just as he invites him to be, being «in his image and likeness», it could not be otherwise with the Decalogue through which he makes a covenant with his people and, beyond them, with all humanity.

The Ten Words are not primarily commandments, impersonal words, as in the version of the catechism which French schoolchildren had to learn by heart:

1. A single God you shall adore	and shall love him perfectly.
2. God's name in vain you shall not swear,	nor others similarly.
3. Sunday you shall commemorate,	serving God devotedly.
4. Father, mother you shall honor,	so as to live lengthily.
5. A murderer you shall not be,	by accident nor purposely.
6. Full of lust you shall not be,	not bodily nor wittingly.
7. Another's goods you shall not take,	nor retain them knowingly.
8. False witness you shall not bear,	nor tell any slightest lie.
9. The flesh you shall only desire,	alone in matrimony.
10. Another's goods you shall not seek	to possess dishonestly.

In French this rhyming, rhythmic text is much easier to memorize than the biblical text[2]. Unfortunately, it is a serious betrayal of the Ten Words of God. The most serious point is that this «poetic» adaptation, with its aim of being memorized and interiorized in childhood, suppresses the first Word of the Decalogue, the basic word — «I am the Lord your God who brought you out of the land of Egypt, of the house of slavery». The speaker and his good things, *freedom from slavery*, disappear and their place is taken by «commandments» alone, which are, therefore, no longer *his* commandments.

In addition, note that, in the real Decalogue, God does not command humanity to love and adore him, as is said in the first commandment of the expurgated version. He says only that humanity is not to «bow down to» idols. Would he demand that we become his slave? We can understand why so many have sent this god to the devil — in fact, it is not worth the effort, as he is already there, for such a divinity *is* the devil. They are better off not having to free themselves from a

2 «A certain memorization of the words of Jesus, of important bible passages, of the Ten Commandments, of the formulas of profession of the faith, of the liturgical texts, of the essential prayers, of key doctrinal ideas, etc., far from being opposed to the dignity of young Christians, or constituting an obstacle to personal dialogue with the Lord, is a real need» (JOHN PAUL II, *Apostolic Exhortation* Catechesi tradendae, 16 October 1979, § 55). This document does not encourage the memorization of falsified texts.

Pharaoh who was much worse than Egypt's Pharaoh, since he does not even give his name. Love does not give orders, neither does the «service» which flows from it and which is the total opposite of slavery, since it is not the consequence of restrictions, but the fruit of love and freedom[3].

In ch. 16 of his Gospel, Luke gives two of Jesus' parables, the parable of the crafty steward, and the parable of the rich man and Lazarus. The first parable is followed by a commentary, and the second one has a sort of introduction given by way of preparation, in which Jesus parallels law with money, which is something of a surprise[4]. What can the two have in common? Both are excellent things. The law is the most precious thing, which the children of Israel, and Jesus' disciples, have. Like money, law can be put to wrong use. Both are means of relationship and exchange between humanity, and between humanity and God, symbols — in the original sense of the term, that is, as means of acknowledgement and signs of alliance. But if they are used for what they are not, if they are held to be absolutes, rather than being symbols, they become idols, those «nothings», as the Bible calls them, which take everything and give nothing. With the capital letter of proper names, money becomes Mammon, and the Law becomes Moloch, who devours children in his fiery mouth.

This is why Jesus rises up against an understanding of the law, and especially the Sabbath, which denatures it and one becomes its slave. This is why Paul, initially blinded by the divine revelation on the road to Damascus, took up again and handed on the flame of the freedom of the children of God. The one who claims to be justified and to be saving himself because he has observed the commandments of the Law is an idolater of the worst kind, because he is putting himself in God's place. True freedom is acknowledging what one really is, one of God's creatures, limited, particularly by a law which is nothing more than an opportunity to exercise one's freedom. It is not the law itself which saves and justifies, but the one God; the one who, from the start of Israel's history has delivered it from slavery, who, rested on the last day of creation, renouncing the exercise of his omnipotence and leaving a space of freedom for all humanity. In agreeing to die on the cross, Jesus went to the very limits of renunciation of omnipotence, thus revealing that the slavery of sin brought death; and in this way, paradoxically, he became able to free from death all those who follow him on the same path.

3 Here it is worth reading ch. 7 of *La Divine Origine*, by Marie BALMARY, entitled «La loi pour l'homme» («The law for humanity»), 219-257.

4 See *Luc*, 646-652.

ALCACÉR J. M., «La historia de la salvación celebrada como Pascua. El "otro" paso del mar: Ap. 15,3-4» in *Escritos del Vedat* 33 (2003) 7-48.

ALONSO MERINO P.J., *El Cántico Nuevo en el Apocalipsis: Perspectiva biblico-teológica*, PUG editrice, Roma 1990.

ALONSO SCHOEKEL L., *Treinta Salmos. Poesía y oración*, Ediciones Cristiandad, Estudios de Antigo Testamento 2, Madrid 1981; Italian translation: *Trenta salmi. Poesia e preghiera*, EDB, Studi biblici 8, Bologna 1982.

ALONSO SCHOEKEL L., and CARNITI C., *I Salmi*, Borla, Commenti biblici I-II, Roma 1992-1993.

AUFFRET P., «Essai sur la structure littéraire d'Ex 14» in *EstBib* 41 (1983) 53-82.

______, «Essai sur la structure littéraire du Psaume 116» in *BN* 23 (1984) 32-47.

______, «"Je marcherai à la face de Yahvé". Étude structurelle du Psaume 116» in *NRTh* 106 (1984) 383-396.

BALMARY M., *La Divine Origine. Dieu n'a pas créé l'homme*, Grasset, Paris 1993.

______, *Abel ou la traversée de l'Éden*, Grasset, Paris 1999.

BAR TURA A., «Uzzî vezimrat Yah» in *BeM* 95 (1983) 330.

BARRÉ M.L., «Psalm 116: Its Structure and Its Enigmas» in *JBL* 109 (1990) 61-78.

BEAUCAMP É., *Le Psautier*, Gabalda, Sources bibliques, Paris 1979.

BEAUCHAMP P., «Propositions sur l'alliance comme structure centrale» in *RSR* 58 (1970) 161-193.

______, *L'Un et l'Autre Testament*, I, Essai de lecture, Éd. du Seuil, Parole de Dieu, Paris 1976.

______, *Psaumes nuit et jour*, Éd. du Seuil, Paris 1980.

______, *L'Un et l'Autre Testament*, II, Accomplir les Écritures, Éd. du Seuil, Parole de Dieu, Paris 1990.

______, *Création et Séparation. Étude exégétique du chapitre premier de la Genèse*, Éd. du Cerf, LeDiv 201, Paris 2005 (first edition: Bruges, Desclée de Brouwer, Bibliothèque de sciences religieuses, 1969).

______, *D'une montagne à l'autre, la Loi de Dieu*, Éd. du Seuil, Paris 1999.

BOGAERT P.-M., «Les Quatre Vivants, l'Évangile et les évangiles» in *RThL* 32 (2001) 457-478.

BONNET L., *Le Nouveau Testament de Notre Seigneur Jésus-Christ expliqué au moyen d'introductions, d'analyses et de notes exégétiques*, IV, *Apocalypse*, Georges Bridel, Lausanne 1905[3], 309-449.

BOVATI P., *Ristabilire la giustizia. Procedure, vocabolario, orientamenti*, Editrice Pontificio Istituto Biblico, AnBib 110, Roma 1986.

______, «Deuterosi e compimento» in *Teologia* 27 (2002) 20-34.

______, *Giustizia e ingiustizia nell'Antico Testamento*, handout, Pontificio Istituto Biblico, Roma 1996.

BOVATI P. and MEYNET R., *Le Livre du prophète Amos*, Éd. du Cerf, RhBib 2, Paris 1994.

BRENNER M.L., *The Song of the Sea, Ex 15:1-21*, De Gruyter, Berlin - New York 1991.

BULLINGER E.W., *Commentary on Revelation*, Kregel Publications, Grand Rapids MI 1984 (Reprint of the third edition of 1935).

BURDEN J.J., «A Stylistic Analysis of Exodus 15:1-21. Theory and Practice» in BURDEN J.J., (ed.), *Exodus 1-15: Text and Context. Proceedings of the 29th annual Congress of the Old Testament Society of South Africa*, OTWSA 29 (1987) 34-72.

CASTELLINO G., «Il ritmo ebraico nel pensiero degli antichi» in *Bib* 15 (1934) 505-516.

CHARPENTIER É., *Pour lire l'Ancien Testament*, Éd. du Cerf, Paris 1980.

COATS G.W., «The Song of the Sea» in *CBQ* 31 (1969) 1-17.

CONDAMIN A., *Poèmes de la Bible, avec une introduction sur la strophique hébraïque*, Beauchesne, Paris 1933.

COSTACURTA B., *La vita minacciata. Il tema della paura nella Bibbia Ebraica*, Editrice Pontificio Istituto Biblico, AnBib 119, Roma 1988. 1997[2].

CRAIGIE P.C., «An Egyptian Expression in the Song of the Sea (Exodus XV 4)» in *VT* 20 (1970) 83-86.

______, *Psalms 1-50*, Word Books, WBC, Waco Texas, 1983.

CROSS F.M., «The Song of the Sea and Canaanite Myth» in *JTC* (1968) 1-25.

CROSS F.M. - FREEDMAN D.N., «The Song of Miriam» in *JNES* 14 (1955) 237-250.

DAHOOD M., *Psalms*, Doubleday, AnB 16.17.17A, Garden City, NY 1965-66, 1968, 1970.

DEISSLER A., *Le Livre des Psaumes*, I-II, Beauchesne, Verbum Salutis, Paris 1968 (original: 1963).

DRIVER S.R., *The Book of Exodus*, University Press, The Cambridge Bible for Schools and Colleges, Cambridge 1911.

PHILO OF CAESAREA, *La Préparation évangélique*, Éd. du Cerf, SC 206,215,228, 262,266,292,307, Paris 1974-1991.

FINKELSTEIN L., «The Origin of the Hallel (Ps 113-118)» in *HUCA* 23, II (1950-51) 319-337.

FLAVIUS JOSEPHUS, *Les Antiquités juives*, Éd. du Cerf, Paris 1990.

FRAENKEL A.A., «Du père au Père» en TAPIERO M. (ed.), *Les Dix Paroles*, Éd. du Cerf, Paris 1995, 301-315.

______, «'Assarah Maamaroth - 'Assarah Dibberot. De la Création à la Révélation» in TAPIERO M. (ed.), *Les Dix Paroles*, Éd. du Cerf, Paris 1995, 59-62.

FREEDMAN D.N., «Strophe and Meter in Ex 15» in BREAM H.N., HEIM R.D., MOORE C.A. (ed.), *A Light unto my Path: OT Studies in Honor of Jacob M. Myers*, Temple University Press, Gettysburg theological studies 4, Philadelphia 1974, 163-203.

______, «Ps 113 and the Song of Hanna» in *Eretz Israel* 14 (1978) 59-69.

GALBIATI E., *La struttura letteraria dell'Esodo*, Editiones Paulinae, Roma 1956.

GAROFALO S., «L'Epinicio di Mosè (Esodo 15)» in *Bib* (1937) 1-22.

GERSTENBERGER E.S., *Psalms. Part I with an Introduction to Cultic Poetry. Part II and Lamentations*, Eerdmans, The Forms of the Old Testament Literature 14-15, Grand Rapids, MI 1988-2001.

GIETMANN G., *De re metrica hebraeorum*, Herder, Fribourg 1880.

GOOD E.M., «Exodus XV 2» in *VT* 20 (1970) 358-359.

HARRINGTON W.J., *The Apocalypse of St. John*, Chapman, London 1969.

HAUPT P., «Moses Song of Triumph» en *AJSL* 20 (1903/4) 149-172.

HOWELL M., «Exodus 15,1b-18. A Poetic Analysis» in *AThL* 65 (1989) 5-42.

HURVITZ A., «Originals and Imitations in Biblical Poetry: a Comparative Examination of 1 Sam 2:1-10 and Ps 113:5-9» in KORT A.-MORSCHAUSER S. (ed.), *Biblical and related studies presented to Samuel Iwry*, Eisenbrauns, Winona Lake, Indiana 1985, 115-121.

JACQUET L., *Les Psaumes et le Cœur de l'homme. Étude textuelle, littéraire et doctrinale*, Duculot, I-III, Gembloux 1975-1979.

JAKOBSON R., «Closing Statements: Linguistics and Poetics» in SEBEOK, T.A., (ed.), *Style in Language*, Technology Press of Massachusetts Institute of Technology, Cambridge 1960; translated from RUWET N., *Essais de linguistique générale*, Éd. de Minuit, Paris 1963.

JENNI E. - WESTERMANN C., *Dizionario teologico dell'Antico Testamento*, Marietti, Torino 1978-1982.

JOÜON P., *Grammaire de l'hébreu biblique*, Institut Biblique Pontifical, Rome 1947.

______, «Respondit et dixit» in *Bib* 13 (1932) 309-314.

LAGRANGE M.-J., «Deux chants de guerre» in *RB* 8 (1899) 532-552.

LE DÉAUT R., *La Nuit pascale. Essai sur la signification de la Pâque juive à partir du Targum d'Exode XII 42*, Institut Biblique Pontifical, AnBib 22, Rome 1963.

LEVINE É., «*Neofiti* 1. A Study of Exodus 15» in *Bib* 54 (1973) 301-330.

LOEWENSTAMM S.E., «The Lord is my Strength and my Glory» in *VT* 19 (1969) 464-470.

LOHFINK N., «De Moysis Epinicio (Ex 15,1-18)» in *VD* 41 (1963) 277-289.

LOISY A., *L'Apocalypse de Jean*, Nourry, Paris 1923.

LOWTH R., *De sacra poesi Hebraeorum praelectiones academicae Oxonii habitae*, Oxford 1753; In French: *Leçons sur la poésie sacrée des Hébreux traduites pour la première fois en français du latin du Dr Lowth*, trad. de M.Sicard, I-II, Lyon 1812 (www.retoricabiblicaesemitica.org).

LUND N.W., «Chiasmus in the Psalms» in *AJSL* 49 (1933) 281-312.

______, *Chiasmus in the New Testament. A Study in Formgeschichte*, Chapel Hill: The University of North Carolina Press, 1942; reprinted as: *Chiasmus in the New Testament. A Study in the Form and Function of Chiastic Structures*, Peabody MA, Hendrickson, 1992.

MESSAS C., «Les dix Paroles» in TAPIERO M. (ed.), *Les Dix Paroles*, Éd. du Cerf, Paris 1995, 17-57.

MEYNET R., *L'Analyse rhétorique. Une nouvelle méthode pour comprendre les textes bibliques: textes fondateurs et exposé systématique*, Éd. du Cerf, Initiations, Paris 1989.

______, «Le cantique de Moïse et le cantique de l'Agneau (Ap 15 et Ex 15)» in *Gr* 73 (1992) 19-55.

______, *«E ora, scrivete per voi questo cantico». Introduzione pratica all'analisi retorica*, 1. *Detti e proverbi*, Edizioni Dehoniane, ReBib 3, Roma 1996; French edition: *«Et maintenant, écrivez pour vous ce cantique». Exercices pratiques d'analyse rhétorique. 1. Dictons et proverbes.* Cfr. www. retoricabiblicaesemitica.org: L'analyse rhétorique, Des exercices.

______, «I due decaloghi, legge di libertà (Es 20,2-17 & Dt 5,6-21)» in *Gr* 81 (2000) 659-692.

______, «Les deux Décalogues, loi de liberté», *StRh* 8 (11.04.2002; 27.09.2005).

______, *Lire la Bible*, Flammarion, Champs 537, Paris 2003.

______, «Le Passage de la mer (Ex 14). Analyse rhétorique» in *RTLu* 9 (2004) 569-590.

______, «Two Decalogues, Law of Freedom (Ex 20:2-17 & Dt 6:6-21)», *StRh* 16 (02.11.2004)

______, *L'Évangile de Luc*, Lethielleux, RhSem 1, Paris 2005.

______, «Es 25,10-40. A proposito del libro di Giorgio Paximadi, *E io dimorerò in mezzo a loro*», *StRh* 21 (29.11.2005; 04.11.2006).

______, *Traité de rhétorique biblique*, Lethielleux, RhSem 4, Paris 2007.

MINELLA M.J., «A Christian Look at Psalm 113» in BiTod 72 (1974) 1613-1618.

MOWINCKEL S., *The Psalms in Israel's Worship*, Blackwell, Oxford 1962.

MUILENBURG J., «A Liturgy on the Triumphs of Yahweh» in *Studia Biblica et Semitica Th. C. Vierzen dedicata*, Veenman & Zonen, Wageningen 1966, 233-251.

MÜLLER D.H., *Die Propheten in ihrer ursprünglicheren Form*, Hoelder, Vienne 1896.

OUAKNINE M.-A. et ROTNEMER D., *La Bible de l'humour juif*, I, Ramsay, Paris 1995.

PAXIMADI G., *E io dimorerò in mezzo a loro. Composizione e interpretazione di Es 25-31*, EDB, ReBib 8, Bologna 2004.

PHILO OF ALEXANDRIA, *De agricultura*, Les Œuvres de Philon d'Alexandrie 9, Éd. du Cerf, Paris 1961.

PLANTIER H., *Études littéraires sur les poètes bibliques*, I-II, Gervais-Bedot, Nîmes 1881[3].

PRINSLOO W.S., «Psalm 116: Disconnected Text or symmetrical Whole?» in *Bib* 74 (1993) 71-82.

RATZINGER J., *Jesus of Nazareth*, Bloomsbury, London 2007.

RAVASI G., *Il libro dei Salmi. Commento e attualizzazione*, EDB, Lettura pastorale della Bibbia 17-19, I-III, Bologna 1985.

RENAUD B., «Les deux lectures du Ps 114» in *RevSR* 52 (1978) 14-28.

ROZELAAR M., «The Song of the Sea (Exodus XV,1b-18)» in *VT* 2 (1952) 221-228.

SKA J.-L., *Le Passage de la mer. Étude de la construction, du style et de la symbolique de Ex 14,1-31*, Institut Biblique Pontifical, AnBib 109, Roma 1986, 1997[2].

______, *Introduction à la lecture du Pentateuque. Clés pour l'interprétation des cinq premiers livres de la Bible*, Lessius, Le livre et le rouleau 5, Bruxelles 2000.

SWETE H.B., *The Apocalypse of St John*, Macmillan, London 1907.

TAPIERO M., «Honore ton père et ta mère» in TAPIERO M. (ed.), *Les Dix Paroles*, Éd. du Cerf, Paris 1995, 265-299.

TEXTOS FUENTES: *Le Psautier: version œcuménique, texte liturgique*, Éd. du Cerf, Paris 1977.

TOURNAY R., «Recherche sur la chronologie des Psaumes» in *RB* 65 (1958) 321-357; 66 (1959) 161-190.

VANHOYE A., «L'utilisation du livre d'Ézéchiel dans l'Apocalypse» in *Bib* 43 (1962) 436-472.

VANNI U., *La struttura letteraria dell'Apocalisse*, Morcelliana, Brescia 1980[2].

______, *L'Apocalisse: ermeneutica, esegesi, teologia*, EDB, Supplementi alla Rivista Biblica 17, Bologna 1988.

VATTIONI F., «Aspetti del culto del Signore dei cieli» in *Aug* 12 (1972) 479-515; 13 (1973) 37-74.

VERVENNE M., «The Sea Narrative Revisited» in *Bib* 75 (1994) 80-98.

WALDMANN N., «A Comparative Note on Exodus 15:14-16» in *JQR* 66 (1975-76) 189-192.

WALVOORD J.F., *The Revelation of Jesus Christ*, Marshall, Morgan & Scott, London 1966.

WATSON W.G.E., «Reversed Rootplay in Ps 145» in *Bib* 62 (1981) 101-102.

WATSON W.G.E., *Classical Hebrew Poetry. A Guide to its Techniques*, JSOT Press, Sheffield 1984.

WATTS J.D.W., «The Song of the Sea, Ex XV» in *VT* 7 (1957) 371-380.

WÉNIN A., «Naître à la liberté et à la vie. Le passage de la Mer (Ex 14)» in ID., *L'Homme biblique. Anthropologie et éthique dans le Premier Testament*, Éd. du Cerf, Théologies Bibliques, Paris 1995, 79-103.

______, «Le Décalogue. Approche contextuelle, théologie et anthropologie» in FOCANT C. (ed.), *La Loi dans l'Un et l'Autre Testament*, Éd. du Cerf, LeDiv 168, Paris 1997, 9-43.

______, «Le Décalogue, révélation de Dieu et chemin de bonheur?», *StRh* 3 (06.04.2002)

WIENNER C., *Le livre de l'Exode*, Éd. du Cerf, CEv 54, Paris 1985.

Index of authors

G

H

I

J

K

L

M

O

P

R

S

T

V

W

ROLAND MEYNET
OTHER PUBLICATIONS IN
THE BIBLE CONTEXT

Quelle est donc cette Parole? Lecture «rhétorique» de l'Évangile selon saint Luc (1-9 et 22-24), Éd. du Cerf, LeDiv 99 A.B., Paris 1979.

Initiation à la rhétorique biblique. Qui donc est le plus grand?, I-II, Éd. du Cerf, Initiations, Paris 1982.

L'Évangile selon saint Luc. Analyse rhétorique, I-II, Éd. du Cerf, RhBib 1, Paris 1988. In Italian: *Il vangelo secondo Luca*, ED, ReBib 1, Roma 1993.

L'Analyse rhétorique. Une nouvelle méthode pour comprendre la Bible. Textes fondateurs et exposé systématique, Éd. du Cerf, Initiations, Paris 1989. In Italian: *L'analisi retorica*, Queriniana, BiBi 8, Brescia 1992. In English: *Rhetorical Analysis. An Introduction to Biblical Rhetoric*, Sheffield Academic Press JSOT. S 256, Sheffield 1998.

Avez-vous lu saint Luc? Guide pour la rencontre, Éd. du Cerf, LiBi 88, Paris 1990. In Polish: *Czytaliscie Sw. Łukasza? Przewodnik, który prowadzi do Spotkania*, Kraków, Wam 1998.

Passion de Notre Seigneur Jésus Christ selon les évangiles synoptiques, Éd. du Cerf, LiBi 99, Paris 1993.

Con N. Farouki, L. Pouzet y A. Sinno, *Méthode rhétorique et herméneutique, Analyse de textes de la Bible et de la Tradition musulmane*, Dar el-Machreq, Beyrouth 1993 (en árabe): In French: *Rhétorique sémitique. Textes de la Bible et de la Tradition musulmane*, Éd. du Cerf, Patrimoines. Religions du Livre, Paris 1998.

Con P. Bovati, *Le Livre du prophète Amos*, Éd. du Cerf, RhBib 2, Paris 1994. In Italian: *Il libro del profeta Amos*, ED, ReBib 2, Roma 1995.

Con P. Bovati, *La Fin d'Israël. Paroles d'Amos*, Éd. du Cerf, LiBi 101, Paris 1994.

Lire la Bible, Paris, Flammarion, Dominos 92, 1996. In Italian: *Leggere la Bibbia*, Il Saggiatore/Flammarion, Due punti 57, Milano 1998.

«E ora, scrivete per voi questo cantico». Introduzione pratica all'analisi retorica, 1. *Detti e proverbi*, ED, ReBib 3, Roma 1996.

Jésus passe. Testament, procès, exécution et résurrection du Seigneur Jésus dans les évangiles synoptiques, PUG Editrice/Éd. du Cerf, RhBib 3, Rome/Paris 1999. In Italian: *La Pasqua del Signore. Testamento, processo, esecuzione e risurrezione di Gesù nei vangeli sinottici*, EDB, ReBib 5, Bologna 2002.

«Vedi questa donna?» Saggio sulla comunicazione per mezzo delle parabole, Edizioni Paoline, Fede e comunicazione 9, Milano 2000. In French: *«Tu vois cette femme?» Parler en paraboles*, Éd. du Cerf, LiBi 121, Paris 2001.

Wprowadzenie do hebrajskiej retoryki biblijnej (*Études de rhétorique biblique*), Kraków, Wam, Myśl Teologiczna 30, 2001.

Una nuova introduzione ai vangeli sinottici, EDB, ReBib 4, 9, Bologna 2001, 2006. In English: *A New Introduction to the Synoptic Gospels*, India Claretian Communications, Chennai 2005.

Mort et ressuscité selon les Écritures, Bayard, Paris 2003. In Italian: *Morto e risorto secondo le Scritture*, EDB, Biblica, Bologna 2003.

Lire la Bible, Flammarion, Champs 537, Paris 2003. In Italian: *Leggere la Bibbia. Un'introduzione all'esegesi*, EDB, Collana biblica, Bologna 2004.

Il vangelo secondo Luca, EDB, ReBib 7, Bologna 2003.

L'Évangile de Luc, Lethielleux, RhSem 1, Paris 2005 (Grand Prix de philosophie de l'Académie française 2006).

La Bible, Le Cavalier bleu, Idées reçues 94, Paris 2005.

Język Przypowieści biblijnych, Kraków, Wydawnictwo Wam, Myśl Teologiczna 50, 2005.

Traité de rhétorique biblique, Lethielleux, RhSem 4, Paris 2007.

Appelés à la liberté, Lethielleux, RhSem 5, Paris 2008.

Called to freedom

This book was printed on *thin opaque smooth white Bible paper,* using the *Minion* and *Type Embellishments One* font families.
This edition was printed in D'VINNI, S.A., in Bogotá, Colombia, during the last weeks of the sixth month of year two thousand nine.

Ad publicam lucem datus mense junii Sacri Cordis Iesus